# GEORGIA GUN LAW
## Armed And Educated

A Complete Guide To Gun Law In Georgia

Written by Attorneys Matthew Kilgo and
Michael Hawkins

Written by Matt Kilgo and Michael Hawkins and published in the United States of America By U.S. Law Shield, LLP

ISBN 978-0-692-50650-9

To order additional books by phone or for wholesale orders, call (877) 448-6839.

# TABLE OF CONTENTS

# PREFACE

At the time my partner Mike Hawkins and I were first approached to draft a book on Georgia's gun laws, I was a gun owner. I was a lawyer who was a gun owner. I was a lawyer who was a gun owner who had a successful criminal practice and thought he knew everything he needed to know about Georgia's gun laws.

Wow.

Drafting this book over the past year has been a true scholar's journey: although I'm quickly approaching my second decade as a Georgia lawyer, my intensive study of Georgia's gun laws has taught me just how complex and too-often confusing those laws can be. It's taught me that, even as a lawyer, there's always something new to learn about the law, and if a lawyer can learn something new, it's my job to make sure my clients can understand those laws as well.

The goal in drafting this book was to put Georgia's gun laws and the gun laws of our federal government in the hands of Georgia's law-abiding gun owners, in a way that is easy to understand. All too often those who want to practice safe, lawful protection for themselves and their families are caught in a situation where a better understanding of the laws (something that isn't always easy) could keep them out of harm's way. With many years experience in prosecuting and defending those accused of gun crimes, my partner and I feel it's our duty to create a resource that will empower Georgia's residents to arm themselves with that kind of knowledge. As the title states, we believe every citizen has a right to be armed and a duty to be educated: our hope is this book will provide you with the essential tools to make you (or anyone) an informed, educated, law-abiding gun owner.

Our firm is committed to protecting the Second Amendment rights of ALL Georgia's citizens. Whether it is in the courtroom, or on the pages of this book, we want everyone to be empowered to protect themselves, and to know the law. We stand by our work, and we stand ready to assist those who need our counsel, so here's our first bit of advice: know the law! You will find we reference the old adage "Ignorance is no excuse" early in the book: that's because it's the law in Georgia! Take this information, use our real-world applications, and become that gun owner who both knows and understands the law. Citizens of Georgia have had the right to protect themselves and their families with firearms since 1791: exercise that right, and use this book to help you. — *Matthew Kilgo*

# SPECIAL ACKNOWLEDGEMENT

The authors wish to express their gratitude and sincere thanks to Michael Banja, full-time law enforcement officer and Georgia weapons expert. Mike's willingness to share his knowledge, his tireless assistance, and his wise counsel on content and presentation helped make this work possible. Thank you, Mike!

# CHAPTER ONE

## BRIEF LEGAL HISTORY OF THE RIGHT TO BEAR ARMS AND THE LAWS REGULATING FIREARMS

### I.    Introduction and overview

To fully understand gun rights today in Georgia or the United States, we should start first at the beginning: the founding document for our system of government, the United States Constitution. The Constitution was written without any individual rights specifically guaranteed: the founding fathers thought it obvious that individuals had "inalienable," universally accepted rights. Because these rights were universal, there was no reason to list them in a document meant to impose restrictions upon the government. James Madison, often viewed as the 'architect' of the Constitution, felt that naming certain rights would imply those to be the only rights an individual possessed.

After much discussion among our Founding Fathers—and a complete change of opinion by Madison—the lack of enumerated rights in the Constitution was remedied in the first Congressional session and the state ratification process. When the dust settled, ten amendments were added to the Constitution: these ten amendments are known as the Bill of Rights. The Second Amendment specifically concerns firearms, and will be the main focus of our attention as we discuss the right to bear arms. Throughout this book, however, we will reference many other vitally important amendments and statutes, including the Fourth and Fifth Amendments, that both affect your right to bear arms and the fundamental rights for us all.

### II.   Do I have a constitutional right as an individual to keep and bear arms?

Yes; the Bill of Rights guarantees your right to keep and bear arms, and the United States Supreme Court has decided that an individual has a constitutionally granted right that flows from the Second Amendment, which states simply:

> *A well-regulated Militia, being necessary to the security of a free State, the right of the people to keep and bear Arms, shall not be infringed.*

From a plain reading, there are two important parts to this amendment: first, that a well-regulated militia is necessary to the security of a free state; and second, that there is a right of the people to keep and bear arms. For years before the issue was conclusively decided, anti-gun activists argued the Second Amendment only applied to "militias" and not to individuals. Fortunately, this argument is not the law. Nevertheless, and despite the Supreme Court rulings stating otherwise, this myth seems to persist. What do these parts of the Second Amendment mean? Are they the same, or are they different?

A.  *What is a "Well-Regulated Militia?"*
The first clause of the Second Amendment references a "well-regulated militia." What is a well-regulated militia? The U.S. Supreme Court has held what this phrase does and does not mean. In 1939, in the case of *United States v. Miller,* 307 U.S. 174 (1939) (ironically, a ruling that upheld firearms regulation), the court defined a Militia as comprising of "all males physically capable of acting in concert for the common defense." Based on how the amendment was drafted, the Court stated, it was clear that the Militia pre-dated Article I of the Constitution, because unlike armies and navies, it did not have to be created by Congress. What then is "well-regulated" per the court? It is exactly what it sounds like: the imposition of discipline and training. So, is this just the National Guard? No.

In the case of *District of Columbia v. Heller,* 554 U.S. 570 (2008), the Supreme Court found a well-regulated militia is not the state's military forces, but a separate entity altogether. The Supreme Court defined the "militia" as the body of the people, and they—the people—were required to keep a centralized government in check. The Supreme Court considered and rejected the position that the National Guard is the current militia under the Second Amendment.

B.  *How has the phrase "right to keep and bear arms" been interpreted by the courts?*
One of the first cases to directly deal with the Second Amendment was the *Miller* case discussed briefly above. In *Miller*, the Supreme Court found that the National Firearms Act ("NFA"), which imposed registration requirements on machine guns, short-barreled weapons, destructive devices, and other similarly unique firearms, did not violate the Second Amendment. The Court used the reasoning that possession of weapons regulated by the NFA did not reasonably

relate to the preservation or efficiency of a well-regulated militia; consequently, the NFA was held constitutional.

**Court fight where it all began: *United States v. Miller***
An interesting quirk of history in the *Miller* case (and not a shining moment for the legal system) is that Miller's attorney never appeared at the arguments before the U.S. Supreme Court because he was court-appointed and had not been paid. There was no written brief and no legal representation at oral arguments by the party arguing that the law was unconstitutional. The Court only heard the government's side. To make matters worse, Miller was shot to death before the decision was rendered.

> ***United States v. Miller, 307 U.S. 174 (1939)***
>
> ***The facts:***
> Defendants, Miller and Layton, transported a double barrel 12-gauge shotgun with a barrel length of less than 18 inches from Oklahoma to Arkansas, and were being prosecuted under the National Firearms Act (which required certain types of firearms to be registered and a tax to be paid). Defendants challenged the NFA as an unconstitutional violation of the Second Amendment.
>
> ***The legal holdings:***
> Upheld the National Firearms Act as Constitutional.

C.   *69 years later, the Supreme Court interprets the Second Amendment again: D.C. v. Heller*
It would be 69 years after *Miller* until the U.S. Supreme Court addressed the Second Amendment directly again, except this time the Court would hear both the government's and the defendant's arguments. Fortunately, freedom and Second Amendment rights prevailed in court that day. The Court held that individuals have a right to keep and bear arms.

Keep in mind *D.C. v. Heller* was a split 5-4 decision, only one justice away from a completely different outcome, where the Second

Amendment (according to the dissent) had "outlived its usefulness and should be ignored."

> **District of Columbia v. Heller, 544 U.S. 570 (2008)**
> **The facts:**
> Heller applied for a handgun ownership permit and was denied; without such a permit, the District of Columbia required that all firearms (including rifles and shotguns) be kept unloaded and disassembled, or bound by a trigger lock, even in a person's own home.
>
> **The legal holdings:**
> 1. The Supreme Court found that the Second Amendment protects an individual right of firearms ownership for purposes of self-defense, not connected with any militia or military purposes; it further elaborated that individual self-defense is "the central component" of the Second Amendment. Further, handguns are the primary defensive weapon of choice and are protected by the Second Amendment.
> 2. A well-regulated militia is not the state's military forces.
> 3. The Court also discussed what the phrase "bear arms" meant: "wear, bear, or carry... upon the person or in clothing or in a pocket, for the purpose... of being armed and ready for offensive or defensive action in a case of conflict with another person."
> 4. The D.C. regulation was held to be unconstitutional.
> 5. The Court concluded that like other rights, the right to bear arms is not completely absolute. Reasonable provisions and restrictions have been upheld.

D. _Can states ignore the Second Amendment? McDonald v. City of Chicago_

_D.C. v. Heller_ was a brave step forward, but the decision was limited: the District of Columbia is under the exclusive jurisdiction of Congress and is not part of any state. Therefore, the case shed no light on the question of what states are allowed to do when it comes to regulating or banning firearms. How do state constitutions interact with the Second Amendment and can states ban guns outright? The _McDonald v. City of Chicago_ case sought to answer these questions.

*McDonald v. City of Chicago, 561 U.S. 742 (2010)*
**The facts:**
*McDonald v. City of Chicago* addressed a Chicago city ordinance banning handgun possession (among other gun regulations). McDonald was a 76-year-old retired maintenance engineer who wanted a handgun for self-defense. Chicago required that all handguns had to be registered, but refused all handgun registration after a 1982 citywide handgun ban.

**The legal holdings:**
The Supreme Court held that the Second Amendment is fully applicable to the states and that individual self-defense is "the central component" of the Second Amendment. Therefore, the Second Amendment prohibits states (and cities) from enacting bans on handguns for self-protection in the home.

E.  *Legal limitations of the right to keep and bear arms*
The U.S. Supreme Court has stated: "Of course the right [to keep and bear arms] was not unlimited, just as the First Amendment's right of free speech was not." Courts may have struggled over the years with what the Second Amendment means, but they have been resolute that there is an element of self-defense. The *Heller* Court found that, "The Second Amendment does not protect the right to carry arms for any sort of confrontation," focusing their decision on self-defense. Further, the *Miller* Court held that the weapons protected were those "in common use at the time" of the decision. This is supported by historical traditions of prohibiting the carry of "dangerous and unusual weapons" that are commonly used by criminals offensively, as opposed to by law-abiding citizens for defensive purposes.

The Second Amendment does not protect against prohibitions on firearm possession by felons and the mentally ill; the Court made this point clear in the *Heller* decision, and many circuit court cases such as *U.S. v. Everist* follow the same reasoning. The Court of Appeals in *Everist* stated the Second Amendment is subject to, "limited narrowly tailored specific exceptions or restrictions for particular cases that are reasonable; it is clear that felons, infants and those of unsound mind may be prohibited from possessing firearms." *U.S. v. Everist,* 368 F.3d 517, 519 (5th Cir. 2004). Along those same lines, the *Heller* Court did not want to eliminate laws that imposed conditions and qualifications on the commercial sales of firearms.

It also does not mean that the Second Amendment includes the right to carry a firearm anywhere you may desire. The *Heller* Court stated that their opinion was not meant to allow the carrying of firearms in sensitive places such as schools and certain government buildings.

### PRACTICAL LEGAL TIP

Currently, the two most important court decisions fortifying our gun rights are *Heller* and *McDonald*. But those cases were very, very close to going the other way! Both were decided by a 5-4 majority, meaning that if only one other Supreme Court Justice had decided differently, our individual right to possess and carry firearms could have been severely limited. — *Matt*

### III.  Major firearms statutes every gun owner needs to know

At the federal level, there are plenty of laws and regulations that concern firearms, but this section will focus on some of the more major legislative actions that all gun owners need to know.

#### A.  *Gun Control Act of 1968*

The Gun Control Act of 1968 ("GCA") was enacted by Congress to "provide for better control of the interstate traffic of firearms." This law is primarily focused on regulating interstate commerce in firearms by generally prohibiting interstate firearms transfers except among licensed manufacturers, dealers, and importers. Interstate commerce, however, has been held by the courts to include nearly everything: it also contains classes of individuals to whom firearms should not be sold.

For the specifics of who can and can't purchase a firearm, please refer to Chapter 3. Among other things, the GCA created the Federal Firearms License ("FFL") system, imposed importation restrictions on military surplus rifles (adding a "sporting purpose test" and a "points system" for handguns) and marking requirements.

## B. *The Brady Handgun Violence Prevention Act*

The Brady Handgun Violence Prevention Act, commonly referred to as the Brady Law, instituted federal background checks (the National Instant Criminal Background Check System or NICS) for firearm purchasers in the United States. It further prohibited certain persons from purchasing firearms; for more information on who can or cannot purchase a firearm, see Chapter 3.

## C. *The Firearm Owners' Protection Act*

The Firearm Owners' Protection Act ("FOPA") revised many provisions of the original Gun Control Act, including "reforms" on the inspection of FFLs. This same Act updated the list of individuals prohibited from purchasing firearms that was introduced by the GCA. The FOPA also banned the ownership by civilians of any machine gun that was not registered under the NFA as of May 19, 1986. FOPA created what is called a "safe passage" provision of the law, which allows for traveling across states with a firearm. Finally, FOPA prohibited a registry for non-NFA items that directly linked firearms to their owners.

## D. *The Public Safety and Recreational Firearms Use Protection Act*

The Public Safety and Recreational Firearms Use Protection Act, commonly referred to as the *Federal Assault Weapons Ban,* was a subsection of the Violent Crime Control and Law Enforcement Act of 1994. It banned outright the manufacture and transfer of certain semi-automatic firearms and magazines. This ban grandfathered-in previously legally owned weapons, but no prohibited firearm could be acquired or manufactured after September 13, 1994. With great foresight, the drafters of this law included a so-called "sunset provision," that stated the ban would expire ten years later unless renewed. The ban expired in 2004 and all attempts to renew have been unsuccessful.

## E. *The National Firearms Act*

The National Firearms Act ("NFA") regulates and imposes a statutory excise tax on the manufacture and transfer of certain types of firearms and weapons: machine guns, short-barreled weapons, suppressors, explosive devices, and "any other weapons" (AOWs can range from everyday objects that are actually firearms, such as an umbrella that can fire a round, to other weapons the ATF decides to place in this category). The tax is $200 if you make or transfer an item (other than for the transfer of AOWs); the tax for transferring

AOWs is $5. The NFA is also referred to as Title II of the federal fire-arms laws. For more information on how to navigate the NFA while remaining legal, please see Chapter 14.

## IV. Do Georgians have a right to keep and bear arms in the Georgia Constitution?

Yes. The Georgia Constitution acknowledges the right to keep and bear arms in Article I, Section 1, Paragraph VIII:

> *The right of the people to keep and bear arms shall not be infringed, but the General Assembly shall power to prescribe the manner in which arms may be borne.*

You can see that, as opposed to the Second Amendment of the United States Constitution, this description specifically allows for legislation. The courts in Georgia have acknowledged the right of the General Assembly (the name for Georgia's legislature) to create laws prohibiting certain types of weapons, and, among other things, have upheld regulations on licensing (*see Hertz v. Bennett,* 294 Ga. 62 (2013)), as well as the restriction of the right to carry by convicted felons (*Landers v. State,* 250 Ga. 501 (1983)).

### A. *Can Georgia prohibit local municipalities from making certain gun laws?*

Yes. The Georgia Legislature can and does prohibit local municipal-ities from making certain gun laws by the legal doctrine known as "preemption." A preemption statute is a mechanism by which the Georgia legislature sets certain areas off limits to local governments, which helps ensure the uniformity of law across the state, in this case, firearms law.

### B. *What local governments may not regulate*

Two separate Georgia statutes deal with firearms preemption. O.C.G.A. § 16-11-130.2, which governs the carrying of weapons at commercial airports, specifically preempts any "ordinance, reso-lution, regulation, or policy" of a county or municipal government concerning carrying weapons at the airport. More broadly, O.C.G.A. § 16-11-173 declares the regulation of firearms and weapons as solely the duty of the General Assembly, and prohibits counties and municipalities, as well as any other authority "other than the General Assembly" from passing laws that impact weapons and your right to carry them. Local municipalities cannot regulate:

- Gun shows;
- "The possession, ownership, transport, carrying, transfer, sale, purchase, licensing, or registration of firearms or other weapons or components of firearms or other weapons;"
- Firearms dealers; or
- Dealers in components of firearms.

C.  *What local governments may regulate*
Local municipalities under state law are empowered to and may regulate "the transport, carrying, or possession of firearms by employees... of government... in the course of their employment," as well as government volunteers. O.C.G.A. § 16-11-173(c)(1). Under this code section, municipalities may also prohibit discharging firearms within the city or county by virtue of an ordinance, and can—ironically—require the heads of household in their jurisdiction to own guns (as in Kennesaw, Georgia, which has an ordinance requiring firearm and ammunition ownership by heads of household). O.G.C.A. § 16-11-173(d),(e).

Preemption applies to municipal housing authorities and their municipal housing codes as well as mass transit authorities; for example, it would be unlawful for a public housing project to prohibit the possession of firearms, evicting anyone who violated such prohibition, as the preemption statute above prohibits such regulations.

# CHAPTER TWO
## LEGAL DEFINITIONS AND CLASSIFICATIONS OF FIREARMS:
### WHAT IS LEGAL?

## I.   Introduction and overview

Before discussing the law of firearms and all its different facets, it is important first to understand what the law defines as a "firearm." Firearms laws are governed on both the federal and state levels; throughout this chapter we will explore the interactions federal and state law have on the purchase and possession of firearms.

### A.   *What is a firearm?*
#### Federal definition

Under federal law, a firearm is defined as "any weapon (including a starter gun) which will or is designed to or may readily be converted to expel a projectile by the action of an explosive." 18 U.S.C. § 921(a)(3). The federal definition of a firearm also includes the frame or receiver of any such weapon, any firearm muffler or silencer, or any "destructive device." The Georgia definition for firearm varies slightly.

#### Georgia definition

In the State of Georgia, for purposes of applying state and not federal law, a firearm is defined by O.C.G.A. § 16-11-103 (the statute prohibiting discharge of a gun near a public highway) as "any handgun, rifle, or shotgun." As contemplated in Georgia law, "firearm" includes a handgun (revolver or semiautomatic) and a long gun (firearm with a barrel length of at least 18 inches that fires shotgun shells or rifle cartridges). The same statute goes further by defining a knife (a blade greater than five inches), and the more general term "weapon" (which includes knives and handguns, but not long guns).

Why might it be important to know the different ways the term "firearm" is defined under federal and state law? Should you find yourself charged with a crime by federal authorities, the federal definition of a firearm will apply. Likewise, if the charge is under a violation of state law, then the Georgia definition will apply. Thus, the primary difference in the definitions and their impact on a defendant charged with a crime involving a firearm lies with how a person may be in trouble with the law. As we will see in the next section, the definitions of what does and does not constitute a firearm, although similar in many aspects, contain an array of differences that make violating the law unwittingly easy.

### B. *Definitions for handguns, rifles, and shotguns*

In addition to defining what constitutes a firearm, federal and Georgia law further classify and define firearms into categories of handguns and long guns (rifles and shotguns). This section will provide an overview of how federal and state laws classify firearms as well as the physical requirements for a firearm to be legal.

### 1. What is a handgun?

At its most basic, a "handgun" simply refers to any firearm designed to be fired by using only one hand. While it is true that most individuals will use two hands when firing a handgun for safety and accuracy purposes, the distinction in the legal definition of a handgun, as opposed to a "long gun," rests in its size and design, which allows it to be held or fired with a single hand.

#### Federal definition

The United States Code of Federal Regulations defines a handgun as "(a) any firearm which has a short stock and is designed to be held and fired by the use of a single hand; and (b) any combination of parts from which a firearm described in paragraph (a) can be assembled." 27 CFR § 478.11.

#### Georgia definition

A handgun is defined in O.C.G.A. § 16-11-125.1 (found under "Carrying and Possession of Firearms") as "a firearm of any description, loaded or unloaded, from which any shot, bullet, or other missile can be discharged by an action of an explosive where the length of the barrel, not including any revolving, detachable, or magazine breech, does not exceed 12 inches." This definition does not include single-shot devices that fire rounds of .46 centimeters or less in diameter. While the Georgia definition makes no mention of how many hands you must use to determine whether your firearm is a handgun, the length of the barrel controls the answer.

### 2. What is a rifle?

Federal law defines a rifle as "a weapon designed or redesigned, made or remade, and intended to be fired from the shoulder, and designed or redesigned and made or remade to use the energy of the explosive in a fixed metallic cartridge to fire only a single projectile through a rifled bore for each single pull of the trigger." 27 CFR § 478.11. In addition, a legal rifle must have a barrel length of 16 inches or greater, and includes any weapon made from a rifle which is at least 26 inches overall in length. Georgia law does not lean upon a definition of "rifle" within the Official Code of Georgia, but rather encompasses the federal definition of "rifle" by the term "long gun," using language similar to the federal law's definition of rifle: "a firearm with a barrel length of at least 18 inches and overall length of 26 inches designed or made and intended to be fired from the shoulder and designed or made to use the energy of the explosive in a fixed... [m]etallic cartridge to fire only a single projectile through a rifle bore for each single pull of the trigger."

*Minimum lengths*
In order for a rifle to not be subject to the National Firearms Act or classified as a "sawed-off rifle" (the term for short-barreled rifles under Georgia law, found in O.C.G.A. § 16-11-121), the firearm must have a <u>barrel</u> of at least 16 inches in length. The ATF procedure for measuring barrel length is accomplished by measuring from the closed bolt (or breech-face) to the furthermost end of the barrel or permanently attached muzzle device. Below is an example of a rifle that does not meet the minimum barrel-length requirement:

The barrel is measured by inserting a dowel rod into the barrel until the rod stops against the bolt or breech-face. The rod is then marked at the furthermost end of the barrel or permanently attached muzzle device, withdrawn from the barrel, and then measured. Any measurement of less than 16 inches will classify the rifle as being "sawed-off" under Georgia law, and "short-barreled" under federal law and subject the firearm to the NFA. For short-barreled rifles and other non-compliant firearms, see Chapter 14, which discusses the NFA. Note: for overall length, rifles with collapsible/folding-stocks are measured from the "extreme ends," unless the stock is "easily detachable," in which case it is measured without the stock.

### 3. What is a shotgun?

The federal definition of a shotgun is "a weapon designed or redesigned, made or remade, and intended to be fired from the shoulder, and designed or redesigned and made or remade to use the energy of the explosive in a fixed shotgun shell to fire through a smooth bore either a number of ball shot or a single projectile for each single pull of the trigger." 27 CFR § 478.11. Like rifles, legal shotguns have requirements for minimum barrel and overall lengths. Shotgun barrels must be at least 18 inches long and must also comply with the same 26-inch overall length requirement. Under Georgia law, shotguns are classified in the same manner as they are under federal law. *See* O.C.G.A. § 16-11-121(6).

*Minimum lengths*

In order for a shotgun to fall outside the National Firearms Act or classification as a short-barreled firearm under Georgia law, it must have a barrel of at least 18 inches in length. The ATF procedure for measuring the barrel length of a shotgun is the same as it is for a rifle. Below is an example of a shotgun that does not meet the minimum barrel length requirement after measurement:

Any measurement of less than 18 inches will classify the shotgun as a short-barreled weapon by federal standards and a "sawed-off shotgun" under Georgia law, and illegal under both Georgia and federal law unless the requirements of the NFA are satisfied. For short-barreled shotguns and other non-compliant firearms, see Chapter 14. Note: the collapsible/folding-stock rule that applies to rifles applies to shotguns as well.

## C. *Antique firearms and replica firearms*

When is a firearm not legally a "firearm?" It is when the law defines it as not being one, such as with "antique" firearms.

### 1. Federal definition of "antique firearm"

*1898 or prior*

The federal definition of firearm under Title 18, Section 921 of the United States Code excludes "antique firearms." Even though an antique firearm still functions ballistically similar to a "modern" firearm, under federal law, antique firearms are regulated differently, if at all. An antique firearm under federal law includes any firearm with a matchlock, flintlock, or percussion cap, or similar type of ignition system manufactured in or before 1898 or any replica of a firearm just described so long as the replica "is not designed or redesigned for using rimfire or conventional centerfire fixed ammunition, or uses rimfire or centerfire ammunition that is no longer manufactured in the United States and is not readily available in ordinary channels of commerce." 18 U.S.C. §§ 921(a)(16)(A), (B). So, an "antique firearm" is not a "firearm" for purposes of federal regulation; it is an "antique firearm."

*Muzzle loading*

In addition, federal law does not consider "any muzzle loading rifle, muzzle loading shotgun, or muzzle loading pistol, which is designed to use black powder, or a black powder substitute, and which cannot use fixed ammunition" as a firearm. Be aware, however, that the term "antique firearm" does not include any weapon which incorporates a firearm frame or receiver, any firearm which is converted into a muzzle loading weapon, or any muzzle loading weapon which can be readily converted to fire fixed ammunition by replacing the barrel, bolt, breech-lock, or any combination of these parts. 18 U.S.C. § 921(a)(16)(C).

### 2. Georgia definition of "antique firearm"

*Pre-1898*

While not explicitly referring to certain firearms as "antiques," Georgia law excludes from Brady Law regulations and National Instant Criminal Background Check mandates "[a]ny firearm, including any handgun with a matchlock, flintlock, percussion cap, or similar type of ignition system, manufactured in or before 1898." O.C.G.A. § 16-11-172. If this language looks familiar, it is because the statute closely tracks the federal definition of antique firearm. So, while Georgia does not deal directly with the notion of antique firearms, it does exclude from Brady regulations those firearms that fit the federal definition of an antique.

D.  *What firearms are illegal?*
Under O.C.G.A. § 16-11-122, certain firearms are prohibited or illegal under Georgia law. These firearms include:

- Sawed-off shotguns (having a barrel length of less than 18 inches or total length less than 26 inches);
- Sawed-off rifles (having a barrel length of less than 16 inches or total length less than 26 inches);
- Machine guns (any weapon designed to fire more than six shots, without manual reloading, by pulling the trigger once);
- Dangerous weapons (literally defined as a rocket launcher, bazooka, recoilless rifle, mortars, and hand grenades); and
- Silencers (any device for silencing or diminishing the report of any portable weapon).

The restriction of these items is subject to exception, however: O.C.G.A. § 16-11-124 exempts peace officers and members of the National Guard or armed forces (as well as nuclear power facility guards) from the prohibition against carrying these types of weapons, and allows any of these specifically listed weapons that have been rendered inoperative (usually by filling the barrel with lead). Furthermore, anyone who has properly registered a sawed-off shotgun, sawed-off rifle, machine gun, dangerous weapon, or silencer under the NFA is authorized by state law to possess those items.

Under federal law, the National Firearms Act regulates many of the same firearms that are prohibited weapons under state law. These firearms include:

- Short-barreled shotguns (referred to as "sawed-off shotguns" in Georgia);
- Short-barreled rifles (referred to as "sawed-off rifles" in Georgia);
- Machine guns;
- Firearm silencers or suppressors;
- Weapons or devices capable of being concealed on the person from which a shot can be fired;
- Pistols or revolvers having a smooth bore (as opposed to rifled bore) barrel designed to fire a fixed shotgun shell;

- Pistols or revolvers with a vertical handgrip;
- Destructive devices; and
- Weapons classified as "Any Other Weapon," or AOWs.

*See* 26 U.S.C. § 5845. For more information on these weapons, see Chapter 14 discussing the National Firearms Act.

E.  *How big of a gun can a person possess?*
Federal law dictates that any firearm which has any barrel with a bore of more than one-half inch in diameter is a "destructive device" and is subject to the National Firearms Act. Possession of any such firearm without the proper paperwork associated with NFA firearms is illegal. Note, however, that some shotguns are regulated differently. For more information on destructive devices and the NFA, see Chapter 14.

## II.  **Ammunition and the law**
No discussion concerning firearms laws would be complete without examining laws concerning the ammunition that goes into a firearm. Just like firearms, the law regulates the possession, sale, and even composition of "legal" ammunition. This section addresses the essential aspects of the law concerning ammunition and what gun owners need to know, both under federal and Georgia law.

A.  *How does the law define ammunition?*
Under federal law, the term "ammunition" is defined under 18 U.S.C. § 921(a)(17)(A) and means "ammunition or cartridge cases, primers, bullets, or propellant powder designed for use in any firearm." Thus, the federal definition of ammunition includes the finished product and all of the components in making a round of ammunition. However, the federal definition of ammunition does not include (1) any shotgun shot or pellet not designed for use as the single, complete projectile load for one shotgun hull or casing, or (2) any unloaded, non-metallic shotgun hull or casing not having a primer. *See* 27 CFR § 478.11. In other words, individual ammunition components are legally defined as ammunition themselves, even if they are simply parts, except that shotgun ammunition components, if not completely assembled, are not ammunition. Under Georgia law, there is neither specific regulation on ammunition that can be sold or possessed in the state, nor is there a statutory definition for mere "ammunition."

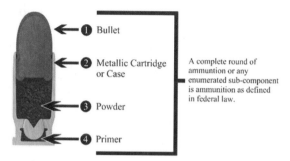

Bullet

Metallic Cartridge or Case

Powder

Primer

A complete round of ammunition or any enumerated sub-component is ammunition as defined in federal law.

## B. *Is there a difference in ammunition that is used in different types of firearms?*

Yes. Ammunition can be divided into two classifications: ammunition for handguns and ammunition for long guns. Long gun ammunition can be further divided into ammunition for rifles and ammunition for shotguns.

Handgun ammunition means ammunition that is meant to be fired from a handgun, and it comes in many different calibers. Rifle ammunition is meant to be fired from a rifle and is similar to handgun ammunition in that it comes in many different calibers. Shotgun ammunition, on the other hand, comes in self-contained cartridges loaded with some form of shot or a shotgun slug which is designed to be fired from a shotgun.

### PRACTICAL LEGAL TIP

Even with firearms, having the right tool for the job is important. Practically speaking, you should choose the firearm and ammo that you feel most comfortable using. At the end of the day, why you started shooting is always more important than what you chose to shoot with. — *Matt*

## C. *What ammunition is illegal?*

Armor-piercing handgun ammunition is the only ammunition that has explicit prohibitions under federal law; there is virtually no regulation of ammunition under Georgia law. The federal definition of armor-piercing ammunition is found in 18 U.S.C. § 921(a)(17)(B) and means "[1] a projectile or projectile core which may be used in a handgun and which is constructed entirely (excluding the presence of traces of other substances) from one or a combination of tungsten alloys, steel, iron, brass, bronze, beryllium copper, or depleted uranium; or [2] a full jacketed projectile larger than .22 caliber designed and intended for use in a handgun and whose jacket has a weight of more than 25 percent of the total weight of the projectile."

Federal law
Under federal law, while there is no blanket prohibition on the mere possession of armor-piercing ammunition, it is prohibited under four conditions:

1. *Prohibition one: it is illegal to make or import armor-piercing ammunition.* Under 18 U.S.C. § 922(a)(7) it is unlawful for any person to manufacture or import armor-piercing ammunition unless (1) the manufacture of such ammunition is for the use of the United States, any department or agency of the United States, any state, or any department, agency, or political subdivision of a state; (2) the manufacture of such ammunition is for the purpose of exportation; or (3) the manufacture or importation of such ammunition is for the purpose of testing or experimentation and has been authorized by the United States Attorney General.

2. *Prohibition two: it is illegal for manufacturers and importers to sell or deliver armor-piercing ammunition.* Federal law makes it unlawful for any manufacturer or importer to sell or deliver armor-piercing ammunition unless such sale or delivery is (1) for the use of the United States, any department or agency of the United States, any state, or any department, agency, or political subdivision of a state; (2) for the purpose of exportation; or (3) for the purpose of testing or experimentation and has been authorized by the United States Attorney General. *See* 18 U.S.C. § 922(a)(8).

3. *Prohibition three: an FFL or other license-holder cannot sell or deliver armor-piercing ammunition without the proper documentation.* Under 18 U.S.C. § 922(b)(5), it is unlawful for any licensed importer, licensed manufacturer, licensed dealer, or licensed collector to sell or deliver armor-piercing ammunition to any person unless the licensee notes in his records, as required under 18 U.S.C. § 923, the name, age, and place of residence of such person if the person is an individual, or the identity and principal and local places of business of such person if the person is a corporation or other business entity.

4. *Prohibition four: it is illegal to possess armor-piercing ammuni-*

*tion if a person is involved in a crime of violence or a drug-trafficking crime.* Pursuant to 18 U.S.C. § 924(c)(5), it is unlawful for "any person who, during and in relation to any crime of violence or drug trafficking crime (including a crime of violence or drug trafficking crime that provides for an enhanced punishment if committed by the use of a deadly or dangerous weapon or device) for which the person may be prosecuted in a court of the United States, uses or carries armor-piercing ammunition." Individuals who use or carry armor-piercing ammunition in the commission of a crime of violence or during a drug-trafficking crime are subject to heightened sentencing standards should they be found guilty.

As you can see, while possession of armor-piercing ammunition itself is not illegal, obtaining armor-piercing ammunition without violating one of the foregoing prohibitions is almost impossible.

Finally, it should be noted that not all ammunition that can pierce armor is actually armor-piercing. The definition of armor-piercing rounds found within federal law contains specific requirements for a particular round of ammunition's composition in order to make it armor-piercing. Federal law requires that the ammunition be comprised of certain alloys: for instance, 5.7 millimeter ammunition for an FN "FiveseveN" handgun or a PS90 rifle, while capable of piercing armor based on its size and velocity, is not ammunition that is armor-piercing as defined under the law because such ammunition, sold commercially, is primarily for sporting purposes according to the ATF.

**Above left, the 5.7x28mm cartridge shown at actual size. Right, the FN PS90 semi-automatic rifle, which fires the 5.7x28 round.**

D. *Does modifying traditional ammunition make it illegal?*
No, outside of armor-piercing ammunition, there is no handgun or long gun ammunition that is prohibited under either federal

or Georgia law. In fact, there are many examples of hollow-point rounds which are modified in a way to become more lethal such as the R.I.P. ammunition, Black Talons, *etc.,* which star outward upon impact in order to do more internal damage. Such ammunition, though it looks different from traditional ammunition rounds, is perfectly legal.

**Right: Unfired 40 S&W cartridge with hollow-point bullet; left, expanded hollow-point bullet after firing.**

E.  *Is it legal to use ammunition that works in both handguns and rifles?*
Yes, except for armor-piercing ammunition that is used principally in handguns. This is because the federal definition of armor-piercing ammunition contemplates handguns only. Armor-piercing ammunition for a rifle is perfectly legal, though it may complicate matters at trial in trying to demonstrate to the jury any differentiation. Beyond armor-piercing ammunition, it is legal to use ammunition that is available in common calibers and that functions in both handguns and rifles.

With a solid understanding of what is and is not a firearm and ammunition, as well as what firearms and ammunition a person may legally possess without the necessity of obtaining additional documentation, we are now ready to move to the next chapter discussing the purchase and possession of firearms.

# CHAPTER THREE

PURCHASING, TRANSFERRING, AND
POSSESSING FIREARMS

## I.   Laws of purchasing and possessing: the basics

The laws of purchasing, selling, gifting, or otherwise transferring a firearm are distinct and different from the laws of possessing a firearm. It may be legal for someone to possess a firearm, and it still be illegal for them to "purchase" the firearm. Further, each of these sets of laws for "purchasing" or "possessing" has a federal and a state component both of which must be satisfied in order to start on the right side of the law.

On the federal level, the Bureau of Alcohol, Tobacco, Firearms and Explosives ("ATF") is charged with regulating firearms including sales, purchases, and transfers through Federal Firearms Licensees ("FFLs" or "dealers"), however, a multitude of federal agencies can be involved in any given firearms law investigation or police function most currently falling under a branch of the U.S. Department of Homeland Security. Georgia has no direct state-level counterpart to the ATF.

### A.   *What is an FFL?*

FFL or Federal Firearms License is a license required by federal law for those persons or entities that are engaged in the business of buying and selling firearms. A federal firearms licensee is often called an "FFL" or "dealer." When an individual purchases, sells, or transfers a firearm through a dealer, the FFL and the individual must both comply with specific federal law requirements, paperwork, and procedures concerning the buying, selling, or transferring of those firearms. These requirements will be addressed throughout this chapter.

### B.   *Who must obtain an FFL?*

Federal law requires a federal firearms license if a person is engaged in business as a firearms dealer, manufacturer, or importer. For the purposes of our discussion in this chapter, a person is engaged in the business when the person "devotes time, attention, and labor to dealing in firearms as a regular course of trade or business with the principal objective of livelihood and profit through the repetitive purchase and resale of firearms, but such term shall not include a person who makes occasional sales, exchanges, or purchases of firearms for the enhancement of a personal collection or for a hobby, or who sells all or part of his personal collection of firearms." 18 U.S.C. § 921(a)(21)(C).

C. *What is a private sale?*
A private sale is just what it sounds like: a sale, purchase, or transfer of a firearm by parties that are not licensed dealers. A private sale is perfectly legal for both handguns and long guns in Georgia, as long as all other legal requirements are met. We will discuss the ins-and-outs of private sales in detail in this chapter under Section IV.

D. *What is the legal age to purchase and possess a firearm?*
Federal law controls all FFL firearms transactions and requires that a person be 21 years of age or older before they may purchase a handgun or 18 for the purchase of a long gun. However, under Georgia law, a handgun or long gun may be purchased in a private sale by a person who is age 18. Official Code of Georgia Annotated § 16-11-101.1(b) makes it a crime for an individual to "Intentionally, knowingly, or recklessly... sell or furnish a pistol or revolver to a minor."

| Required Age To Purchase Firearms | Federal Law: From Dealer | Georgia Law: Private Sale |
|---|---|---|
| Handgun | 21 | 18 |
| Long Gun | 18 | 18 |

Under federal law, a person must be at least 18 years of age in order to possess a handgun or ammunition for a handgun. *See* 18 U.S.C. § 922(x)(2). Unlike the law on purchasing a long gun, there is no federal age requirement for the possession of a rifle or shotgun. There is no age restriction on the possession of rifles or shotguns in Georgia.

E. *Criminal liability for allowing a minor access to firearms*
Georgia law makes it a crime for an individual to "intentionally, knowingly, or recklessly... sell or furnish a pistol or revolver to a minor." O.C.G.A. § 16-11-101.1(b). A parent or legal guardian may legally permit a minor to possess a firearm under exceptions found in O.C.G.A. § 16-11-132 (including but not limited to hunter safety courses and while on the parents' property; all exceptions are discussed later in this chapter), but it is unlawful for a parent to furnish

a pistol to a minor if the parent knows the minor has violated any permissible exception. Furthermore, it is unlawful for a parent to intentionally, knowingly, or recklessly furnish a pistol or revolver to a minor if the parent or guardian "is aware of a substantial risk that such minor will use a pistol or revolver to commit a felony," or if the parent is aware of that risk and fails to take steps to stop the minor. O.C.G.A. § 16-11-101.1(c)(2). A parent is also in violation if he or she furnishes a pistol to a minor who has been convicted of a forcible felony or forcible misdemeanor or has been adjudicated for a delinquent act that would be considered a forcible felony or forcible misdemeanor if the minor were an adult. Any adult violating this code section is guilty of a felony.

## F. *When may children legally possess firearms?*

We begin with the notion that Georgia law makes it a crime "for any person under the age of 18 years to possess or have under such person's control a handgun." O.C.G.A. § 16-11-132(b). This crime is a misdemeanor, punishable by up to 12 months in custody, or a $1000 fine, or both. Keep in mind, however, this statute does NOT apply to long guns (rifles and shotguns). A second violation is a felony, punishable by up to three years incarceration and a $5000 fine.

Georgia law does allow, however, for the legal possession of firearms under specific exceptions included in the law. These exceptions include anyone under 18 who:

### 1. Attends a hunter education or firearms safety course

The first exception to the rule that minors may not possess handguns is that the minor's access to the firearm was while "[a]ttending a hunter education course or firearms safety course." This is a common sense rule that allows minors to learn the safe handling and operation of firearms from trained professionals in a classroom setting. The next exception for minors possessing handguns fits within the same category of common sense education.

### 2. Practices shooting at an established gun range

The second exception to the law prohibiting minors from possessing handguns applies to minors "[e]ngaging in practice in the use of a firearm or target shooting at an established range." O.C.G.A. § 16-11-132(c)(1)(B). The range must be authorized by the local jurisdiction—meaning it can't just be in the backyard.

### 3. Engages in an organized shooting competition

The law forbidding minors to possess handguns excepts when minors are involved in "an organized competition involving the use of a firearm or practicing in or practicing for a performance" for a non-profit group sponsoring such an event or team. O.C.G.A. § 16-11-132(c)(1)(C).

### 4. Hunts or fishes

O.C.G.A. § 16-11-132(c)(1)(D) allows for the carrying of handguns by minors when "[h]unting or fishing pursuant to a valid license if such person has in his or her possession such a valid hunting or fishing license if required; is engaged in legal hunting or fishing; has permission of the owner of the land on which the activities are being conducted; and the handgun, whenever loaded, is carried only in an open and fully exposed manner."

### 5. Is found on parents' property

O.C.G.A. § 16-11-132(c)(2) allows anyone under the age of 18 to possess a handgun "who is on real property under the control of such person's parent, legal guardian, or grandparent and who has the permission of such person's parent or legal guardian to possess a handgun." This would conceivably cover the possession of a handgun by a minor for any potential use, when on parents' real property (excluding the home, which is considered a "habitation" and discussed in later chapters) and with their permission.

### 6. Uses a handgun in self-defense

Georgia law provides a powerful exception to minors who protect themselves (or others) with a handgun in their own home. Subsection (c)(3) of O.C.G.A. § 16-11-132 allows the possession of a handgun to "[a]ny person under the age of 18 years who is at such person's residence and who, with the permission of such person's parent or legal guardian, possesses a handgun for the purpose of exercising the rights authorized in Code Section 16-3-21 ('Use of force in the defense of self or others') or 16-3-23 ('Use of force in defense of habitation')." These laws permit the use of force against an assailant who threatens people or property, and are discussed in depth in Chapters 4, 5, and 7.

Example:

> One night, armed intruders break into Timmy's home and hold Timmy's parents at gunpoint while burglarizing the home. Timmy, who is 14, covertly sees what is transpiring from the top of the stairs. Timmy has been trained in firearm safety and can shoot his father's handgun, which is loaded in his father's nightstand. Timmy retrieves the weapon and shoots the burglar threatening his parents.

Two questions arise in this scenario: first, is Timmy legally justified in shooting the armed burglar? As we will see later in Chapters 4, 5, and 7, yes, he is. Timmy is justified in defending a third person and property with deadly force under the circumstances. Second, is Timmy's father in trouble legally for leaving his firearm accessible to Timmy? No, he is not in trouble. Timmy has been trained in the safe use of a handgun, and we may safely assume Timmy's parents would permit him to use the handgun to protect himself or to protect his family. Moreover, for obvious reasons, if a child uses a firearm in self-defense, or in defense of another person or property, there is a general public policy interest in not prosecuting those persons. There is no statute criminalizing a parent's negligent storage of a firearm in Georgia.

## G. _Special duty of firearms dealers involving minors_

Federal law requires that FFLs who deliver handguns to non-licensees display at their licensed premises (including temporary business locations at gun shows) a sign that customers can readily see. These signs are provided by the ATF and contain the following language:

(1) The misuse of handguns is a leading contributor to juvenile violence and fatalities.

(2) Safely storing and securing firearms away from children will help prevent the unlawful possession of handguns by juveniles, stop accidents, and save lives.

(3) Federal law prohibits, except in certain limited circumstances, anyone under 18 years of age from knowingly possessing a handgun, or any person from transferring a handgun to a person under 18.

(4) A knowing violation of the prohibition against selling, delivering, or otherwise transferring a handgun to a person under the age of 18 is, under certain circumstances, punishable by up to 10 years in prison.

In addition to the displayed sign, federal law requires FFLs to pro-vide non-licensee customers with a written notification containing the same four points as listed above as well as sections 922(x) and 924(a)(6) of Title 18, Chapter 44 of the United States Code. This writ-ten notification is available as a pamphlet published by the ATF en-titled "Youth Handgun Safety Act Notice" and is sometimes referred to as ATF information 5300.2. Alternatively, this written notification may be delivered to customers on another type of written notifica-tion, such as a manufacturer's brochure accompanying the hand-gun or a sales receipt or invoice applied to the handgun package. Any written notification delivered to a customer other than the one provided by the ATF must include the language described here, and must be "legible, clear, and conspicuous, and the required language shall appear in type size no smaller than 10-point type." 27 CFR § 478.103(c).

## II. Federal law disqualifications for purchasing and possessing firearms

Federal law lists categories of persons disqualified from legally pur-chasing and possessing a firearm. This list comprises disqualifica-tions that come from several different pieces of federal legislation including the Gun Control Act of 1968, the Brady Handgun Violence Protection Act, and the Violence Against Women Act. If a person buys or attempts to buy a firearm from an FFL, they must not be disqualified under any of the laws. Before an FFL may sell or oth-erwise transfer a firearm, the purchaser must fill out an ATF Form 4473. This form has questions concerning each of the criteria that disqualify a person to purchase a firearm under federal law. These disqualifications include:

(1) if the person is not the actual purchaser of the firearm—also known as a "straw man purchaser;"

(2) if the person is under indictment or information in any court for a felony or any other crime for which the judge could imprison the person for more than one year;

(3) if the person has ever been convicted in any court for a felony or other crime for which the judge could imprison the person for more than one year;

(4) if the person is a fugitive from justice;

(5) if the person is an unlawful user of, or addicted to, mari-juana, or any depressant, stimulant, narcotic drug, or con-trolled substance;

(6)   if the person has ever been adjudicated as mentally defec-
      tive or has been committed to a mental institution;
(7)   if the person has been dishonorably discharged from the
      Armed Forces;
(8)   if the person is subject to an active protective order re-
      straining the person from harassing, stalking, or threaten-
      ing the person's child, or an intimate partner or child of
      such partner;
(9)   if the person has been convicted in any court for a misde-
      meanor crime of domestic violence;
(10)  if the person has ever renounced their United States citi-
      zenship;
(11)  if the person is an alien illegally in the United States; and
(12)  if the person is admitted under a non-immigrant visa and
      does not qualify for an exception.

The purchaser must legally affirm that they are not subject to any
of the criteria listed above before they may purchase a firearm. If a
prospective purchaser answers any question on the form in a manner that indicates they are legally disqualified, it is illegal for the FFL
to sell that person the firearm, and it is illegal for the purchaser to
complete the transaction or possess the firearm.

A.   *Understanding who is disqualified*
     1.   Can I buy a firearm for another person?
No. This would be a "straw man" purchase. In order to legally purchase a firearm from a dealer, you must be the "actual purchaser
or transferee." If you are not the actual purchaser or transferee, it
is illegal for you to complete the transfer or sale under federal law.
Purchases for third persons are often called "straw man" purchases
and are illegal. If you are not the actual purchaser, beware!

In fact, the ATF has a campaign called "Don't Lie for the Other Guy"
that is targeted at (as they term it on their website) detection and
deterrence of "straw man" purchases. The ATF website lists numerous examples of prosecutions for "straw man" purchases and a United States Supreme Court case examined and upheld federal law on
this matter. *Abramski v. United States,* 134 S.Ct. 2259 (2014).

So who is the "actual" buyer or transferee so as not to be a "straw
man?" The ATF states that you are the actual "transferee/buyer if
you are purchasing the firearm for yourself or otherwise acquiring

the firearm for yourself (*e.g.*, redeeming the firearm from pawn/ retrieving it from consignment, firearm raffle winner)." The ATF goes on to state "you are also the actual transferee/buyer if you are legitimately purchasing the firearm as a gift for a third party."

Example:

*Mr. Smith asks Mr. Jones to purchase a firearm for Mr. Smith. Mr. Smith gives Mr. Jones the money for the firearm. Mr. Jones then buys the firearm with Mr. Smith's money and gives Mr. Smith the firearm.*

Mr. Jones is not the "actual buyer" (he is legally a "straw man") of the firearm and if Mr. Jones indicates that he is the "actual buyer" of the firearm on ATF Form 4473, he has committed a federal crime. The Supreme Court ruling in *Abramski,* however, did not make "gifts" of firearms illegal.

When completing ATF Form 4473: if a person checks "yes" to the box asking if the person is the "actual purchaser," then that person cannot have engaged in a separate transaction to sell or transfer the firearm privately. Please note: the Supreme Court's ruling held that a person cannot legally purchase a firearm on behalf of another even if the person receiving the firearm would not otherwise be prohibited from making the purchase themselves. So don't buy a firearm for another person no matter how good a friend, relative, or person they are—it is a crime!

---

**FREQUENTLY ASKED QUESTIONS FROM ATF WEBSITE**

*Q: May I buy a firearm from an FFL as a "gift" for another person?*

**A:** Yes. [*Editor's note: Instead of the previous example on page 30, in which Mr. Smith paid Mr. Jones to purchase a firearm for him, if Mr. Jones decides to buy a firearm with his own money and then give the firearm to Mr. Smith as a present, then Mr. Jones is the actual buyer/transferee of the firearm. Since Mr. Jones is the actual buyer, there exists no sham or "straw man," and the purchase is legal.*]

*Q: May a parent or guardian purchase a firearm as a gift for a juvenile?*

**A:** Yes, however, possession of handguns by juveniles is generally unlawful under federal law. Juveniles may only receive and possess handguns with the written permission of a parent or guardian for limited purposes, *e.g.*, employment, ranching, farming, target practice, or hunting.

*For more information, see www.atf.gov.*

---

2.  <u>A person cannot purchase a firearm if they have been convicted or are under "indictment or information" for a felony or certain misdemeanors</u>

If a person has been convicted of a felony or other crime for which a judge may sentence, or could have sentenced the person to more than one year imprisonment, that person may not legally purchase a firearm (unless the crime was a state misdemeanor punishable by imprisonment of two years or less). *See* 18 U.S.C. § 921(a)(20)(B). Likewise, if a person is under "indictment" or "information" for a felony, or any other crime for which a judge may sentence the person to more than one year imprisonment, that person is disqualified from purchasing a firearm. An "indictment" or "information" is a formal accusation of a crime punishable by imprisonment for a term exceeding one year. It is important to see that the <u>actual sentence</u> received is not the determining factor for disqualification, rather, it is the possible maximum sentence. A person may have only been sentenced to 30 days imprisonment, but if the crime for which they were charged allowed a maximum penalty of five years, then that person is disqualified. *See Schrader v. Holder,* 831 F.Supp.2d 304 (D.D.C. 2011, *aff'd,* 704 F.3d 980 (D.C. Cir. 2013)).

3. What does it mean to be a "fugitive from justice" so as to be disqualified from purchasing a firearm?

A "fugitive from justice" is a person who, after having committed a crime, flees from the jurisdiction of the court where the crime was committed. A fugitive from justice may also be a person who goes into hiding to avoid facing charges for the crime of which he or she is accused. Such individuals are not eligible to purchase or possess firearms.

4. Unlawful users of or persons addicted to drugs are disqualified from purchasing firearms

Federal law is very broad in that it disqualifies persons from the purchase of firearms if they are either users of or addicted to marijuana or any depressant, stimulant, narcotic drug, or any controlled substance. Under federal law, an "addict" is defined as a person that "habitually uses any narcotic so as to endanger the public morals, health, safety, or welfare, or who is so far addicted to the use of narcotic drugs as to have lost the power of self-control with reference to his addiction." 21 U.S.C. § 802(1). However, in using the terms "users of," no such frequency or dependence seems contemplated in the words, nor did Congress give further guidance. Illegal users and addicts are prohibited from purchasing firearms from any person under federal law, and are likewise prohibited from possessing firearms. *See* 18 U.S.C. §§ 922(d) and (g).

5. A person can't legally buy or possess firearms if they are "mentally defective"

What does "mentally defective" mean? A person is considered to have been adjudicated as "mentally defective" if there has been a "determination by a court, board, commission, or other lawful authority that a person, as a result of marked subnormal intelligence, or mental illness, incompetency, condition, or disease: is a danger to himself or others, or lacks the mental capacity to contract or manage his own affairs." The term "mentally defective" includes "a finding of insanity by a court in a criminal case, and those persons found incompetent to stand trial or found not guilty by reason of insanity or lack of mental responsibility." 27 CFR § 478.11.

"Mentally defective" also includes a person who has been committed to a mental institution by a court, board, commission, or other lawful authority, or a commitment to a mental institution involuntarily. The term includes commitment for mental defectiveness or mental illness, and also includes commitment for other reasons, such as drug use. However, it does not include a person in a mental institution for observation or a voluntary admission to a mental institution. Individuals who have been adjudicated as mentally defective are also prohibited from possessing firearms under federal law. *See* 18 U.S.C. § 922(g)(4).

6. A person subject to a restraining order may not purchase or possess a firearm

Under 18 U.S.C. § 922(g)(8), firearms may not be sold to or received by persons subject to a court order that: (a) was issued after a hearing which the person received actual notice of and had an opportunity to participate in; (b) restrains the person from harassing, stalking, or threatening an intimate partner or child of such intimate partner or person, or engaging in other conduct that would place an intimate partner in reasonable fear of bodily injury to the partner or child; and (c) includes a finding that such person represents a credible threat to the physical safety of such intimate partner or child; or by its terms explicitly prohibits the use, attempted use, or threatened use of physical force against such intimate partner or child that a person would reasonably be expected to cause bodily injury. An "intimate partner" of a person is the spouse or former spouse of the person, the parent of a child of the person, or an individual who cohabitates with the person.

7. Domestic violence issues and disqualifications

A person who has ever been convicted of the crime of domestic violence may not purchase or possess firearms under federal law. These restrictions were passed in what is known as the Violence Against Women Act in 1994 and amended in 1996. This is an often misunderstood law, and, in fact, the ATF has numerous "Frequently Asked Questions" concerning this disqualification on its website: www.atf. gov. The ATF does a good job of explaining the scope of this subject in their FAQs. Due to the complexity of this issue, ATF examples are cited on the following four pages:

## FREQUENTLY ASKED QUESTIONS FROM ATF WEBSITE

**Q: What is a "misdemeanor crime of domestic violence?"**

**A:** A "misdemeanor crime of domestic violence" means an offense that:

1. is a misdemeanor under federal or State law;
2. has, as an element, the use or attempted use of physical force, or the threatened use of a deadly weapon; and
3. was committed by a current or former spouse, parent, or guardian of the victim, by a person with whom the victim shares a child in common, by a person who is cohabiting with or has cohabited with the victim as a spouse, parent, or guardian, or by a person similarly situated to a spouse, parent, or guardian of the victim.

However, a person is not considered to have been convicted of a misdemeanor crime of domestic violence unless:

1. the person was represented by counsel in the case, or knowingly and intelligently waived the right of counsel in the case; and
2. in the case of a prosecution for which a person was entitled to a jury trial in the jurisdiction in which the case was tried, either —
   1. the case was tried by a jury, or
   2. the person knowingly and intelligently waived the right to have the case tried by a jury, by guilty plea or otherwise.

In addition, a conviction would not be disabling if it has been expunged or set aside, or is an offense for which the person has been pardoned or has had civil rights restored (if the law of the jurisdiction in which the proceedings were held provides for the loss of civil rights upon conviction for such an offense) unless the pardon, expunction, or restoration of civil rights expressly provides that the person may not ship, transport, possess, or receive firearms, and the person is not otherwise prohibited by the law of the jurisdiction in which the proceedings were held from receiving or possessing firearms. 18 U.S.C. 921(a)(33), 27 CFR 478.11.

*[Editor's note: A significant number of people make the mistake of overlooking or forgetting about a court issue or family law judicial proceeding. However, if you meet the above criteria, you are federally disqualified from possessing a firearm.*

## FREQUENTLY ASKED QUESTIONS FROM ATF WEBSITE

*The fact that it may have happened a long time ago, or that you did not understand the ramifications, is legally irrelevant.*

**Q: What is the effective date of this disability?**
**A:** The law was effective September 30, 1996. However, the prohibition applies to persons convicted of such misdemeanors at any time, even if the conviction occurred prior to the law's effective date.

*[Editor's note: For those wondering why this is not an unconstitutional ex-post facto law, multiple federal appeals courts have ruled against that argument and the Supreme Court has consistently declined to review any of those cases, effectively accepting the ruling of the courts of appeals and upholding the law.]*

**Q: X was convicted of misdemeanor assault on October 10, 1996, for beating his wife. Assault has as an element the use of physical force, but is not specifically a domestic violence offense. May X lawfully possess firearms or ammunition?**
**A:** No. X may not legally possess firearms or ammunition. 18 U.S.C. 922(g)(9), 27 CFR 478.32(a)(9).

*[Editor's note: In this situation because X's conviction for assault was against a person in the statute's protected class, the conviction would be, for purposes of firearms purchasing disqualification, a domestic violence conviction.]*

**Q: X was convicted of a misdemeanor crime of domestic violence on September 20, 1996, 10 days before the effective date of the statute. He possesses a firearm on October 10, 2004. Does X lawfully possess the firearm?**
**A:** No. If a person was convicted of a misdemeanor crime of domestic violence at any time, he or she may not lawfully possess firearms or ammunition on or after September 30, 1996. 18 U.S.C. 922(g)(9), 27 CFR 478.32(a)(9).

**Q: In determining whether a conviction in a State court is a "conviction" of a misdemeanor crime of domestic violence, does Federal or State law apply? (continued on next page)**

## FREQUENTLY ASKED QUESTIONS FROM ATF WEBSITE

**A:** State law applies. Therefore, if the State does not consider the person to be convicted, the person would not have the Federal disability. 18 U.S.C. 921(a)(33), 27 CFR 478.11.

*Q: Is a person who received "probation before judgment" or some other type of deferred adjudication subject to the disability?*
**A:** What is a conviction is determined by the law of the jurisdiction in which the proceedings were held. If the State law where the proceedings were held does not consider probation before judgment or deferred adjudication to be a conviction, the person would not be subject to the disability. 18 U.S.C. 921(a)(33), 27 CFR 478.11.

*Q: What State and local offenses are "misdemeanors" for purposes of 18 U.S.C. 922(d)(9) and (g)(9)?*
**A:** The definition of misdemeanor crime of domestic violence in the GCA (the Gun Control Act of 1968) includes any offense classified as a "misdemeanor" under Federal or State law. In States that do not classify offenses as misdemeanors, the definition includes any State or local offense punishable by imprisonment for a term of 1 year or less or punishable by a fine. For example, if State A has an offense classified as a "domestic violence misdemeanor" that is punishable by up to 5 years imprisonment, it would be a misdemeanor crime of domestic violence. If State B does not characterize offenses as misdemeanors, but has a domestic violence offense that is punishable by no more than 1 year imprisonment, this offense would be a misdemeanor crime of domestic violence. 18 U.S.C. 921(a)(33), 27 CFR 478.11.

*Q: Are local criminal ordinances "misdemeanors under State law" for purposes of sections 922(d)(9) and (g)(9)?*
**A:** Yes, assuming a violation of the ordinance meets the definition of "misdemeanor crime of domestic violence" in all other respects.

*Q: For an offense to qualify as a "misdemeanor crime of domestic violence," must it have as an element the relationship part of the definition (e.g., committed by a spouse, parent, or guardian)?*

## FREQUENTLY ASKED QUESTIONS FROM ATF WEBSITE

**A:** No. The "as an element" language in the definition of "misdemeanor crime of domestic violence" only applies to the use of force provision of the statute and not the relationship provision. However, to be disabling, the offense must have been committed by one of the defined parties. 18 U.S.C. 921(a)(33), 27 CFR 478.11.

*[Editor's note: This basically means that if illegal force was used against another person, regardless of the language in the underlying statute, if the illegal force was used against a member of the protected class under the statute, federal law will deem this as satisfying the requirements and disqualify the individual from purchasing and possessing firearms.]*

*Q: What should an individual do if he or she has been convicted of a misdemeanor crime of domestic violence?*
**A:** Individuals subject to this disability should immediately dispose of their firearms and ammunition. ATF recommends that such persons transfer their firearms and ammunition to a third party who may lawfully receive and possess them, such as their attorney, a local police agency, or a Federal firearms dealer. The continued possession of firearms and ammunition by persons under this disability is a violation of law and may subject the possessor to criminal penalties. In addition, such firearms and ammunition are subject to seizure and forfeiture. 18 U.S.C. 922(g)(9) and 924(d)(1), 27 CFR 478.152.

*Q: Does the disability apply to law enforcement officers?*
**A:** Yes. The Gun Control Act was amended so that employees of government agencies convicted of misdemeanor crimes of domestic violence would not be exempt from disabilities with respect to their receipt or possession of firearms or ammunition. Thus, law enforcement officers and other government officials who have been convicted of a disqualifying misdemeanor may not lawfully possess or receive firearms or ammunition for any purpose, including performance of their official duties. The disability applies to firearms and ammunition issued by government agencies, purchased by government employees for use in performing their official duties, and personal firearms and

**FREQUENTLY ASKED QUESTIONS FROM ATF WEBSITE**

ammunition possessed by such employees. 18 U.S.C. 922(g)(9) and 925(a)(1), 27 CFR 478.32(a)(9) and 478.141.

*Q: Is an individual who has been pardoned, or whose conviction was expunged or set aside, or whose civil rights have been restored, considered convicted of a misdemeanor crime of domestic violence?*
A: No, as long as the pardon, expungement, or restoration does not expressly provide that the person may not ship, transport, possess, or receive firearms.

*For more information, see www.atf.gov.*

**PRACTICAL LEGAL TIP**

If you or a loved one are going through court proceedings involving family issues and a restraining or protective order is entered in your case, it can suspend your ability to purchase or possess firearms. Language in the court order prohibiting any acts of family violence, whether or not family violence actually occurred,  make it so the person whom the other impacts is legally barred from the purchase or possession of any firearm. Believe it or not, the Family Courts have the ability to suspend your Second Amendment rights. — *Matt*

8. <u>Illegal aliens or aliens admitted under a non-immigrant visa</u>
Persons who are illegally in the United States may not legally purchase, possess, or transport firearms. Generally, non-immigrant aliens are also prohibited from legally purchasing, possessing, or transporting firearms.

*Exceptions for nonimmigrant aliens*
However, a nonimmigrant alien who has been admitted under a non-immigrant visa is not prohibited from purchasing, receiving, or possessing a

firearm if the person falls within one of the following exceptions:

1.   if the person was admitted to the United States for lawful hunting or sporting purposes or is in possession of a hunting license or permit lawfully issued in the United States;
2.   if the person is an official representative of a foreign government who is accredited to the United States Government or the Government's mission to an international organization having its headquarters in the United States;
3.   if the person is an official representative of a foreign government who is *en route* to or from another county to which that alien is accredited;
4.   if the person is an official of a foreign government or a distinguished foreign visitor who has been so designated by the Department of State;
5.   if the person is a foreign law enforcement officer of a friendly foreign government entering the United States on official law enforcement business;
6.   if the person has received a waiver from the prohibition from the Attorney General of the United States.

*See* 18 U.S.C. § 922(y).

## III.   State law disqualifications: who cannot buy a firearm under state law?

As mentioned earlier, Georgia has restrictions on the sale, transfer, and possession of firearms that are separate and distinct from the federal restrictions. If a person runs afoul of the law, they could potentially face prosecution in both state and federal court.

### A.   *Georgia law disqualifications for "purchasing" a firearm*

As previously explained, minors in Georgia (those individuals under the age of 18) may not purchase a firearm (meaning handgun or long gun) under Georgia (or federal) law, but under certain exceptions may possess handguns, and are under no restrictions to possess long guns, even though they may not purchase them. Georgia also restricts the purchase of firearms by convicted felons or individuals serving a probationary sentence as a 'first offender'. A convicted felon is easy enough to understand, but what is a first offender?

The law in Georgia allows an individual who has pled guilty or been found guilty of a first felony conviction to undergo a period of probation, with oversight by a probation officer under the First Offender

Act, O.C.G.A. § 42-8-60. If the probationer completes all the conditions of his or her sentence successfully and without reoffending, the judge will discharge the defendant without a sentence of guilt. There is no conviction (O.C.G.A. § 42-8-62).

While on probation, however, a first offender probationer "who receives, possesses, or transports a firearm" is guilty of a felony, and may be sentenced from one to five years in prison. O.C.G.A. § 16-11-131. The same rule—and punishment—applies to a convicted felon: no receipt, possession, or transport of a firearm. The "felony" may be any felony in Georgia, any of the other 49 states, any federal law violation, or a felony violation in a foreign country. If the offense for which the defendant has been convicted or placed on first offender probation is a forcible felony, there is a mandatory five-year sentence.

B.  *Georgia law disqualifications for "possessing" firearms*
Similar to the disqualifications for purchasing firearms under federal law, the Official Code of Georgia also includes prohibitions on the possession of firearms. We know that convicted felons and first offender probationers may not possess firearms in Georgia. We also know that O.C.G.A. § 16-11-132 prohibits minors from possessing handguns; it does not prohibit minors from possessing long guns, however. In addition, there are the exceptions we have previously discussed that allow a minor to possess a handgun in Georgia (see section I(F) earlier in this chapter).

Note: even though a person may not be disqualified from possession of a firearm under state law, that person may nevertheless still be disqualified to possess a firearm under federal law.

1.  Illegal to sell to felons
If a seller knows that a buyer has been convicted of a felony, they may not legally sell that other person a firearm under federal law. Those who violate this law may be found guilty of unlawfully transferring a firearm to a felon under federal law.

2.  Will my juvenile record prevent me from purchasing and possessing a firearm?
Generally, if any person, including a juvenile, has been convicted of a crime which carries a punishment of imprisonment for more than one year, then that person will not be permitted to purchase a firearm under either federal or Georgia law unless their firearm rights are re-

stored. *See* 18 U.S.C. § 922(g); and *United States v. Walters,* 359 F.3d 340 (4th Cir. 2004).

## IV. Understanding "private sales" laws

As mentioned earlier, Georgia has restrictions on the sale, transfer, and possession of firearms that are separate and distinct from the federal restrictions. If a person runs afoul of the law, they could potentially face prosecution in both state and federal court.

### A. *What are the legal restrictions on "private sales" of firearms?*

Private individuals may legally buy, sell, gift, or otherwise transfer firearms to another private individual in Georgia. However, when doing so, careful attention needs to be paid to not violate the laws regulating these transactions. So what are the legal restrictions? First, the ATF website has an informative pamphlet entitled "Best Practices: Transfers of Firearms by Private Sellers" located on its website. This pamphlet should be a must-read before entering into a "private sale" transaction involving a firearm. So what are the rules in Georgia regarding private sales?

#### 1. Residency requirements

Georgia law allows residents of Georgia to purchase rifles and shotguns in "any state of the United States," so long as the resident complies with all federal laws and laws of Georgia and the purchaser's state (O.C.G.A. § 10-1-100), and non-residents may purchase rifles and shotguns in Georgia (O.C.G.A. § 10-1-101). In order for the private sale of a handgun to be legal in Georgia, however, both parties must reside in the same state. This means, for our purposes, that both the buyer and seller of the handgun must be Georgia residents. Similarly, under federal law, an unlicensed (non-dealer) may only "transfer" a firearm to another unlicensed person in the same state. This means that if a person is a resident of Georgia, federal law prohibits the person from directly (not through a dealer) selling or transferring the firearm to a resident of another state.

Federal law makes these transactions illegal from both the buyer/transferee and seller/transferor perspective. It is illegal for a private individual to transport into or receive within his own state a firearm which was purchased in another state from a private seller. *See* 18 U.S.C. § 922(a)(3). Likewise, it is illegal for a private seller to sell or deliver a firearm to an individual whom the private seller knows or has reason to believe is not a resident of the seller's state. *See* 18 U.S.C. § 922(a)(5).

Example:

> *Bob is visiting his best friend from high school, Jim. Ten years ago after high school was over, Bob moved to Nebraska from Georgia. One night, Bob and Jim decide to go to the shooting range during Bob's trip, and Bob borrows one of Jim's handguns. After shooting at the range, impressed with both the feel and action of Jim's handgun, Bob asks Jim if he could buy it from him. Since they've been friends for so many years, Jim says yes, and even offers him a good price for the transaction. Before leaving to go home to Nebraska, Bob pays Jim and packs his new handgun.*

Has Jim committed a crime in selling the handgun to Bob? Has Bob committed a crime in purchasing the handgun from Jim? The answer to both questions is yes! Under federal law, Bob is not allowed to privately purchase a handgun in another state and transport it back to his home state. Likewise, Jim is not allowed to sell a firearm legally to a person he knows lives in another state. In this example, both Bob and Jim know that Bob is not a Georgia resident—the place where Jim has sold his firearm. Bob has committed the crime of willful receipt of a firearm from out-of-state by an unlicensed person, while Jim has committed the federal crime of willful sale of a firearm to an out-of-state resident. *See* 18 U.S.C. § 924(a)(1)(D). The penalties for these crimes include jail time up to 5 years and/or a fine of $250,000!

What if the situation is less obvious? Let's take a look at an example where "reasonable cause to believe" comes into play.

Example:

> *Frank, a Georgia resident, recently posted his Glock 19 for sale on an internet message board in Georgia. Frank receives an email from a person named Ted who would like to buy the handgun. Frank and Ted agree, via email, on a purchase price and arrange to meet at a place in Georgia one week later to facilitate the transfer. When Ted pulls up in his 1978 Ford LTD Wagon, Frank notices the car's Tennessee license plates. Nevertheless, Frank shrugs and sells Ted the gun anyway without going through any of the formalities of a bill-of-sale, or asking for identification. Two weeks later, Frank finds himself at an FBI field office in Atlanta an-*

*swering questions about a shooting that took place with his (former) Glock 19.*

Is Frank in trouble? It is highly likely. Although Frank is not the center of the shooting investigation, Frank is probably the center of an investigation for illegally selling the firearm to an out-of-state resident under federal law.

### 2. Private sales: don't knowingly sell to the "wrong" people

A private individual may sell a firearm to a private buyer in the same state so long as the seller does not know or have reasonable cause to believe that the person purchasing the firearm is prohibited from possessing or receiving a firearm under federal or state law. *See* 18 U.S.C. § 922(d). Also, see discussion in the previous sections on "disqualifications."

Example:

> *Gordon and Josh are friends and Josh tells Gordon that he has just attempted to buy a gun from a local FFL and that he was denied because he was disqualified for some reason under federal law (something about a conviction or restraining order or drug use or psychiatric problems—Josh was too mad to remember!). Gordon says, "no problem, I'll just sell you one of mine," and he does.*

Gordon has just committed a federal and state crime, because he knew (or at least had reasonable cause to believe) that Josh was prohibited from purchasing a firearm under the law. See our earlier discussion concerning disqualifications.

### B. *How does the law determine a person's residence when buying or selling a firearm?*

#### 1. Individuals with one residence

For the purpose of firearms purchases, the person's state of residence is the state in which the person is present and where the individual has an intention of making a home. 27 CFR § 478.11.

#### 2. What if a person maintains a home in two states?

If a person maintains a home in two (or more) states and resides in those states for periods of the year, he or she may, during the period of time the person actually resides in a particular state, purchase a firearm in that state. However, simply owning property in another state does not qualify a person as a resident of that state so as to purchase a firearm in that state. To meet the residency requirements, a person must actually maintain a home in a state which includes an intention to make a particular state a residence. *See* 27 CFR § 478.11. This issue may ultimately be a fact question with evidence of residency being things like a driver's license, insurance records, recurring expenses in the state, as well as other things related to making a particular state a person's residence.

### 3.   Members of the Armed Forces

A member of the Armed Forces on active duty is a resident of the state in which his or her permanent duty station is located. If a member of the Armed Forces maintains a home in one state and the member's permanent duty station is in a nearby state to which he or she commutes each day, then the member has two states of residence and may purchase a firearm in either the state where the duty station is located or the state where the home is maintained. *See* 18 U.S.C. § 921(b). *See also* ATF FAQs on residency at www.atf.gov.

### 4.   Nonimmigrant aliens

Persons who are legally present in the United States are residents of the state in which they reside and where they intend to make a home. Such persons, provided they meet all other requirements and are not otherwise prohibited from purchasing a firearm are lawfully permitted to purchase a firearm.

### C.   *Suggestion on how to document a private firearms sale*

Protect yourself! This is practical advice that should not be ignored. If you engage in the private sale of a firearm, here are some practical tips:

- Ask for identification whether you are the buyer/transferee or seller/transferor to establish residency;
- Get and/or give a "bill of sale" for the transfer and keep a copy—identify the firearm including make, model, and serial number, as well as the date and place of transfer;
- Put the residency information on the "bill of sale" including names, addresses, and phone numbers;
- Do not sell or transfer a firearm or ammunition if you think the person may not be permitted or is prohibited from receiving the firearm.

Why do this? Not only will it help establish residency, but if you unfortunately happen to buy or sell a firearm that was previously used in a crime, or if you sell or transfer a gun that is later used in a crime, you want to be able to establish when you did and did not own or possess the firearm.

Further, as a matter of good course, if you are a seller or transferor in a private sale, you might ask whether there is any reason the buyer/transferee cannot own a firearm. Why? So that if there is an issue later, you can at a minimum say that you had no reason to know the buyer could not legally possess firearms. However, do not overlook behavior that may indicate the buyer is not telling you the truth, because law enforcement will not overlook facts that show you did know, or should have had reasonable cause to believe that the buyer/transferee could not own a firearm at the time of the transfer if a legal issue arises later.

## V.   Buying, selling, and transferring through an FFL
### A.   *Basic procedures*
Persons purchasing firearms through dealers must comply with all legal requirements imposed by federal law. These include both paperwork, and appropriate background checks or screenings to ensure that the purchaser is not prohibited from the purchase or possession of a firearm under federal law.

When purchasing through a dealer, the first thing a prospective buyer will do is select a firearm. Once a selection has been made, the prospective purchaser is required to show proper identification and complete ATF Form 4473. This form requires the applicant, under penalty of law, to provide accurate identifying information, as well as answer certain questions in order to establish whether a person may legally purchase a firearm. The information provided on Form 4473 is then provided to the National Instant Criminal Background Check System (NICS) for processing and approval in order to proceed with the transfer (however, no NICS background may be required if the transferee is legally exempt for reasons such as possessing a state-issued firearms license like a Georgia Weapons Carry License). A FFL dealer can submit the check to NICS either by telephone or through the online website and only after the FFL completes all of these steps successfully is a purchaser/transferee allowed to take possession of the firearm.

B. *What is Form 4473?*
ATF Form 4473 is the ATF's form known as a Firearms Transaction Record that must be completed when a person purchases a firearm from an FFL. *See* 27 CFR § 478.124. Form 4473 requires the applicant to provide their name, address, birth date, state of residence, and other information including government issued photo identification. The form also contains information blanks to be filled-in including the NICS background check transaction number, the make, model, and serial number of the firearm to be purchased, and a series of questions that a person must answer. *See* 27 CFR § 478.124(c). This series of questions and the corresponding answers help determine a purchaser's eligibility under federal law to purchase a firearm. Once the form is completed, the prospective purchaser will sign the form and attest that the information provided thereon is truthful and accurate under penalty of federal law. This means that if you lie or make false statements on this form, the Feds can and will prosecute you for a crime!

Likewise, the dealer must also sign Form 4473 and retain it for at least 20 years. The ATF is permitted to inspect, as well as receive a copy of Form 4473 from the dealer both during audits and during the course of a criminal investigation. The 4473 records must be surrendered to the Bureau of Alcohol, Tobacco, Firearms and Explosives in the event the FFL dealer retires or ceases business.

C. *How are background checks administered when purchasing a firearm?*
    1. NICS: National Instant Criminal Background Check System
Background checks by dealers when transferring firearms are completed through the National Instant Criminal Background Check System or NICS, if required, prior to the transfer of a firearm from an FFL dealer to a non-dealer. When the prospective purchaser/transferee's information is given to NICS, the system will check the applicant against at least three different databases containing various types of records. Applicants are checked against the records maintained by the Interstate Identification Index (III) which contains criminal history records, the National Crime Information Center (NCIC) which contains records including warrants and protective orders, as well as the NICS Index which contains records of individuals who are prohibited from purchasing or possessing firearms under either federal or state law. In addition, if the applicant is not a United States Citizen, the application is processed for an Immigration Alien Query

(IAQ) through the Department of Homeland Security's Immigration and Customs Enforcement Division.

2. Responses from NICS

NICS responses to background checks come in three basic forms: proceed, delay, or deny. The "proceed" response allows for the transfer to be completed. The "delay" response means that the transfer may not legally proceed. If the dealer receives a response of "delay," NICS has three business days to research the applicant further. If the dealer has not received a notice that the transfer is denied after the three business days, then the transfer may proceed. "Deny" means the transfer does not take place; a transferee's options after a "deny" are discussed below.

3. What transactions require background checks?

A background check is required before each and every sale or other transfer of a firearm from an FFL to a non-licensee unless an exception is provided under the law. For every transaction that requires a background check, the purchaser/transferee must also complete ATF Form 4473. This includes:
- The sale or trade of a firearm;
- The return of a consigned firearm;
- The redemption of a pawned firearm;
- The loan or rental of a firearm for use off of an FFL's licensed premises;
- Any other non-exempt transfer of a firearm.

## PRACTICAL LEGAL TIP

Thinking about buying a gun on behalf of your buddy? Not a good idea! One of the purposes of ATF Form 4473 is to conduct a background check on individuals who want to purchase firearms in order to make sure they are legally allowed to do so. Acting as a "straw man" by purchasing it for your buddy circumvents this process and is a crime. — *Matt*

### 4. What transactions do not require background checks?

Under the law, a background check is not required under the following circumstances:

- The sale or transfer of a firearm where the transferee presents a valid state permit/license that allows the transferee to carry a firearm (for example, a Georgia Weapons Carry License) from the state where the FFL is located and the state permit/license is recognized by the ATF as a qualifying alternative to the background check requirement;
- The transfer of a firearm from one FFL to another FFL;
- The sale of a firearm to a law enforcement agency or a law enforcement officer for official duties if the transaction meets the specific requirements of 27 CFR § 478.134 including providing a signed certification from a person in authority on agency letterhead stating that the officer will use the firearm in official duties and where a records check reveals the officer does not have any misdemeanor convictions for domestic violence;
- The return of a repaired firearm to the person from whom it was received;
- The transfer of a replacement firearm of the same kind and type to the person from whom a firearm was received;
- The transfer of a firearm that is subject to the National Firearms Act if the transfer was pre-approved by the ATF.

Note: A Georgia Weapons Carry License currently qualifies as an alternative to the NICS background check requirement as long as the license was issued within 5 years of the date of the transfer. A complete permit chart for all states is available on the ATF's website at www.atf.gov.

### 5. If a person buys multiple handguns, a dealer must report that person to the ATF

Under federal law, FFLs are required to report to the ATF any sale or transfer of two or more pistols, revolvers, or any combination of pistols and revolvers totaling two or more to an unlicensed (non-FFL) individual that takes place at one time or during any five consecutive business days. This report is made to the ATF on Form 3310.4 and is completed in triplicate with the original copy sent to the ATF, one sent to the designated State police or local law enforcement agency in the jurisdiction where the sale took place, and one retained by the dealer and held for no less than five years.

6. **FFLs must report persons who purchase more than one rifle in southwest border states**

In Texas, Arizona, New Mexico, and California, dealers are required to report the sale or other transfer of more than one semiautomatic rifle capable of accepting a detachable magazine and with a caliber greater than .22 (including .223 caliber/5.56 millimeter) to an unlicensed person at one time or during any five consecutive business days. *See* 18 U.S.C. § 923(g)(3)(A). This report is made via ATF Form 3310.12 and must be reported no later than the close of business on the day the multiple sale or other disposition took place. This requirement includes (but is not limited to) purchases of popular semiautomatic rifles such as AR-15s, AK-47s, Ruger Mini-14s, and Tavor bullpup rifles.

## VI.  What if I'm denied the right to purchase a firearm?

A.  *If I am denied the right to purchase, how do I appeal?*

Persons who believe they have been erroneously denied or delayed a firearm transfer based on a match to a record returned by the NICS may request an appeal of their "deny" or "delay" decision. All appeal inquiries must be submitted to the NICS Section's Appeal Service Team (AST) in writing, either online or via mail on the FBI's website at www.fbi.gov. An appellant must provide their complete name, complete mailing address, and NICS Transaction Number. For persons appealing a delayed transaction, a fingerprint card is required and must be submitted with the appeal, although the fingerprint card is merely recommended on appeals for denied applications. This may seem counter-intuitive, but it is required per the FBI's website.

B.  *What if I keep getting erroneously delayed or denied when I am attempting to buy a firearm?*

Apply for a PIN (personal identification number) that is designed to solve this issue. Some individuals may have a name which is common enough (or happens to be flagged for other reasons) that it causes undue delays or denials in the background check verification process through NICS. For that reason, NICS maintains the Voluntary Appeal File database (VAF) which allows any applicant to apply by submitting an appeal request and then obtain a UPIN or Unique Personal Identification Number. A person who has been cleared through the VAF and receives a UPIN will then be able to use their UPIN when completing Form 4473 in order to help avoid further erroneous denials or extended delays. A person can obtain a UPIN by following the procedures outlined on the FBI's website at www.fbi.gov.

## VII. Additional considerations in firearms purchasing and possession laws

A. *How can I legally purchase a firearm from someone in another state?*

Any individual who wishes to purchase a firearm from a person that lives in another state than the purchaser must complete the transaction through an FFL.

Sellers or transferors are legally authorized to facilitate a private transaction or transfer by shipping the firearm to the purchaser's FFL in the recipient/buyer's state, where the FFL will complete the transfer process. It is a federal crime to sell or transfer a firearm between persons who are residents of different states, or where a transfer takes place in a state other than the transferee/transferor's singular state of residence.

B. *Can I purchase firearms on the Internet?*

Yes. However, all legal requirements for a transfer must be followed. If the buyer and seller are both residents of Georgia, then the two may lawfully conduct a private sale so long as all other legal issues are satisfied (see our earlier discussion on disqualifications to purchasing and possessing firearms in this chapter). However, if buyer and seller are not residents of the same state, the transaction can only be legally facilitated through the intervention of an FFL.

C. *Shipping firearms*

1. Can I ship my firearm through the postal service?

Long guns: yes. Handguns: no. Under federal law, a non-licensed individual may not transfer (and this would include shipping to someone) a firearm to a non-licensed resident (non-FFL) of another state. However, a non-licensed individual may mail a long gun to a resident of his or her own state, and they may also mail a long gun to an FFL of another state. To that end, the USPS recommends that long guns be mailed via registered mail and that the packaging used to mail the long gun be ambiguous so as to not identify the contents. Handguns are not allowed to be mailed through USPS. *See* 18 U.S.C. §§ 1715, 922(a)(3), 922(a)(5), and 922(a)(2)(A). Rather, handguns must be shipped using a common or contract carrier (*e.g.*, UPS or FedEx).

### 2. Shipping handguns and other firearms through a common or contract carrier

Under federal law, a non-licensed individual may ship a firearm (including a handgun) by a common or contract carrier (*i.e.,* UPS or FedEx) to a resident of his or her own state, or to a licensed individual (FFL) in another state. However, it is illegal to ship any firearm to a non-FFL in another state. It is a requirement that the carrier be notified that the shipment contains a firearm, however, carriers are prohibited from requiring any identifying marks on the package which may be used to identify the contents as containing a firearm. *See* 18 U.S.C. §§ 922(a)(2)(A), 922(a)(3), 922(a)(5), 922(e), 27 CFR 478.31 and 478.30.

### D. *Can I ship my firearm to myself for use in another state?*

Yes. In accordance with the law as described in the preceding section, a person may ship a firearm to himself or herself in care of another person in another state where he or she intends to hunt or engage in other lawful activity. The package should be addressed to the owner and persons other than the owner should not open the package and take possession of the firearm.

### E. *If I am moving out of the state of Georgia, may I have movers move my firearms?*

Yes, a person who lawfully possesses firearms may transport or ship the firearms interstate when changing the person's state of residence so long as the person complies with the requirements for shipping and transporting firearms as outlined earlier. *See* 18 U.S.C. § 922(e) and 27 CFR § 478.31. However, certain NFA items such as destructive devices, machine guns, short-barreled shotguns or rifles, and so forth require approval from the ATF before they can be moved interstate. *See* 18 U.S.C. § 922(a)(4) and 27 CFR § 478.28. It is important that the person seeking to move the firearms also check state and local laws where the firearms will be relocated to ensure that the movement of the firearms into the new state does not violate any state law or local ordinance.

### F. *May I loan my firearm to another person?*

There is no prohibition on loaning a firearm to another person, so long as the person receiving the firearm may lawfully possess one. However, under Georgia law, O.C.G.A. § 16-11-101.1(b) states that it is unlawful for a person intentionally, knowingly, or recklessly to sell or furnish a pistol to any child younger than 18 years of age.

G. *What happens to my firearms when I die?*

Depending on the manner in which a person leaves his or her estate behind, firearms may be bequeathed in a customary manner like other personal property. However, firearms held in an estate are still subject to the laws of transfer and possession. This careful consideration needs to be given in estate planning for firearms law of both the jurisdiction in which the estate is located as well as to who is to receive the firearms.

## VIII. Ammunition: the law of purchasing and possession

A. *Who is legally prohibited from purchasing ammunition under federal law?*

Under federal law, there are six primary situations where a person is prohibited from buying, selling, or possessing ammunition (beyond armor-piercing ammunition which was discussed in chapter 2).

1. Under 18 U.S.C. § 922(b)(1), it is unlawful for a person to sell long gun ammunition to a person under the age of 18;
2. Under 18 U.S.C. § 922(b)(1), it is unlawful for a person to sell handgun ammunition to a person under the age of 21;
3. Under 18 U.S.C. § 922(x)(2)(B), it is unlawful for a juvenile to possess handgun ammunition;
4. Under 18 U.S.C. § 922(d), it is unlawful to sell ammunition to a person who is prohibited from purchasing firearms;
5. Under 18 U.S.C. § 922(g), it is unlawful for a person who is disqualified from purchasing or possessing firearms to possess firearm ammunition if such ammunition has moved in interstate commerce (which is nearly all ammunition); and
6. Under 18 U.S.C. § 922(h), it is unlawful for a person who is employed by a person who is disqualified from purchasing or possessing ammunition to possess or transport ammunition for the disqualified individual.

For the statutes that involve juveniles, there are a couple of notable exceptions to the law: first, the law against selling handgun ammunition to a juvenile and possession of handgun ammunition by a juvenile does not apply to a temporary transfer of ammunition to a juvenile or to the possession or use of ammunition by a juvenile if the handgun and ammunition are possessed and used by the juvenile in the course of employment, in the course of ranching or farming-related activities at the residence of the juvenile (or on property used for ranching or farming at which the juvenile, with the permission of the property owner or lessee, is performing activities related to the operation of the farm or ranch), target practice, hunting, or a course of instruction in the safe and lawful use of a handgun. The law also does not apply to the temporary transfer to or use of ammunition by a juvenile if the juvenile has been provided with prior written consent by his or her parent or guardian who is not prohibited by federal, state, or local law from possessing firearms. *See* 18 U.S.C. § 922(x)(3).

Additionally, juveniles who (1) are members of the Armed Forces of the United States or the National Guard who possess or are armed with a handgun in the line of duty, (2) receive ammunition by inheritance, or (3) possess ammunition in the course of self-defense or defense of others are permitted to possess ammunition.

<u>There are no real restrictions to the purchase, possession, or sale of ammunition in Georgia.</u>

B.  *Can a person be disqualified from purchasing ammunition if they are disqualified from purchasing firearms?*
Yes, under federal law. Under 18 U.S.C. § 922(g) it is unlawful for a person who is disqualified from purchasing or possessing firearms if the ammunition has moved in interstate commerce. Since nearly all ammunition or ammunition components move through interstate commerce in one form or another, this disqualification includes essentially all ammunition.

C.  *Can a person purchase ammunition that is labeled "law enforcement use only?"*
Yes. Although some handgun ammunition is sold with a label "law enforcement use," such a label has no legal meaning and is only reflective of a company policy or, viewed less positively, as a marketing strategy.

# CHAPTER FOUR

## WHEN CAN I LEGALLY USE MY GUN: PART I.
## UNDERSTANDING THE LAW OF JUSTIFICATION;
## SOME BASIC LEGAL CONCEPTS

### I. Ignorance of the law is NEVER an excuse!

Now we start to get into the meat of our discussion: when is it legal to use a gun as a weapon? The purpose of this chapter is to look at the essential, basic legal concepts of the law of when and under what circumstances a person is legally justified in using force or deadly force against other persons or animals. Know when you may legally shoot, because Georgia law is clear: ignorance is never an excuse! That is why it is critical you know the law so that you are in the best possible situation to preserve your legal rights if you ever need them.

### II. Gun owners need to know the law

Of particular importance to Georgia gun owners are the defenses found in Title 16, Chapter 3 of the Official Code of Georgia, entitled "Defenses To Criminal Prosecution," which we cover in detail throughout this book. The full text of relevant provisions of that chapter of the Official Code of Georgia are found in the Appendix.

### III. To legally use force or deadly force, you must be "justified." What is legal justification?

A. *Basic definition of justification: a legal excuse*

So, when is it legal to use force or deadly force against another person? When is it legal to even threaten to use force or deadly force against another? The answer is when there is a legal "justification." A legal justification is an acceptable reason or excuse under the law for taking an action that would otherwise be a crime. In Georgia, legal justification is a defense to specific types of conduct that might otherwise be a crime.

Example:
> *Mike is forced to change a flat tire on the interstate and, while he is standing near his car, a vicious dog appears from the woods and is clearly about to attack. Mike draws his handgun and shoots the dog.*

Mike has discharged his firearm while standing near a public high-way, which is ordinarily a crime. Why will Mike likely be not guilty of the crime of "discharge of a gun or pistol near a public highway?" Because he was legally justified in shooting the dog! That is, the law will likely say Mike's excuse for discharging his firearm near the high-way—protecting himself from a vicious animal—makes Mike's ac-tion of discharging a firearm near a public highway reasonable and, therefore, legally justified.

---

### PRACTICAL LEGAL TIP

A defense to prosecution is not the same as a bar to prosecution. A "bar to prosecution" is where a person can't be prosecuted for engaging in certain conduct, whereas a "de-fense to prosecution" allows prosecution for the conduct, but offers defendants a justifi-cation that must be demonstrated with evi-dence in court. —*Matt*

---

B.  *Basic requirement: you must admit your action*
If a person wants the potential protection of legal justification in Georgia — in order to raise the defense of justification in court — a person is required to admit all of the elements of the crime for which they are charged except the intent to commit the crime. In other words: you must admit to committing the act, without admit-ting you intended to do so. Then, the person must present evidence of justification before a jury will be given an instruction that "a per-son is legally justified to use force if..." In plain English, a person will not be allowed to say "I didn't do it, but if I did do it, I was justified!" You must admit the underlying elements of the charge.

Example:
*Jane is walking home one night, when a man jumps out of the bushes and demands her purse. Jane pulls out her handgun and points it at the man, who then runs away. Unfortunately, Jane does not call the police, but the crimi-nal immediately does, reporting a crazy woman threaten-ing him with a gun. Jane ends up charged with aggravated assault, even though Jane was the victim.*

Justification is a legal defense in Georgia. If Jane is tried for aggravated assault, she must admit in court that she did pull her handgun and point it at the would-be robber in order to offer a legal justification. Then, in order for the jury to consider a legal justification defense (*i.e.*, receive a jury instruction from the judge), she must offer some evidence of why she is legally justified under the law for having pulled her weapon (in this example, Jane believed she was being robbed). The result is that Jane is entitled to have the judge instruct the jury that they may find Jane not guilty because she was justified in her action. The jury will then decide whether they believe Jane and whether she is guilty or not guilty of the crime of aggravated assault.

---

**PRACTICAL LEGAL TIP**

A jury instruction is a statement or "charge" given to the jury by the judge in a case, informing them of the particular laws that apply in the case. —*Matt*

---

On the other hand, if Jane does not admit to the elements of the criminal offense she is charged with, she will not be allowed to offer a legal justification defense under Georgia law. Legal justification is, therefore, literally the law of "Yes, I did it, BUT...!" Once Jane has admitted the elements of the offense and offered evidence of her justification, the prosecutor must prove her LACK of a justification beyond a reasonable doubt: the burden is always on the state to disprove a defense of justification (more on this later in the book). *See Hall v. State,* 235 Ga. App. 44 (1998).

## IV. Categories of force for justification

Anytime a person makes intentional physical contact with another person, he (or she) has used force. The Official Code of Georgia (our set of laws) divides or categorizes uses of force into different levels. Whether or not a use of force was justified under the law often depends on how that force is categorized. These categories, which we will address throughout this book, are: 1) the threat of force, 2) force, and 3) deadly force.

### A. *What if a person uses greater force than the law allows?*
The use of a legally appropriate level of force is important because if

a person uses more force than is "reasonably believed to be necessary" (see Section V), that person may not be legally justified in using that level of force. It is important to understand the differences in the levels of force and the circumstances under which the law allows the use of each.

For example, if a person uses deadly force, and the law allows only for the use of force, that person will not be legally justified. Likewise, if a person uses force when no force is legally allowed, that use of force will not be legally justified.

Example:
> *Harry Homeowner looks out his window and sees a person standing on his front lawn. Harry yells at the fellow to get off his land. The fellow on the lawn does not respond. Harry rushes out to confront the fellow and demands that he leave Harry's lawn.*

Because this gentleman has remained on Harry's property after Harry has given him an order to leave, he is a trespasser! But what degree of force may Harry use to remove the trespasser? The law, as discussed later, will show that Harry is only allowed to use that degree of force necessary to end the trespass. If Harry uses deadly force against the trespasser, he will not be legally justified and could be found guilty of using unlawful force against the trespasser. Ultimately, using the correct degree of force is critical in determining whether a person has committed a crime or a legally justified action.

## B. *"Force" and "deadly force"*
In order to understand "the threat of force," it's important to start with the concept of force. "Force" is not defined in the Official Code of Georgia; "deadly force," on the other hand, is defined. The State of Georgia has defined deadly force by statute in Official Code of Georgia Annotated § 16-3-21(a) as "force which is intended or likely to cause death or great bodily harm."

### 1. Deadly force does not have to cause death!
On the surface, the legal definition of deadly force seems simple. However, the meaning of what is and is not deadly force can be legally tricky. A particular action does not necessarily have to result in death to be legally defined as deadly force—it just needs to be capable of causing death or great bodily harm.

Example:
> *Jim is being robbed and beaten by a group of individuals when he manages to draw his handgun and fire it at one of the most aggressive assailants. His shot misses his intended target but breaks the group up, causing the would-be robbers to flee.*

In our example, even though the bullet did not kill or even strike any of his assailants, Jim legally used deadly force because his conduct fit the legal definition of "intended or likely to cause death or great bodily harm." Thus, death is not a prerequisite for the existence of deadly force! Likewise, almost any object can be used as a weapon in a particular circumstance. Therefore, in this section of the law, the focus is on the object's intended use and not just on the object itself.

### 2. "Intended or likely" as a component of deadly force
Deadly force, by its legal definition, occurs when a person takes an action that is *intended* or *likely* by the actor to cause death or great bodily harm. This knowledge or intention to cause serious bodily harm or death is called a person's mental state. A prosecutor must prove beyond a reasonable doubt that a person possessed a particular mental state applicable to a crime in order to meet the state's burden of proof and convict someone of a crime.

Often a person's intent is easy to judge by circumstances. For example, if a person is the would-be victim of robbery, and the person resists by pulling his or her gun and firing at the robber, the law will likely find the victim used justifiable deadly force, because the victim of the crime resisted and used force that the victim intended to cause death or great bodily harm.

However, the weapon used is not always dispositive evidence of someone's intent to use deadly force. Hammers, toasters, knives, baseball bats, tire irons, and almost any other object can be "capable of causing" great bodily harm or death under a particular circumstance. The case legally turns, then, on how the person is using the force.

### C. *What are threats of force? "Stop or I will..."*
The law in Georgia allows for the use of force when an individual reasonably believes it necessary to defend himself (or another) against "the imminent use of unlawful force" (*see* O.C.G.A. § 16-3-21, "Use of force in defense of self or others"). Likewise, given the

right circumstances, you may legally threaten the use of deadly force to defend yourself from death, great bodily injury, or from the commission of what is known as a "forcible felony."

Example:

> Billy is walking to his car after work when three individuals with baseball bats confront him in the parking lot and surround him in an aggressive manner. Fearing that they are about to assault him with the bats, Billy draws his gun and clearly demands that the aggressors leave him alone, at which point they all flee from the scene.

Has Billy legally used deadly force by showing his gun? No: Billy has used the threat of deadly force. Billy's threat was to create apprehension that he would use deadly force if necessary. If Billy believed these misguided ballplayers intended the imminent use of force, he could threaten the use of force – and in this case, the use of deadly force – to prevent the attack.

## D.   _Warning shots_

Warning shots get a lot of good folks in legal trouble! Warning shots are commonly portrayed in movies and television as a good idea— and people like to mimic what they see in movies and on TV! Leaving completely aside all practical issues of whether under a particular set of circumstances a warning shot is a good idea (and experience has taught us that very rarely are they a good idea), what does Georgia law say about warning shots?

### 1.   Are warning shots a use of deadly force?

First, the term "warning shot" does not appear in the Official Code of Georgia. Without clear guidance from statutory law, courts are left to determine if the action of firing a warning shot is to be considered under either the use of force standard or the use of deadly force standard.

Although the firing of a warning shot is not _per se_ legally forbidden, you should be aware that if you fire a warning shot, it is highly likely that your conduct will be judged under the legal standard that you have used deadly force and not just mere force. This means that a person may only be allowed the legal argument of justification if a warning shot is fired in situations in which deadly force is justified under the law. There is little appellate court case law demonstrating how Georgia courts have addressed the issue of warning shots. Every gun owner should be aware that one likely argument a prosecutor may put forth against a defendant at trial is that the simple discharge of a firearm is an action that is capable of causing death or serious bodily harm. Such an argument, if successful, will shift the analysis of warning shots into the use of deadly force arena of whether a person intended that action or not.

Why is it important whether the law classifies a warning shot as a use of force or a use of deadly force, even if no one is injured? Let's take a look at an example:

Example:
> *Harry Homeowner looks outside during broad daylight and sees a trespasser on his property. Not knowing what the trespasser is doing, Harry grabs his firearm to investigate. Harry confronts the trespasser and demands that he leave the property, but the trespasser ignores Harry. Being both scared and agitated, Harry fires a "warning shot" to get the trespasser's attention and compliance.*

Does Harry's discharging his gun fit the definition of the use of deadly force? Likely, yes. Harry very likely may be guilty of a crime and not have a justification available as a defense, because he used a higher degree of force than the law allows.

2. Warning shots: "But, I never meant to hurt anyone!"
Going back to our example, assume Harry will say he fired the warning shot, but that he never aimed at or even meant to hit anyone. In fact, assume Harry will say he only shot into the dirt to get the trespasser to leave. How will the law view Harry's "warning shot?"

First, Harry Homeowner was confronted in this example with a mere trespasser and under Georgia law as we will see later, a person may legally use force, but not deadly force to remove a trespasser. Based on our facts, there is no reason for Harry to believe the trespasser intended to commit a forcible felony, which is a requirement for the use of deadly force to prevent a trespass.

Therefore, if the "warning shot" that was fired by Harry is legally classified as deadly force under the law, Harry will not be legally justified, and instead, a jury may decide he is guilty of a crime such as aggravated assault. So, the classification is the difference between guilt and innocence in this example. Now, let us change the example a bit to see how things may get even more complicated:

Example:

> Harry Homeowner confronts the same trespasser (Tom) as before and fires a warning shot. This time, however, the shot startled Tom out of his zoned state of self-meditation and wandering in which he likes to contemplate the universe. Tom was so deep in his personal world, he didn't realize he had accidentally wandered onto Harry's property. In fact, Tom the trespasser was so deep in meditative strolling and enjoying the Georgia air that he didn't even hear Harry's verbal demands, but, the sound of Harry's 30.06 hunting rifle got Tom's full attention! As a result, Tom does exactly what his 25 years of police training have taught him—he draws and fires at Harry, believing that Harry's shot had meant to end his days of strolling and meditation!

Where do we start the legal analysis? First, Harry Homeowner is in what lawyers often call a "big mess!" Harry has very likely used unlawful deadly force against a mere trespasser. After Harry's shot, does this turn our absent-minded wandering Tom into a victim who reasonably believes his life is threatened? Does this fact then allow Tom the trespasser some legal justification to return fire, *etc.*?

Continuing the issue, if our wandering Tom Trespasser then returns fire at Harry, is Harry then legally justified in using deadly force to defend himself? Or, because Tom is an accidental trespasser, is Tom required to retreat first before he takes any action? Keep in mind that Harry knows nothing about Tom's meditation or walks—he is just confronted with a trespasser who did not respond to verbal requests, but has now responded to Harry's "warning shot" with muzzle flashes from a pistol. Ultimately, you can see how messy this type of scenario can become, which all started with a well-intentioned "warning shot."

After the dust clears (assuming perfect knowledge), Harry likely used a higher degree of force than the law allows. But who decides if a "warning shot" is a "warning shot" and not a shot at someone that simply missed? Who decides if a response to a situation is reasonable? In the vast majority of cases in Georgia, a jury ultimately decides. There are no bright lines on warning shots, so be advised that a warning shot can potentially be viewed as a use of deadly force, whether you subjectively intended it to or not, and, therefore, should never be used without careful consideration.

## V. In the law, what does it mean to "reasonably believe force is necessary?"

In Georgia, the legal standard for a justified use of force is generally expressed as a person must "<u>reasonably</u>" believe that the use of force is "<u>necessary</u>" to defend against another's "imminent use of unlawful force."

But what does "reasonable" mean? Further, when is something "necessary"—and who decides whether it is or not? The answers to these questions are how the legal process decides guilt or justification. For all gun owners, these concepts are critical.

### A. *How does the law determine "reasonable?"*

In determining what is reasonable, the law often uses a standard known as the "reasonable person" standard to evaluate a person's conduct. It uses a hypothetical "reasonable person." Who is a reasonable person, and how does he or she act? The reasonable person isn't you; he or she isn't the party you have protected yourself against; the reasonable person isn't even the juror determining what is reasonable. The reasonable person is a hypothetical person who only acts upon deliberation and contemplation: one who acts "reasonably," given all the circumstances. Ultimately, a reasonable person is whoever a jury says it is.

The legal analysis behind the reasonable person goes like this: if a person used force or even deadly force, they must act like a reasonable person would have acted under the same or similar circumstances in order to be legally justified! However, if a person fails to act like a reasonable person, their conduct will fall below the acceptable legal standard and will not be justified. The reasonable person standard is the law's attempt to make the concept of reasonableness an objective and measurable test.

Under this standard, the law does not focus on whether you subjectively (or personally) believed force was reasonable, but whether a "reasonable person" would have considered it reasonable, an objective standard. If the legal system (and ultimately, again, this could be a jury) determines that a reasonable person would have believed that force was necessary in response to another person using unlawful force against you, then you will be found legally justified in using force.

Keep in mind, however, that judges, juries, and prosecutors are simply human beings, and people can have vastly different ideas of how a reasonable person should act under any given circumstances. This is particularly true if asked to decide whether force or deadly force was necessary or not.

> **PRACTICAL LEGAL TIP**
>
> Throughout this book, we refer to juries making the ultimate determination of fact. There are, however, some limited occasions where a judge makes the determinations. For example, if all parties waive their right to a jury, the Court may conduct what is called a "bench trial." —*Matt*

B.  *What does "necessary" mean under the law?*
When does someone have a reasonable belief that force is "necessary"? In Georgia, it ultimately may be a jury that is tasked with determining whether someone had a reasonable belief if an action was necessary or not, given all the circumstances. Clearly, "necessary" attempts to convey a sense of urgency for the use of force, but again, it usually falls back to the jury to decide if this standard was met in a particular case.

C.  *There is no presumption of what is "reasonable": prosecutors are allowed to second-guess*
As we have discussed, the issue of whether a belief of the necessity to use force or deadly force was or was not reasonable is left to the jury, and prosecutors are allowed to question and "second-guess" the reasonableness of the timing and/or degree of force used by a defendant.

Accordingly, because there is no statute in Georgia law that will automatically presume you have acted reasonably when using force or deadly force, a prosecutor has the opportunity to argue that a person's use of that force was neither necessary nor reasonable, given the circumstances. While there is no "duty to retreat" in Georgia

(Georgia in fact has a "stand your ground" law we will discuss later), the lack of a presumption of reasonableness allows for arguments by prosecutors in court like "should have used lesser force," and so forth. In these circumstances, a jury will decide the issue of the reasonableness of a person's belief and whether the force used was necessary, deciding ultimately, whether or not a person is guilty of a crime. As we shall see, though, no matter how much a prosecutor may remonstrate against the acts of a gun owner acting in self-defense or defense of others or property, it is still the government's burden to prove the defendant guilty beyond a reasonable doubt, and to disprove a defendant's defense of justification, if properly submitted to a jury.

## VI.  The burden of proof in criminal cases

In criminal cases, the prosecution (the attorneys who act on behalf of the state) have the burden of proof. This means that it is the State's responsibility to present enough evidence to prove the defendant committed a crime. This burden of proof that the prosecutor bears is a standard called "beyond a reasonable doubt." It is the highest level of proof used in the American justice system. The state's job at trial in attempting to prove the defendant's guilt includes eliminating any reasonable doubt that the defendant's conduct was justified.

We are now ready to look at under what circumstances Georgia law allows a person to use deadly force to protect themselves and others in the next chapter.

### PRACTICAL LEGAL TIP

A word about juries. Juries are not "picked" in Georgia. Rather, they are the first six people that are not "struck" from the pool of folks called a jury pool. Most of the time, in my opinion, juries get it "right," but after years of practice, some juries' decisions leave you scratching your head... That is why these legal presumptions can be critical. — *Matt*

# CHAPTER FIVE

WHEN CAN I LEGALLY USE MY GUN: PART II.
SELF-DEFENSE AND DEFENSE OF OTHERS;
UNDERSTANDING WHEN FORCE AND DEADLY FORCE
CAN BE LEGALLY USED AGAINST ANOTHER PERSON

## I.  Introduction and overview

The question of when a person may legally use deadly force against another is critically important if you are a legal Georgia gun owner. Although a firearm is nothing more than a tool, it is a tool that by its very nature has the ability to deliver deadly force. Thus, all responsible firearms owners should understand when they are justified in using force or deadly force under the law. Failure to understand the law gets lots of good folks in serious trouble!

The primary Georgia statutes dealing with self-defense and defense of other people are contained in three sections of the Official Code of Georgia:

§ 16-3-24.2: Immunity From Prosecution
§ 16-3-21: Use of Force in Defense of Self or Others
§ 16-3-23.1: No Duty to Retreat Prior to Use of Force

The law of justified self-defense found in section 21 includes the use of mere threats of force, the use of force, and the use of deadly force, and the law contained in sections 23.1 and 24.2 clarifies the rights and duties of those who justifiably use any of the three—threats, force, or deadly force. The language of these sections contains Georgia's version of "Stand Your Ground" laws (Georgia's version of the "Castle Doctrine" is found in the Code section dealing with use of force in the defense of habitation, O.C.G.A. § 16-3-23), using the specific term "stand your ground" within the text of the statute.

In the previous chapter, several legal concepts, such as reasonableness, necessity, and the categorization of force and deadly force were discussed. Those concepts have practical applications in this chapter. In this chapter, we will expand upon those topics to include when a person may be justified in using force or deadly force in self-defense, as well as those circumstances when the law specifically prohibits the use of force or deadly force. We will discuss how changes in Georgia law have even granted immunity from prosecution to those who properly rely on these statutes to protect themselves and others from harm.

## II.   O.C.G.A. § 16-3-24.2: Immunity from Prosecution

| IMMUNITY FROM PROSECUTION; EXCEPTION |
| --- |
| **O.C.G.A. § 16-3-24.2.** A person who uses threats or force in accordance with Code Section 16-3-21, 16-3-23, 16-3-23.1, or 16-3-24 shall be immune from criminal prosecution therefor unless in the use of deadly force, such person utilizes a weapon the carrying or possession of which is unlawful by such person under Part 2 of Article 4 of Chapter 11 of this title. |

As a general proposition, Georgia law provides immunity from prosecution for those who use threats or force – and deadly force – in situations where they defend themselves, others, their homes, or their property, in situations where there is no "duty to retreat." Given the proper, lawful circumstances, there would be no question of guilt or innocence: the law would not allow your prosecution, much less authorize a jury to return a verdict.

Shouldn't this be the end of the story—or at least the end of the chapter? It would seem an immunity from prosecution would make any discussion of legal justification and self-defense unnecessary. Unfortunately, that just isn't so. An immunity from prosecution doesn't relieve you from the criminal process in the event you have used your firearm in defense of yourself, others, or your property. A court of competent jurisdiction must determine that you are immune, which means (almost without question) some form of criminal proceeding has begun.

Consider the circumstances: a police officer arrives at your home after you've called 911 to report shooting an armed intruder. You've eliminated the threat to your family; you've called the authorities; you've secured your firearm; and you fully intend to cooperate with the police. Your attacker dies from his wounds before police arrive.

The problem here is simple: only two people know the full story, your assailant and you. At least one of you (the person foolish enough to break into your home) isn't talking. Police only know what you tell them, but law enforcement officers on the scene can't (or won't) typically make a determination you've acted "in the right" without turning the scene over to a supervisor or a detective; procedure must be followed. The detective has rules he or she must follow, so a full investigation begins, and the prosecuting attorney is contacted. Perhaps the prosecutor isn't willing to make a unilateral decision to find you reasonably and justifiably acted in self-defense, so the prosecutor turns the case over to a panel of grand jurors, none of whom were present when your life was threatened.

Who talks to the grand jury? Certainly not you: in Georgia, the subject of a grand jury proceeding is not afforded the right to participate in the proceedings or give evidence to a grand jury (unless that individual is a law enforcement officer who has been accused of a crime during the course of employment as a law enforcement officer; even then, he or she is only allowed to make a statement, and cannot bring an attorney into the proceedings). Your fate at this point is in the hands of strangers who were not present when you acted, and who will not benefit from your first-hand experience. All too often, this scenario results in an indictment for serious felony charges.

Why then is there even the possibility of immunity from prosecution? In Georgia, to prevail on a claim of immunity and avoid trial, a defendant (notice we've said "defendant," a person *accused of a crime,* meaning the criminal process has already begun) bears a burden of showing he or she is entitled to immunity under O.C.G.A. § 16-3-24.2 by a "preponderance of the evidence" standard. *Bunn v. State,* 284 Ga. 410 (2008). A preponderance of the evidence is a level of proof much less than beyond reasonable doubt (what is required for a determination of guilt) but more than probable cause, which is the level of evidence necessary to determine a crime may have been committed, thereby authorizing an arrest. Nevertheless, it is a burden the **defendant** must meet, which is normally not the case in a criminal proceeding, as the defendant has no burden of proof; the burden of proof always rests with the prosecution to prove the offense, as we have discussed.

The decision whether a person is immune from prosecution must be determined by the trial court before the trial commences. *See Bunn* at 412-413. If the judge determines there is no immunity in the defendant's actions during the pre-trial phase (and this decision will be by the judge, not a jury, since juries determine guilt or innocence), he or she may still pursue a justification defense during trial with the jury by using the same evidence, even though these affirmative defenses may be based on the same statutory provisions underlying a prior pre-trial immunity motion. When a defendant raises an affirmative defense and offers evidence in support thereof, the State still has the burden of disproving that defense beyond a reasonable doubt. *Id.* at 413.

The simplest method of discussing immunity, then, is to emphasize it as a bar to prosecution, not arrest. Immunity from prosecution for the proper use of force must be determined by a judge, and if a judge is involved, you have been investigated, possibly arrested, and most certainly indicted and hauled into court. If immunity fails, you can still rely on the defense of justification to your actions in protecting yourself, your family, other persons, and property.

---

### PRACTICAL LEGAL TIP

People often misconstrue immunity from prosecution or justification for an action with freedom from arrest. Remember, police officers usually weren't present to see what happened, and doing their job means securing the scene and those in it. If you find yourself being questioned or under arrest, remain calm and professional; request your attorney; and let your lawyer make the arguments. You stay quiet. —*Matt*

---

## III. Defending people with force or deadly force

### A. *General self-defense justification*

The primary self-defense statute in Georgia is O.C.G.A. § 16-3-21, "Use of force in defense of self or others...." This section establishes that a person is legally justified in using the threat of force, or actual force against another "when and to the extent that he or she reasonably believes that such threat or force is necessary to defend himself or herself or a third person against such other's imminent use of unlawful force."

Likewise, O.C.G.A. § 16-3-21 establishes the general standard for the justified use of deadly force. A person is legally justified in using deadly force ("force which is intended or likely to cause death or great bodily harm") for self-defense "only if he or she reasonably believes that such force is necessary" to protect himself or herself against death "or great bodily injury," or the commission of a forcible felony, which we will discuss soon. As detailed in the previous chapter, what a person believes is necessary and whether that belief is reasonable is the difference between justification (not guilty) and conviction (guilty).

Who decides whether an actor's belief is or is not reasonable that force or deadly force is necessary? Who decides if the degree of force used by someone was reasonable under a particular set of circumstances? The answer to both of these questions is the jury.

Therefore, if a person finds himself or herself facing a criminal charge and is claiming self-defense under the general self-defense provisions of § 16-3-21, the jury will decide if that person's belief was or was not reasonable regarding the immediate necessity of the use of force or deadly force by that person. As can be imagined, this leaves a lot of room for juries to interpret what actions are reasonable or not. It also leaves the door open for legal second-guessing by prosecutors as to when and how much force was used, including arguments that there was no imminent threat and as such, the force or deadly force was not really "necessary." If the prosecutor convinces a jury that a person used force or deadly force when or to a degree that was not "reasonably" believed to be necessary, a person's use of force or deadly force will not be legally justified, and that person could be found guilty by using unlawful force or deadly force.

### B. *Prevention of a "forcible felony"*
If a person is a victim or would-be victim of unlawful force or deadly force, Georgia law allows for the justified use of force or deadly force when and to the degree that the person reasonably believes that it is necessary to protect himself or herself from unlawful force, death, or great bodily injury. Georgia law also justifies the use of deadly force to protect yourself from what is known as a "forcible felony." But what constitutes a forcible felony in Georgia?

### 1. What does forcible felony mean?
To understand "forcible felony," you must first understand what constitutes a felony. In broad terms, crimes in Georgia fall into two categories: misdemeanors and felonies. Misdemeanors carry a maximum fine of $1000 and maximum sentence of twelve months in

custody (there are some special crimes in Georgia called 'high and aggravated misdemeanors' that allow for higher fines but still only a year in jail), and most of the crimes in Georgia fall into this category. Felonies, on the other hand, start with punishment at one year in custody, and can result—in certain circumstances—in an imposition of life in prison, or of the death penalty. The General Assembly (our body of state lawmakers) defines in Georgia whether each criminal charge is a misdemeanor or a felony, and usually includes the designation of each crime in the statute defining that crime.

O.C.G.A. § 16-1-3(5) defines a felony as "a crime punishable by death, by imprisonment for life, or by imprisonment for more than 12 months." A "forcible felony" is described by subsection 6 of the same statute as "any felony which involves the use or threat of physical force or violence against any person." So we know, a forcible felony consists of any crime which threatens or uses physical force or violence, and can be punished by more than 12 months in jail. Wouldn't it be great if our lawmakers would just give us a list of forcible felonies?

## 2.  Georgia has no list of forcible felonies

No such luck: there is no complete list of what are considered forcible felonies in Georgia law. Neither our state lawmakers nor our courts have provided us with a comprehensive idea of what is considered a forcible felony, but some laws point us in the right direction. Let's consider O.C.G.A. § 16-11-131(e), which defines the crime of possession of a firearm by a convicted felon. According to the statute, the term "forcible felony" means:

> any felony which involves the use or threat of physical force or violence against any person and further includes, without limitation, murder; murder in the second degree; burglary in any degree; robbery; armed robbery; home invasion in any degree; kidnapping; hijacking of an aircraft or motor vehicle; aggravated stalking; rape; aggravated child molestation; aggravated sexual battery; arson in the first degree; the manufacturing, transporting, distribution, or possession of explosives with intent to kill, injure, or intimidate individuals or destroy a public building; terroristic threats; or acts of treason or insurrection. O.C.G.A. § 16-11-131(e)

It's not an exhaustive list – it does say "without limitation" – but it gives us a better understanding of what forcible felony means. Let's take a closer look at some of the most well known (and unfortunately common) examples of a forcible felony in Georgia.

### 3. Murder

So, what is murder? O.C.G.A. § 16-5-1 defines murder as any time a person:

- unlawfully and with malice aforethought, either express or implied, causes the death of another human being;
- when, in the commission of a felony... causes the death of another human being; or
- when, in the commission of cruelty to children in the second degree. . . causes the death of another human being (second degree cruelty to children occurs when a person with criminal negligence causes someone under 18 "cruel or excessive physical or mental pain").

How should the law under § 16-3-21 be applied after a self-defense shooting?

Example:
> One busy day at his job, David is working quietly at his desk when he hears an angry voice yell out, "I hate this company, and I'm going to kill every one of you!" About that time, David spots a machete in a deranged-looking stranger's hand. The stranger turns toward David with an evil look. David draws a gun from his desk drawer. As the man continues toward David with the machete raised, David fires two shots at the attacker, killing him.

In this scenario, David would be justified in using force or deadly force when and to the degree he reasonably believes it is necessary to defend himself (or anyone else in harm's way). Here, David skipped mere force and immediately used deadly force. Was this reasonable? Should David have first used non-deadly force? Should he have used a method of dispute resolution? If he could have retreated out of a back door, was his use of deadly force really necessary? These are the types of questions and issues that will be presented to the jury to determine.

However, in this example, because David is about to be a victim of murder, David acted in self-defense, and his use of deadly force should be justified! How do we know David acted in self-defense? In this example, the attacker makes it easy, because he cleared up any ambiguity of his intentions when he declared "I am going to kill every one of you" while wielding a machete. David, as a would-be victim of murder, had a reasonable belief that it was necessary to use force or deadly force against the attacker to prevent his own murder. Therefore, David is legally justified in using deadly force. See also the discussion on "stand your ground" later in this chapter.

If, for some reason, David was ever charged with a crime for killing the would-be murderer, and David puts forth "some evidence" in trial that he was about to be the victim of murder, the jury would then be given a "jury charge"—an instruction from the judge—on self-defense, and then decide whether David acted in self-defense under O.C.G.A. § 16-3-21. For a discussion of the legal concept of "some evidence," see Section C. The jury will be told that if David reasonably believed he was about to be murdered, he was justified in the use of deadly force. The prosecution would then have the burden of establishing beyond a reasonable doubt that David did not act in self-defense (*i.e.,* David did not know or have reason to believe he was about to be murdered). If the jury finds that the prosecution did not meet this burden of proof, it will decide his use of deadly force was legally justified.

But, how does the self-defense statute work when the example is not so clear?

Example:
> Police respond to a two-car collision in a parking lot. When the police arrive, they discover that the collision has sparked a violent road-rage incident. At the scene, one man is dead on the ground with a tire iron beside him. The remaining driver—the shooter—Michael, a man with no previous criminal record, fired two shots and is now a suspect in a murder investigation. Michael claims that the other driver became irate after the collision, threatened him, and aggressively came toward him with the tire iron raised in his hand. However, the position of the physical evidence makes it so that determination of who was the true victim in this incident is unclear. In fact, one investigator thinks Michael is lying. There are no other witnesses.

If Michael ultimately faces criminal charges for murder and claims self-defense at his trial, how does the determination of legal justification work in practice?

In order to receive a jury charge on justification, Michael has the initial burden of producing "some evidence" in court to support that he "knew or had reason to believe" that he was about to be the victim of murder (*e.g.*, the man screamed threats at him and was about to strike him with the tire iron, and Michael was in fear of his life, so he shot the man). If Michael puts forth "some evidence" that the dead man was about to murder him, the law requires the prosecution to then prove beyond a reasonable doubt that the accused (in this case, Michael) did not act in self-defense. *See Anderson v. State,* 262 Ga. 7, 413 S.E.2d 722 (1992), overruled on other grounds, 264 Ga. 253, 443 S.E.2d 626 (1994). The prosecution will have an opportunity to put forth evidence that Michael was not about to be the victim of murder based on the physical evidence found at the scene as well as the investigating officer's testimony, but again, must disprove the defense of justification beyond a reasonable doubt. If the jury believes Michael acted in self-defense to an attempted murder or, more precisely, that the prosecution did not prove beyond a reasonable doubt that Michael did not act in self-defense (read carefully, the law is full of confusing language), he should be found not guilty!

### 4. Kidnapping

If a person is a victim or a would-be victim of kidnapping, a felony in Georgia, he or she will be justified in the use of force or deadly force against the attacker if necessary to defend himself or herself, and if the victim's belief it was necessary was reasonable.

What is kidnapping? Generally, kidnapping occurs anytime a person "abducts or steals away another person without lawful authority... and holds such other person against his or her will." The law finds even "slight movement" of another person against his or her will to be a crime, and violators can be sentenced to life in prison if the crime was committed for ransom, or if the victim received bodily injury during the commission of the kidnapping. This is the definition found in O.C.G.A. § 16-5-40.

Example 1:
> Jane is out jogging one evening, when a white van pulls up
> next to her, and a masked man with a gun jumps out, trying

*to grab her and drag her into his van. Jane pulls out her pepper spray, sprays the man in the face, and runs away to call police.*

Example 2:
*Jane is out jogging one evening, when a white van pulls up next to her, and a masked man with a gun jumps out, trying to grab her and drag her into his van. Jane pulls out her Glock 42 and fires two shots, killing her attacker.*

In the first example, was Jane legally justified in her use of force against the man? What about her use of deadly force in example two? The answer to both is yes. Jane's belief that the use of force (pepper spray) was necessary will justify her actions, because the man in the white van was attempting to commit kidnapping! Likewise, in the second example, Jane's belief that deadly force was necessary would be considered reasonable, and also results in the conclusion that Jane's use of deadly force was justified.

In these hypotheticals, the masked man with the gun was trying to abduct Jane. Whatever his ultimate purpose for trying to grab her, if Jane reasonably believed she was about to be a victim of kidnapping, the law will justify her use of force against the man. These are clear examples, however; we will discuss later how the law is applied in more ambiguous cases.

### 5. Aggravated assault and aggravated battery

Like murder and kidnapping, if a person is the victim of a aggravated assault or aggravated battery, Georgia law allows for the legally justified use of force or deadly force to stop the assault in progress, or prevent its occurrence if it is reasonable to believe the assault is imminent. How does the law define aggravated assault and aggravated battery?

*Aggravated Assault*
O.C.G.A. § 16-5-21 defines aggravated assault as a felony in Georgia. A person commits aggravated assault in the State of Georgia any time that person assaults another a person:
- with the intent to murder, to rape, or to rob;
- with a deadly weapon or with any object... when used offensively... is likely to or actually does result in serious bodily injury; or
- without legal justification by discharging a firearm from

within a motor vehicle toward a person... (otherwise known as a "drive-by shooting").

An individual convicted of aggravated assault may receive up to 20 years in prison for his or her actions, actions for which you may claim a legal justification of self-defense if you oppose, if your defense is a reasonable and necessary reaction to an imminent threat.

*Aggravated Battery*
The crime of aggravated battery under Georgia law is found in § 16-5-24 of the Official Code and is a felony. Aggravated battery is defined as "maliciously causing bodily harm to another by depriving him or her of a member of his or her body, by rendering a member of his or her body useless, or by seriously disfiguring his or her body or a member thereof." O.C.G.A. § 16-5-24. Loss of an eye or finger, a broken bone, even a missing tooth in the proper circumstance may be considered enough to constitute aggravated battery.

   6.  Victims of robbery and armed robbery
Like the other violent crimes found in Georgia law, if a person is a victim or would-be victim of robbery or armed robbery, Georgia law allows the victim to protect himself or herself against the robber with legally justified force or deadly force. Further, like the other crimes listed in these sections, there is no duty to retreat if all statutory requirements are met. How does Georgia law define robbery and armed robbery?

Under O.C.G.A. § 16-8-40, robbery occurs when a person "takes the property of another":
 •  by use of force;
 •  by intimidation, by the use of threat or coercion, or by placing such person in fear of immediate serious bodily injury to himself or to another; or
 •  by sudden snatching.

For a robbery to occur, a robber does not actually have to acquire the property directly from the person: the "immediate presence" of a victim is sufficient, according to statute. Robbery is a forcible felony for which a victim may assert a justification of self-defense under O.C.G.A. § 16-3-21. The same justification will lie in defense of armed robbery, yet another forcible felony defined under O.C.G.A. § 16-8-41 as the taking of property "by use of an offensive weapon, or any replica, article, or device having the appearance of such a weapon." Hand in the pocket that looks like a gun? Armed robbery. Toy gun? Armed robbery. Banana in a paper bag? Armed robbery. The justified use of force will still apply if it is reasonable to believe the use of force or deadly force was necessary to protect against the forcible felony.

Example:
> *Tina is on her way home from work. She stops by a local convenience store for some bread and milk. As she enters the store, a masked man suddenly approaches her with a knife, grabs her by the arm, and demands her money. Tina, scared and shaken, remembers her training, opens her purse and pulls a .357 revolver and fires, killing the masked robber.*

In this example, because an armed robbery was unfolding, Georgia law allows for the justified, legal use of force or deadly force when and to the degree Tina reasonably believes it is necessary to terminate the armed robbery. Thus, her use of deadly force is legally justified. What if the example is less clear?

Example:
> *Hank, a sixty-six year old disabled man, works downtown. He has to park four blocks from his company's office buildings and has to walk through some rough parts of town in order to get to his car. A man suddenly appears in front of him and says, "Hey man—give me some money!" Hank, feeling very frightened and intimidated, walks on with the now more loud and aggressive panhandler demanding, "Hey! Man! I said give me some money!" Hank now becomes extremely concerned for his safety. About that time, Hank makes a wrong turn into an alley where he is cornered. He again hears, "HEY! MAN! I SAID GIVE ME SOME MONEY!" When Hank turns around, he sees the same man, now very aggressive, with something in his hand.*

Is the panhandler just being annoying, or is Hank about to be the victim of robbery or armed robbery? This is the ultimate issue Hank may face if Hank decides to use force or even deadly force against the alleged aggressor. How will the law evaluate a use of deadly force under O.C.G.A. § 16-3-21?

This is an example full of gray area. The man never verbally threatened Hank, nor did he ever physically touch him. All the man said was "give me some money;" he didn't even demand all of Hank's money—just some. Do robbers ever demand just some money? If Hank is in genuine fear of an armed robbery, does he have a duty to retreat? What about the fact that Hank was cornered in an alley? If Hank takes out his legal carry pistol and fires it to defend himself, what happens? Was Hank really about to be robbed, or is he a paranoid trigger-happy fellow as the prosecutor may try to portray him? Beyond that, who decides what the facts really were? This goes to show that there are never bright-line rules in such a situation.

If Hank finds himself charged with unlawfully using force or deadly force against his alleged attacker, he can assert a legal justification based on self-defense. Again, the law will allow Hank to use force or deadly force for self-defense when and to the degree he reasonably believes it is necessary to stop unlawful force—or the use of deadly force—against him. In this example, before a jury will be allowed to decide if Hank acted in self-defense, Hank must present "some evidence" at trial that he reasonably believed he was about to be robbed (see our discussion of what constitutes "some evidence" in Section C). Hank may attempt to satisfy the "some evidence" requirement by testifying that he was in fear for his safety and had seen the panhandler acting violently on the same street many times in the past. Hank may also say the man raised a weapon in his hand and was moving aggressively toward him, and that the assailant out-weighed Hank by 75 pounds and was about a foot taller. Hank will absolutely testify he felt he was being robbed. If Hank puts forth "some evidence" in court that he was the victim of an attempted armed robbery, the jury will get to decide if Hank is credible and if his belief was reasonable, and the law then requires the prosecution to prove beyond a reasonable doubt that Hank did not act in self-defense. However, if Hank fails to put forth "some evidence" that he acted in self-defense, he will not be entitled to a self-defense jury instruction covering O.C.G.A. § 16-3-21, and the jury will not get to decide the issue.

### 7. Hijacking a motor vehicle

Hijacking a motor vehicle (more commonly known as "car-jacking") is yet another forcible felony for which a justification defense may lie in a situation wherein you reasonably believe force or deadly force is necessary to prevent death or great bodily injury. O.C.G.A. § 16-5-44.1 defines hijacking a motor vehicle as an offense where an individual "while in possession of a firearm or weapon obtains a motor vehicle from the person or presence of another by force and violence or intimidation or attempts or conspires to do so." Notice the act must not be completed in order to qualify as a hijacking: a conspiracy or attempt to commit the act will suffice; for purposes of a self-defense justification, this would allow a victim the opportunity to protect himself or herself by use of force—or deadly force, because this is a forcible felony—before the act is complete.

### 8. Burglary

Just as with the other forcible felonies we have discussed, should you find yourself the victim of burglary, Georgia law allows you to protect yourself (and family, home, and property) against the perpetrator with legally justified force or deadly force. It is particularly important to note there is no "duty to retreat" in burglary situations if all statutory requirements are met, and O.C.G.A. § 16-3-23 — Georgia's codification of the Castle Doctrine — will protect you in your home from an attack upon your habitation.

A burglary occurs when, "without authority and with the intent to commit a felony or theft therein, he or she enters or remains within an occupied, unoccupied, or vacant dwelling house of another or any building, vehicle, railroad car, watercraft, aircraft, or other such structure designed for use as the dwelling of another." O.C.G.A. § 16-7-1(b). This is known as burglary in the first degree (one of the few crimes in Georgia to be separated by degree) and may be punished by up to 20 years in prison. Burglary in the second degree occurs when a perpetrator enters a building, structure, vehicle, railroad car, watercraft, or aircraft with the intent to commit a felony or theft. O.C.G.A. § 16-7-1(c). Second-degree burglary may be punished by up to five years in prison.

The definition of second-degree burglary looks just like burglary in the first degree, doesn't it? The difference between the two is the requirement of a "dwelling" in first-degree burglary, a residence, the home of a victim, whereas second-degree burglary contemplates any building not considered a "dwelling" by the definition found in Georgia law.

These crimes merely scratch the surface of what can be considered forcible felonies in Georgia. Arson, terroristic threats (threatening to commit a crime of violence), aggravated stalking (placing another person under surveillance or contacting that person in violation of a court order or restraining order), and sexual offenses such like rape, aggravated child molestation, and aggravated sexual battery are only the beginning to what may be considered forcible felonies in our state. For each of these acts of violence, the law may consider your actions in threatening or using force or deadly force against an assailant when it is reasonable to believe the force you use is necessary to prevent unlawful force, or the prevention of death or great bodily injury. In each case, when the individual seeking the use of a justification defense presents "some evidence" of his or her justification, he or she is entitled to a jury charge on justification, and the prosecution must disprove the justification beyond a reasonable doubt.

C.   *What is "some evidence?"*
So, how much evidence does a person have to offer in a trial to con-stitute "some evidence" in order to be entitled to a jury charge re-garding self-defense? Georgia appeals courts have stated that "[w]here there exists some evidence to support a requested justification charge, it is error to fail to give the charge and the conviction must be reversed. *Jones v. State,* 220 Ga. App. 784 (1996). *See also Williams v. State,* 209 Ga. App. 355 (1993). A defendant could conceivably offer anything as evidence that raises the issue of self-defense, and may then be entitled to receive a jury instruction regarding self-de-fense under O.C.G.A. § 16-3-23. A defendant testifying in court at his own trial that he was attacked first and feared for his life as a result of the attack, would have submitted sufficient evidence—the author believes—to be entitled to a jury instruction on self-defense.

Of course, relying on a defendant's testimony to be the sole source of evidence in order to obtain a jury instruction on self-defense can be fraught with peril as well. All defendants have the right not to tes-tify at their trial—which can be a sound trial tactic in that it prevents the State from examining the defendant under oath and on the wit-ness stand. Once a defendant takes the witness stand, however, that defendant will be subject to examination by not only his attorney, but also by the State, examination which may ultimately contain ev-idence which sways a jury away from seriously considering acquittal on self-defense grounds.

D.   *Georgia's "stand your ground" law*
*In Georgia, "stand your ground" means no duty to retreat!*
"Stand your ground" is a common term for laws that provide an indi-vidual has no legal duty to retreat before using force or deadly force against a person that is a threat. The words "stand your ground" are used in the statute itself, and the language codified in Georgia is

typical of "stand your ground" statutes in many states. In Georgia, you may meet force with force – and deadly force with deadly force – if your actions qualify under the statute. Thus, the existence of no duty to retreat is also a powerful legal tool for any defendant.

The provision establishing no duty to retreat in Georgia is located in the Official Code of Georgia Annotated § 16-3-23.1. This provision will act to limit a prosecutor from arguing in court that a person's use of force or deadly force was not really "necessary" or reasonable because the person could have or should have first retreated.

> A person who uses threats or force in accordance with Code Section 16-3-21, relating to the use of force in self-defense or others, Code Section 16-3-23, relating to the use of force in defense of a habitation, or Code Section 16-3-24, relating to the use of force in defense of property other than a habitation, has no duty to retreat and has the right to stand his or her ground and use force as provided in said Code Sections, *including deadly force.* O.C.G.A. § 16-3-23.1 (emphasis added).

To receive the "Stand Your Ground" protection under this statute, first, a person must satisfy one of the following conditions in the Code:

(1) a use of threat or force (including deadly force) following the rules set out in O.C.G.A. § 16-3-21, which is use of force in self-defense;

(2) a use of threat or force (including deadly force) following the rules set out in O.C.G.A. § 16-3-23, which is use of force in defense of habitation (your home: don't worry, we haven't covered that yet!);

(3) a use of threat or force (including deadly force) following the rules set out in O.C.G.A. § 16-3-24, which is use of force in defense of property other than a habitation (covered in the next chapter with habitations).

At least one of these conditions must be satisfied in order for the "Stand Your Ground" provisions to apply. Further, if a person does not qualify for the "Stand Your Ground" provisions, it does not mean that the person's use of force or deadly force was not legally justified. It simply means that a jury will evaluate whether the person's belief was "reasonable" that the use of force or deadly force was necessary. If a person cannot satisfy at least one requirement, the prosecutor will be free to argue that because the accused could have but did not retreat, the accused's belief that the use of force or deadly force was necessary was not reasonable.

Example:

> One day, looking for a shortcut through the neighborhood, Tom hops a fence (a trespass) and is walking across open property to reach the street on the other side of the property. Tom is confronted by the property owner and tries to explain that he meant no harm and was just taking a shortcut. However, the property owner becomes irate and cocks his gun, aims it at Tom, and says "I'm going to kill you!"

Under this example, Tom is a trespasser, and the property owner has a right to threaten or use force to terminate the trespass to the property. If Tom is walking through the property, however, and has made no overt move to commit a forcible felony, the property owner would not be justified in his threats of the use of deadly force ("I'm going to kill you!"). He may threaten the use of force, but not deadly force, and could not stand behind a justified use of such a threat in this scenario. Now let us take the example one step further:

> Tom is scared out of his mind as he looks down the barrel of the property owner's shotgun. The two are about 20 feet apart. Tom, hearing the property owner's threat to kill him, draws his own firearm and fires two shots, killing the property owner.

Tom is the trespasser, but is the property owner's response disproportionate? In Georgia, the answer is yes. A trespass amounts only to a misdemeanor and does not justify killing the trespasser. *Norrell v. State,* 116 Ga. App. 479 (1967). In our scenario, the property owner has made a disproportionate threat to Tom's act of trespass. But what can Tom do to protect himself? The court in the *Norrell* case has the answer.

> One who provokes a difficulty may yet defend himself against violence on the part of the one provoked, if the violence be disproportionate to the seriousness of the provocation, or greater in degree than the law recognizes as justifiable under the circumstances…. If a person provokes a difficulty and the provocation amounts to no more than

a mere trespass, it would not put him in the wrong in resisting or defending himself against a felonious attack on account of the provocation. *Id.* at 483.

Tom has "provoked a difficulty" by trespassing on land that does not belong to him, but the property owner's response is disproportionate to Tom's trespass, and Tom now finds his life in danger. He now has a right to defend himself against the "felonious attack" of the property owner (remember, the property owner has threatened to kill Tom), and in this situation, would be justified in the use of deadly force to protect himself from the property owner's disproportionate attack.

Would Tom have a duty to retreat? Considering he is justified in the use of deadly force to prevent death to himself, he would be entitled to stand his ground (even though it doesn't belong to him) and defend himself from the unreasonable acts of the property owner. The moral of this story? *Don't take shortcuts!*

E.  *When is the use of force or deadly force explicitly not legally justified under O.C.G.A. § 16-3-21?*
O.C.G.A. § 16-3-21 outlines three specific situations where a person is not justified in using force. Of course, since being justified in the use of force is an absolute prerequisite to the use of deadly force, any time a person is not justified to use force under this Code Section, that person is also automatically disqualified from being justified to use deadly force. Without being justified, a person cannot claim self-defense.

1.  Force never legally justified for initial provocation
If you think back to your childhood, you probably remember saying these words to your parents or a teacher: "But he started it!" In Georgia, those who "pick a fight" by provoking the use of force against them cannot claim justification in the use of force.

**NOT JUSTIFIED IN USING FORCE**

**O.C.G.A. § 16-3-21(b)(1).** A person is not justified in using force... if he... [i]nitially provokes the use of force against himself with the intent to use such force as an excuse to inflict bodily harm upon the assailant;

**O.C.G.A. § 16-3-21(b)(2).** A person is not justified in using force... if he... [i]s attempting to commit, committing, or fleeing after the commission or attempted commission of a felony;

**O.C.G.A. § 16-3-21(b)(3).** A person is not justified in using force... if he... [w]as the aggressor or was engaged in a combat by agreement unless he withdraws... and effectively communicates... his intent to do so.

Example:

> Samantha spots an old high school rival walking to her car in the grocery store parking lot and wants to settle an old score. She pushes a shopping cart into the woman, causing her to fall and spill her groceries. The woman turns to Samantha with hands raised; Samantha steps over her rival's broken eggs and punches the woman in the face.

In this instance, Samantha is not legally justified in her use of force because she initiated the contact, provoking a response from the other woman. Samantha will have problems in court.

2. <u>Force not legally justified when committing a felony</u>

Example:

> Money is tight for Wayne, but he knows his elderly neighbor has a roll of cash under her mattress. While she's out for a walk, he breaks into her home and takes the money. The neighbor catches him in her home and yells for help. Another male neighbor gives chase and Wayne tries to outrun him, but Wayne is tripped and they fall together. In the melee, the neighbor is seriously injured by Wayne, who uses a nearby rock to break his nose.

Wayne is in serious trouble. Not only has he committed a burglary, during the flight from his felony he committed an aggravated battery by breaking the neighbor's nose. Because Wayne was fleeing after the commission of a felony (the burglary), he will not be justified in using force or deadly force against the Good Samaritan neighbor.

### 3. Being the aggressor; or combat by agreement

Example:

> *Andy and Dwight are having an argument about whose fa-vorite football team will win the championship. In the heat of the argument, Andy calls Dwight a derogatory name and Dwight asks if Andy wants to take it outside. Andy agrees, and they both begin fighting in the parking lot. Shortly after they begin fighting, the police show up and arrest them for disorderly conduct and assault.*

This statute serves the purpose of preventing individuals who arrange to fight each other from avoiding criminal responsibility for their actions by claiming self-defense. The statute here is clear: if a person agrees to the force used against him or her by another person, that person cannot later claim that he or she fought back in self-defense! But what if a person who started a fight soon realizes he bit off more than he can chew? Under the law, that person can withdraw or "effectively communicate" his desire to abandon the encounter. If, after a person abandons or attempts to abandon the encounter, the person who was provoked "continues or threatens to continue the use of unlawful force" (as stated in the Code Section) against the provocateur, the provocateur may then be legally justified to fight back.

Example:

> *Dave is at a bar when he notices another man checking-out his girlfriend. Dave tells the other man, "take a hike or you'll regret it" and slightly shoves the admirer. The other man responds by punching Dave in the face. Dave, who didn't really want a confrontation, holds both his hands up in surrender and says, "I don't want any more trouble!" As he turns his back to his former foe, the other man pulls out a knife and lunges at Dave.*

In this scenario, Dave is legally justified to fight back: he attempted to withdraw from the incident and made his intention known to the other person. When the other man continued to attack, Dave is now legally justified to defend himself, even though he made the initial provocation.

### IV. Do I have a legal responsibility to defend another person?

Under Georgia law, the average person has no duty to come to the defense of another. This is true even if a crime is in progress (but note: this lack of a legal duty does not include police officers and other professionals that may have affirmative legal duties to assist). If you see a third person that is the victim of what you believe to be the unlawful use of force or deadly force, you have no legal duty to aid that person—it is your decision. This is equally true if you are legally carrying a gun pursuant to a Weapons Carry License. But what if you decide to help the third person? The same rules of justification apply to the defense of third persons in Georgia.

A.  *When does Georgia law allow for the justifiable use of force or deadly force to protect someone else?*

| USE OF FORCE IN DEFENSE OF SELF OR OTHERS |
| --- |
| **O.C.G.A. § 16-3-21.** A person is justified in threatening or using force against another when and to the extent that he or she reasonably believes that such threat or force is necessary to defend himself or herself *or a third person* against such other's imminent use of unlawful force; however, except as provided in Code Section 16-3-23, a person is justified in using force which is intended or likely to cause death or great bodily harm only if he or she reasonably believes that such force is necessary to prevent death or great bodily injury to himself or herself *or a third person* or to prevent the commission of a forcible felony. |

In the last sections, we addressed the law of legal justification for the use of force or deadly force for self-defense. We now turn to when the law allows the justified use of force or deadly force to protect another person or persons.

In general, if you place yourself in the "shoes" of the third person, and the law would allow the third person to use force or deadly force to protect themselves, then you are legally justified to use the same level of force to protect a third person. O.C.G.A. § 16-3-21 allows a person to protect a third person from the unlawful use of force or deadly force by another in the same circumstances in which a person could justifiably use force under the law to protect themselves, so long as the person reasonably believes that the intervention is "necessary." Georgia law makes the legal analysis for defending third persons the same as for self-defense.

Therefore, the same legal justifications for self-defense are also available for the defense of third persons. If a person decides to aid a third person, the law of justifiable use of force will allow a person to defend a third person to the extent they may defend themselves. As long as the person defending another reasonably believes that the third person would be justified in using force or deadly force to protect him or herself, the person defending may step in and use force or deadly force on that person's behalf. *See Carter v. State,* 285 Ga. 565 (2009). However, please note that the law still imposes a requirement that a person's belief in the necessity of the use of force or deadly force be reasonable, and that the danger is "imminent", or as the Court said in *Carter,* "urgent and pressing." If a person decides to defend a third person, prudence dictates that the person defending must be sure they know what is truly happening in a situation before using force or deadly force. If a belief in the necessity of the use of force or deadly force turns out to be unreasonable, the use of force or deadly force will not be legally justified no matter how well intentioned a person may be.

B.   *What if the situation is not as I thought it appeared to be?*
A third person and a "Good Samaritan" may not potentially see things as they really are. When a person elects to use force or deadly force to defend a third person, it can all go terribly wrong.

Example:
> Peter, a licensed handgun owner, decides to get some lunch, so he pulls into a local burger joint to eat. He parks and exits his vehicle whereupon he witnesses a man walking out of the restaurant and across the parking lot. Suddenly, another man comes running up and points a gun in the first man's face. Peter, not wanting to become a victim of an armed robbery, drops to one knee while drawing his handgun. Still seeing the gun pointed at the first man, Peter decides to protect the would-be victim of robbery and fires his gun striking the robber.

If there was in fact an armed robbery taking place, Peter's use of deadly force is likely legally justified, because if we put Peter in the shoes of the third person (the first man in the example), Peter would be legally justified in using deadly force to stop the armed robbery. Thus, the law will deem Peter's belief that the use of deadly force was immediately necessary as reasonable. But what if there was no armed robbery? In fact, what would happen if in the instant after Peter fires his gun, the man Peter sought to protect immediately turns to help the wounded suspected robber yelling "murderer!" at Peter while screaming in fear and grief, "why did you shoot my friend?" It turns out that there was not a robbery, just a couple of fellows were pranking each other, and the gun Peter saw was a toy. How does the law deal with this scenario?

In such a situation, Peter's perspective and knowledge of the situation are very different from the person he sought to defend. The man clearly knew there was no robbery in progress since he recognized his friend, and that it was a prank. In this situation, if Peter's belief that an armed robbery was in progress was reasonable, then Peter will be legally justified. However, if a jury finds that his belief was unreasonable, Peter will not be legally justified and likely guilty of aggravated assault, or worse.

## C.  *Do I have a duty to report a crime?*
Generally, there is no duty to report a crime under Georgia law. There are specific instances, however where professionals are required to report acts of violence: O.C.G.A. § 19-7-5 requires health professionals, teachers, and law enforcement personnel to report allegations or suspicions of child abuse; and O.C.G.A. § 30-5-4(a)(1) and (b) require the same mandatory reporting by healthcare professionals and law enforcement of suspected elder abuse. As a driver on the streets and highways of Georgia, you are required to report an accident involving injury, death, or property damage to police (O.C.G.A. § 40-6-273), but otherwise, there is no general requirement to report a crime you may have witnessed.

# CHAPTER SIX

## WHEN CAN I LEGALLY USE MY GUN: PART III.
## UNDERSTANDING WHEN DEADLY FORCE
## CAN BE USED AGAINST ANIMALS

## I.   Can I legally use deadly force against animals?

When it comes to the law of the use of force and deadly force to defend yourself, others, or property from animal attacks, Georgia law is a mixture of different laws that are not contained in one section of statutes alone.

### A.   *No general defense against animals statute*

Georgia has no dedicated self-defense or defense of others statute that deals with all animals. There exist statutes that justify – using the term as a defense in the manner we have come to know it – acts against animals in general, and more specific statutes that grant freedom from liability for acts committed against animals involved in specific conduct. This chapter will examine the laws that do exist relating to the use of deadly force against an animal and how your right to self-preservation can best be accomplished.

### B.   *Cruelty to animals*

As we have found in our discussion on justification, Georgia law allows for the justified use of force or deadly force when and to the degree that the person reasonably believes that it is necessary to protect himself or herself from unlawful force, death, or great bodily injury. As this law applies to animal attacks, a person may be legally justified in using force or deadly force (such as firing a gun) against an attacking animal if that person "reasonably believes that such act is necessary to defend against an imminent threat of injury or damage to any person, other animal, or property." O.C.G.A. § 16-12-4(h)(1). However, the threat must be "imminent": our Georgia Court of Appeals has found that, in order to justify the act of killing a dog, even in the defense of yourself, your family, or property (or the person or property of another), "such danger must be imminent, and a real or obviously apparent necessity must exist, and the threatened injury could not otherwise be avoided." *Readd v. State,* 164 Ga. App. 97 (1982).

Example:

> *Jim is walking in his neighborhood when out of nowhere three large pit bulls spot him and immediately begin running toward him barking with sharp fangs showing. Jim barely has time to draw and fire his .40 caliber Glock at the lead dog just before it lunged at him. Having dispatched one dog, the other two dogs flee.*

Jim's conduct would be justified as necessary under these circumstances, either by virtue of the general doctrine of justification, or the explicit wording of the cruelty to animals statute AND the cruelty to dogs statute (which we will discuss later). While the general theory of justification would provide a defense, subsection (h) of the cruelty to animals statute, O.C.G.A. § 16-12-4, discharges Jim of **any criminal responsibility** for the death of the animal he shot, so long as he felt it necessary to protect himself from "an imminent threat of injury." "[A] person who humanely injures or kills an animal under the circumstances indicated in this subsection shall incur no civil liability or criminal responsibility for such injury or death." O.C.G.A. § 16-12-4(h)(3). By virtue of this subsection, and considering our facts, Jim would be free of criminal responsibility for killing the first dog, and would not be liable for monetary damages to the dog's owner for the death.

### PRACTICAL LEGAL TIP

Beware! Using deadly force against a dog or cat that is only digging into your flowerbed or getting into your garbage may not be justified. —*Matt*

C. *Cruelty to dogs*

| CRUELTY TO DOGS; AUTHORIZED KILLING OF DOGS |
| --- |
| **O.C.G.A. § 4-8-5. (a)** No person shall perform a cruel act on any dog; nor shall any person harm, maim, or kill any dog, or attempt to do so, except that a person may:<br>**(1)** Defend his or her person or property, or the person or property of another, from injury or damage being caused by a dog; or<br>**(2)** Kill any dog causing injury or damage to any livestock, poultry, or pet animal.<br>**(b)** The method used for killing the dog shall be designed to be as humane as is possible under the circumstances. A person who humanely kills a dog under the circumstances indicated in subsection (a) of this Code section shall incur no liability for such death. |

The law on permitted action appears to become more permissive when it comes to dogs. While the justification provisions of the cruelty to animals statute, O.C.G.A. § 16-12-4, absolve an individual from criminal responsibility for the death of an animal when "necessary to defend against an imminent threat of injury or damage," the cruelty to dogs statute, O.C.G.A. § 4-8-5, arguably lowers the threshold for freedom from liability for killing a dog, only requiring a showing that an individual has defended his or her person or property "from injury or damage" caused by a dog.

D. *Animals attacking livestock*

The laws of Georgia work together to protect your livestock from opportunistic creatures, and to provide you with cover in the event you must take action to protect what is yours. O.C.G.A. § 16-12-4, the cruelty to animals statute, justifies injury or death to an animal to defend against an "imminent threat" of injury to another animal (by acting prior to the death of the animal protected), while O.C.G.A. § 4-8-5, the cruelty to dogs statute, allows an individual freedom from liability for killing a dog "causing injury or damage to any livestock, poultry, or pet animal."

It would therefore seem Georgia law requires a heightened level of justification in prospectively protecting animals threatened with injury, while (at least in the case of dogs, whom it would seem the General Assembly believes to be more capable of harm to other creatures than most) allowing a much lower level of justification to kill a dog that has already injured or damaged livestock.

E. *Fur-bearing animals*
It's not uncommon to be troubled by fur-bearing pests on your property, such as minks and otters. Many of these animals destroy property, crops, and so forth in their attempt to build their own habitats. It's for that reason that Georgians are afforded the opportunity to dispatch certain animals: to provide you with some recourse in the event a pest troubles you and your property. This appears to be an affirmative authorization to use deadly force against one.

---

**KILLING OR INJURING MINK OR OTTER WITH FIREARM; POSSESSION OR SALE OF MINK OR OTTER, OR PELT THEREOF, KILLED BY FIREARM**

**O.C.G.A. § 27-3-64.** It shall be unlawful to use any... firearm to kill or injure mink or otter... provided that nothing in this Code section shall prevent a person from dispatching a mink or otter found in a trap or from killing any mink or otter while it is destroying or damaging, or about to destroy or damage, the person's crops, domestic fowl, or other personal property.

---

F. *Federal law defenses*
The federal law, in comprehensive fashion, has had the foresight to specifically provide that a person may kill an animal protected by federal law in self-defense, such as the regulations concerning the grizzly bear in 50 CFR § 17.40(b)(1)(i)(B). Unlike Georgia's statutes, this makes the Federal law clear and comprehendible. Therefore, if you are carrying a firearm in a National Park (see Chapters 9 and 10), and you find yourself face to face with a grizzly bear, you will have a legal defense for protecting yourself.

# CHAPTER SEVEN
## WHEN CAN I LEGALLY USE MY GUN: PART IV. UNDERSTANDING WHEN DEADLY FORCE CAN BE USED TO PROTECT PROPERTY

### I.  Overview and location of the law to protect property

Georgia law allows a person to protect, with force, their property from another's unlawful interference or trespass onto their property or the property of another. Further, under certain circumstances, the law will also allow a person to use legally justified deadly force to protect property. The statutes in the Official Code of Georgia dealing with legally justified force or deadly force to defend property we shall discuss are:

O.C.G.A. § 16-3-23: Use of Force in Defense of Habitation
O.C.G.A. § 16-3-24: Use of Force in Defense of Property
      Other Than A Habitation

Protection of property—meaning habitations and real property—will be analyzed under the same "reasonable person" standard discussed in Chapters 4 and 5 and will have the same requirements for a person reasonably believing that the force or deadly force used was "necessary." Let's begin with the use of force in defense of habitation, and Georgia's "castle doctrine."

## II.  Use of force in defense of habitation

### USE OF FORCE IN DEFENSE OF HABITATION

**O.C.G.A. § 16-3-23.** A person is justified in threatening or using force against another when and to the extent that he or she reasonably believes that such threat or force is necessary to prevent or terminate such other's unlawful entry into or attack upon a habitation; however, such person is justified in the use of force which is intended or likely to cause death or great bodily harm only if:

(1) The entry is made or attempted in a violent and tumultuous manner and he or she reasonably believes that the entry is attempted or made for the purpose of assaulting or offering personal violence to any person dwelling or being therein and that such force is necessary to prevent the assault or offer of personal violence;

(2) That force is used against another person who is not a member of the family or household and who unlawfully and forcibly enters or has unlawfully and forcibly entered the residence and the person using such force knew or had reason to believe that an unlawful and forcible entry occurred; or

(3) The person using such force reasonably believes that the entry is made or attempted for the purpose of committing a felony therein and that such force is necessary to prevent the commission of the felony.

The statute detailing a justification defense for the protection of your "habitation" in Georgia is O.C.G.A. § 16-3-23, "Use of force in defense of habitation." An individual is legally justified in using the threat of force, or actual force against another "when and to the extent that he or she reasonably believes that such threat or force is necessary to prevent or terminate such other's unlawful entry into or attack upon a habitation...." Does this language look familiar? It should: it closely tracks the language of O.C.G.A. § 16-3-21, use of force in self-defense. The defense of habitation statue follows the self-defense statute numerically in the Georgia Code, and both statutes are referenced as containing precursor acts that invoke the "stand your ground" provisions of O.C.G.A. § 16-3-23.1, Georgia's "no duty to retreat" law.

Like the use of force in self-defense statute, O.C.G.A. § 16-3-23 establishes the general standard for the justified use of both force and deadly force in protecting the habitation (home). Under the statute, a person is legally justified in using deadly force ("force which is intended or likely to cause death or great bodily harm") only when:

- The entry is made or attempted in a violent and tumultuous manner and he or she reasonably believes that the entry is attempted or made for the purpose of assaulting or offering personal violence to any person dwelling or being therein and that such force is necessary to prevent the assault or offer of personal violence;
- That force is used against another person who is not a member of the family or household and who unlawfully and forcibly enters or has unlawfully and forcibly entered the residence and the person using such force knew or had reason to believe that an unlawful and forcible entry occurred; or
- The person using such force reasonably believes that the entry is made or attempted for the purpose of committing a felony therein and that such force is necessary to prevent the commission of the felony. O.C.G.A. § 16-3-23.

As always, what a person believes is necessary and whether that belief is reasonable is the difference between justification (not guilty) and conviction (guilty).

### A. *O.C.G.A. § 16-3-23 is Georgia's "Castle Doctrine"*
The term "castle doctrine" does not appear in Georgia statutes; the legal concept, however, comes from the philosophy that every person is the king or queen of his or her "castle"—the home. As such, no king or queen is required to retreat before using force or deadly force against an intruder in their castle. In Georgia, the "Castle Doctrine" is codified in O.C.G.A. § 16-3-23, "Use of force in defense of habitation." The doctrine extends to cover a person's "habitation," meaning a dwelling, vehicle, or place of business.

If you are the intended victim of unlawful force or deadly force when you are in your dwelling, motor vehicle, or place of business, these places are your "castle," and the law will provide you protection beyond the general rule. In these "Castle Doctrine" circumstances, the law will justify the use of force or deadly force based upon a person's reasonable belief that force or deadly force was necessary to defend against force. This justification applies to you when:

(a) A person has unlawfully and with force entered, or attempted to enter your: dwelling, motor vehicle, or place of business.

The justification will be further enhanced by having no duty to retreat (remember our discussion of Georgia's "Stand Your Ground" statute) and will help prevent prosecutors in court from second-guessing when or the amount of force that was used.

1. *What is a habitation under the "Castle Doctrine?"*
Georgia law, in defining "Castle Doctrine" rights, does not use the term "home" or "house"; the term employed is "habitation." A "habitation" is defined by O.C.G.A. § 16-3-24.1 as:

*any dwelling, motor vehicle, or place of business.*

A "dwelling" would properly be considered to be any building or part of a building connected to that part of the home in which a person can live. This would seem to mean that structures that are detached from the building where you sleep at night may not be considered your habitation. Therefore, any use of force or deadly force may not qualify as justified use of force in this circumstance. However, if your garage, or front or back porch is connected to the structure containing your sleeping quarters (as exists in many suburban communities), it may be considered part of your habitation as defined by Georgia law.

2. *What is a motor vehicle under the "Castle Doctrine?"*
Georgia "Castle Doctrine" protections are applicable to occupied motor vehicles. If a person is attempting to hijack your motor vehicle (more commonly referred to as "carjacking" and codified as a felony under O.C.G.A. § 16-5-44.1, discussed in Chapter 5), you will fall under the "Castle Doctrine." But what does Georgia define as a motor vehicle?

O.C.G.A. § 40-1-1 begins by defining a "vehicle" as "every device in, upon, or by which any person or property is or may be transported or drawn upon a highway, excepting devices used exclusively upon stationary rails or tracks." O.C.G.A. § 40-1-1(75). This excludes flying machines and trains, but seems to include all manner of wheeled devices, powered or not.

Subsection 33 of the same statute further defines a "motor vehicle" as "every vehicle which is self-propelled other than an electric personal assistive mobility device (EPAMD)." A motor vehicle is more commonly understood to mean a self-propelled vehicle with wheels that is designed to be used, or is ordinarily used, to transport people or property on roads. *Harris v. State,* 286 Ga. 245 (2009). This is a very broad definition and appears to include anything wheeled that carries people or property from one place to another, including cars, motorcycles, trucks, golf carts, and so forth.

## III.  Use of force in defense of property other than habitation
Georgia law also provides substantial protection for property owners acting in defense of property other than a habitation (which we now know to be a dwelling, motor vehicle, or place of business, locations we "inhabit"). Found in O.C.G.A. § 16-3-24, "Use of force in defense of property other than a habitation" (aptly named!), the statute—just as with defense of self and defense of habitation—provides for two tiers of action: threatening or using force against one who commits a trespass or tortious criminal interference to your real property; and the use of deadly force against those who may attempt to commit a forcible felony on that property.

### A.  *How is this property different from a habitation?*
We know a habitation to be a dwelling, motor vehicle, or our place of business under Georgia law, in other words, a physical location we "inhabit," which is under our control. In defining the terms so that we properly understand "habitation," "real property," and "personal property," Georgia law acknowledges a habitation to include those locations we know, and restricts "personal property" to "personal property other than a motor vehicle." O.C.G.A. § 16-3-24.1. The goal is to restrict the justification defenses found in O.C.G.A. § 16-3-23 to habitations, and O.C.G.A. § 16-3-24 to real property. Still confused? The Georgia Department of Revenue defines "real property" as "the bundle of rights, interests, and benefits connected with the ownership of real estate." Ga. Comp. R. & Regs. r. 560-11-10-.02. In other words, O.C.G.A. § 16-3-24 deals with real property, the physical real estate you own, except for the habitation you reside in. This would include tracts of land you may additionally own but do not reside upon, and would necessarily also include any real estate your place of business rests upon (remember, "place of business" is considered part of your habitation).

## IV. When is someone legally justified to use "force" but not "deadly force" to protect their own property?

### A. *Prevent or terminate unlawful entry or attack upon habitation; prevent or terminate a trespass onto real property*

The law answers this question based upon the statutory language of the justified use of force to protect habitation contained in O.C.G.A. § 16-3-24, the "Castle Doctrine", and the justified use of force to protect real property found in O.C.G.A. § 16-3-24. The use of force (but not deadly force) is legally justified in situations where necessary to prevent or terminate another person's unlawful entry into or attack upon a habitation, *e.g.*, entry without authorization, vandalizing property, *etc.*, but also to terminate a trespass to or other tortious or criminal interference with real property (*i.e.* the property you own that your habitation sits on).

*If you catch someone in the act*
In plain terms, if someone has unlawfully attacked your habitation, you are justified in using force (or threats of force) to stop him or her (or them). If someone has trespassed upon your property, you may use force or threats of force—**but not deadly force**—to stop them. Of course, just like instances of self-defense, you must also meet the standard of reasonable belief in the necessity of the use of force.

The analysis so far leads us to the question: if force may legally be used to prevent or terminate trespass or interference with property, what constitutes a trespass or interference with property?

### B. *What is a trespass?*

The commonly understood meaning of trespass is "an unlawful interference with one's person, property, or rights." This definition has been expanded to refer typically to "any unauthorized intrusion or invasion of private premises or land of another." *Black's Law Dictionary, 6th ed.* This commonly understood definition of trespass is slightly different and more expansive than the offense of criminal trespass found in Georgia law. O.C.G.A. § 16-7-21 defines a criminal trespass as any time a person:

(a)... intentionally damages any property of another without consent of that other person and the damage thereto is $500.00 or less or knowingly and maliciously interferes with the possession or use of

the property of another person without consent of that person.
(b)... knowingly and without authority:

    (1) Enters upon the land or premises of another person or into any part of any vehicle, railroad car, aircraft, or watercraft of another person for an unlawful purpose;

    (2) Enters upon the land or premises of another person or into any part of any vehicle, railroad car, aircraft, or watercraft of another person after receiving, prior to such entry, notice from the owner, rightful occupant, or, upon proper identification, an authorized representative of the owner or rightful occupant that such entry is forbidden; or

    (3) Remains upon the land or premises of another person or within the vehicle, railroad car, aircraft, or watercraft of another person after receiving notice from the owner, rightful occupant, or, upon proper identification, an authorized representative of the owner or rightful occupant to depart.

In other words, unlike the common definition of trespass where a person becomes a trespasser whether they realized it or not (unwittingly walking across the King's hunting grounds, for instance), under the Georgia Code, prior to committing a criminal offense, a person must have knowledge that they are in a place they do not belong or are not welcome.

C.   *Trespass, for legal justification, is not just "criminal trespass"*

### USE OF FORCE TO PREVENT TRESPASS

**O.C.G.A. § 16-3-24(b).** The use of force which is intended or likely to cause death or great bodily harm to prevent trespass on or other tortious or criminal interference with real property other than a habitation or personal property is not justified unless the person using such force reasonably believes that it is necessary to prevent the commission of a forcible felony.

How, then, is "trespass" defined in O.C.G.A. § 16-3-24 for purposes of defending property? Because the plain language of the statute refers only to terminating "such other's trespass" and does not reference a "criminal trespass," it is clear that the statute intends to follow a broader definition of trespass than just the offense of criminal trespass found in O.C.G.A. § 16-7-21. In other words, a person may be potentially legally justified in using force against a person found trespassing on their land—even if that person has not committed the crime of criminal trespass, but only so long as the use of force is accompanied with a reasonable belief that it is necessary to terminate the trespass. Without a specific definition of what "trespass" means as found in O.C.G.A. § 16-3-24, in the vast majority of cases, a jury will be the ultimate arbiter of whether or not a person had a reasonable belief that it was immediately necessary to terminate another person's trespass on the land.

D.  *What is unlawful interference with property?*
You have a legal right to prevent or terminate "tortious or criminal interference with real property," but what does this mean? It can be a theft, destruction, vandalism, or anything else that diminishes a person's right to their property. Whether particular conduct rises to "interference with property" is an issue that a jury decides.

E.  *Is there a statutory minimum value of property before force may be legally used to protect it?*
No. There exists no statutory minimum value for real property before force may be used to protect it. Georgia law does not specify that the real property a person seeks to protect must be of a certain minimum dollar value in order for a person to protect it. What the Georgia Code does specify, is that a person must have a reasonable belief that the use of force or deadly force is immediately necessary to protect that property under all attendant circumstances before a person would be justified in using force or deadly force.

V.  **When is someone legally justified in using "deadly force" to protect their own property (other than the home)?**
When a person may legally use deadly force (force that is intended to cause serious bodily injury or death) to defend his or her property is addressed in section 16-3-24(b) of the Georgia Code. As in other situations where deadly force is justified under Georgia law, the use of deadly force is justified when the actor reasonably believes it necessary to prevent the commission of a forcible felony. Remember those? We discussed an expansive list of what may be considered a forcible felony in Chapter 5: it includes such crimes as murder, kidnapping, aggravated assault and aggravated battery, robbery and armed robbery, hijacking a motor vehicle, burglary, arson, and any number of sexual offenses. An individual who acts in accordance with the restriction of the use of deadly force in protection of real property would be immune from prosecution under O.C.G.A. § 16-3-24.2, just as in the case of one who uses deadly force in de-

fense of himself or herself or a third person. Additionally, there is no duty to retreat for one who lawfully uses deadly force in defense of real property. Georgia's "stand your ground" statute, O.C.G.A. § 16-3-23.1, would protect anyone who follows the law in using deadly force to protect property in that situation, just as in situations where deadly force is used in self-defense or the defense of third parties.

## VI. Can I protect another person's property?

Yes! O.C.G.A. § 16-3-24 provides that a person is justified in threatening or using force – but not deadly force – to protect a third person's property to the same extent as the law allows the protection of their own property against unlawful entry or criminal or other tortious interference, if the person has a legal duty to protect the property of the third person or is a member of the third person's immediate family. Remember, however, that this is "real property": the land or real estate upon which another person's habitation resides.

But what about the use of deadly force? Georgia law appears to depart from the restriction allowing the use of force only upon property you have a duty to protect when dealing with forcible felonies. Under O.C.G.A. § 16-3-24(b), deadly force may be used to prevent a trespass on real property when "the person using such force reasonably believes that it is necessary to prevent the commission of a forcible felony." The use of deadly force in prevention of such an act does not appear to be restricted only to real property lawfully in your possession, the possession of your immediate family, or property you have a legal duty to protect.

Example:
> After a long day at work, Gordon pulls into his own driveway one night and witnesses two men climbing out of his neighbor's window which appears to be broken and with what looks to be his neighbor's television (Gordon is not related to his neighbor). Gordon exits his vehicle gun drawn and demands the two men stop. When the men ignore his command, Gordon shoots and wounds both men.

Is Gordon legally justified in using deadly force under this scenario? Let's analyze the facts. Gordon would have been justified in using deadly force if the property he was protecting was his own: if arriving to witness a burglary in progress, Gordon would have been justified in the use of deadly force by virtue of O.C.G.A. § 16-3-23(2) or

(3). In this scenario, Gordon does not appear to be in possession of the property (it's his neighbor's), and there is no indication he owes a legal duty to his neighbor, since they are not immediate members of the same family. Even if Gordon's neighbor had not specifically asked Gordon to protect his property, because Gordon's belief that a forcible felony of burglary was being committed, his actions are likely to be viewed as reasonably necessary to prevent the burglary. If Gordon presents "some evidence" to substantiate his belief a forcible felony was being committed, the jury will be authorized to receive an instruction on defense of property other than habitation, and Gordon may be justified in his actions.

## VII.  How can I assist law enforcement?
Almost without fail, as an attorney I am regularly asked about whether you can make a citizen's arrest, and how you can best assist law enforcement in dangerous situations. Since every legal situation is unique, here is a brief summary of the general law, as well as reference some of the statutes governing the use of citizen's arrests and how to assist authorities.

### A.  *Citizen's Arrest*
The law in Georgia does allow for a private citizen to make an arrest – a citizen's arrest, if you will. O.C.G.A. § 17-4-60, "Arrest by Private Persons" provides "a private person may arrest an offender if the offense is committed in his presence or within his immediate knowledge. If the offense is a felony and the offender is escaping or attempting to escape, a private person may arrest him upon reasonable and probable grounds of suspicion." A private citizen in Georgia has as much power to arrest a fugitive felon, when the emergency calls for immediate action, as a public officer, and while so doing, is equally under the protection of the law. *Johnson v. Jackson,* 140 Ga. App. 252 (1976).

A private citizen's powers with respect to arresting a felon are clear. But what about a misdemeanor? A private person may make an arrest for a misdemeanor offense only when that offense occurs in his presence.

Moreover, the arrest must occur immediately after the perpetration of the offense. If the observer fails to make the arrest immediately after the commission of the offense his power to do so is extinguished, and a subsequent arrest is illegal. *McWilliams v.*

*Interstate Bakeries, Inc.,* 439 F.2d 16, 16 (5th Cir. 1971). *See also Williams v. State,* 171 Ga. App. 807 (1984). For purposes of a short answer, then: a private citizen may make an arrest for a misdemeanor or a felony committed "within his presence" or immediate knowledge. If the suspect is escaping, however, only in the event of a felony may a private citizen apprehend "upon reasonable and probable grounds of suspicion."

B.  *Shopkeepers arresting shoplifters*
These protections extend to shopkeepers and their employees tasked with loss-prevention, stopping those who would take what doesn't belong to them from a shopkeeper's store. Moreover, Georgia law contains a statute protecting shopkeepers who apprehend shoplifters from civil liability. Found in O.C.G.A. § 51-7-60, the law precludes a recovery for false imprisonment when it is shown that the owner or operator of a store reasonably believed the person detained was engaged in shoplifting. *Kemp v. Rouse-Atlanta, Inc.,* 207 Ga. App. 876 (1993). The law thus implicitly recognizes the right of a shop owner to protect himself from shoplifting by detaining a customer who has acted in a suspicious manner. *Id.* at 879.

C.  *Assisting police officers*

---

**IMMUNITY FROM CRIMINAL LIABILITY OF PERSONS RENDERING ASSISTANCE TO LAW ENFORCEMENT OFFICERS**

**O.C.G.A. § 16-3-22.** (a) Any person who renders assistance reasonably and in good faith to any law enforcement officer who is being hindered in the performance of his official duties or whose life is being endangered by the conduct of any other person or persons while performing his official duties shall be immune to the same extent as the law enforcement officer from any criminal liability that might otherwise be incurred or imposed as a result of rendering assistance to the law enforcement officer.

---

Sometimes, even professionals need help; law enforcement officers are no exception. Should there come a time when you find yourself in such a situation, the law in Georgia will protect you from criminal liability for your actions in assisting an officer obstructed in performing his duties—or whose life is in danger—to the same extent the law enforcement officer is protected, if you act "reasonably and in good faith" to assist that officer. This Code section acts to convey immunity to a private citizen as if the citizen were a law enforcement officer, but keep in mind: a defendant accepts a burden in proving immunity from criminal liability. Should you be denied immunity (and subsequently prosecuted), you may still rely upon the justification of defense of a third party (the officer, in this case). If you propound "some evidence" of a justification defense (for instance, the testimony of a grateful police officer), you will be entitled to a jury instruction on defense of third parties, and the prosecution must disprove your justification defense beyond a reasonable doubt.

### VIII. What crimes can I be charged with when my use of deadly force is not justified?

Before moving onto our next topic, it's time to give a brief summary of where you'll find yourself in legal trouble if you don't meet the elements of justification as we've described throughout this book. The following table lists just some of the crimes involving the use of deadly force or a firearm and where relevant provisions may be found in Georgia law. The facts of any individual case may support one of more of these or other charges you may face in situations where you may have used any level of force without justification.

| CRIMES INVOLVING DEADLY FORCE OR A FIREARM |
| --- |
| 1. Murder: **O.C.G.A. § 16-5-1** |
| 2. Voluntary Manslaughter: **O.C.G.A. § 16-5-2** |
| 3. Involuntary Manslaughter: **O.C.G.A. § 16-5-3** |
| 4. Aggravated Assault: **O.C.G.A. § 16-5-21** |
| 5. Aggravated Battery: **O.C.G.A. § 16-5-24** |
| 6. Pointing Pistol at Another: **O.C.G.A. § 16-11-102** |
| 7. Discharging Pistol Near a Highway: **O.C.G.A. § 16-11-103** |
| 8. Discharging Firearm on Property of Another: **O.C.G.A. § 16-11-104** |

## WHAT DO I DO IMMEDIATELY AFTER I USE MY FIREARM?

1. Make sure that the threat is contained or neutralized;
2. Return your firearm to safekeeping;
3. Call 911 and tell them you (or another person) has been the victim of a crime. Give the operator your location and description. Avoid giving any unnecessary information, and avoid telling them you shot someone. It may be wise to suggest an ambulance is needed. Then hang up with 911.
4. Call the Law Shield Emergency Hotline and follow the instructions your program attorney gives you;
5. Wait for police and do not touch any evidence;
6. If directed by your attorney, provide police only simple details of the crime against you;
7. Be careful of police questions and always be ready to invoke your right to silence and your right to counsel at any time.

# CHAPTER EIGHT

## LAW OF CONCEALED CARRY: PART I.
## THE LICENSE QUALIFICATIONS, REQUIREMENTS, APPEALS, AND REGULATIONS

Georgia law has regulated the possession and carry of firearms since shortly after the state's birth. In Georgia, qualified individuals may obtain a Weapons Carry License (our shorthand will be "WCL"), which allows the carrying of a handgun—openly or concealed— on their person in any location authorized by law. To obtain a WCL, a person must meet certain requirements and submit an application to the probate court in the county in which he or she resides. This chapter deals exclusively with the licensed carrying of a handgun in Georgia. A valid WCL allows the holder to carry any weapon in any county of the state.

### I.   Georgia's current weapons carry laws

Georgia experienced a sea change in firearms laws in 2014. With the passage of General Assembly House Bill 60, officially entitled the "Safe Carry and Protection Act" but referred to by many as the "Guns Everywhere Law," it has been said the rights of lawful gun owners and possessors in Georgia to carry—either concealed or openly—expanded over the horizon. Gone were prohibitions on carrying firearms into government buildings and bars; with permission, Weapons Carry License holders could carry firearms into houses of worship. Schools could also authorize individuals on-campus to carry firearms. And while many believe it expanded citizen carry in Georgia, what HB 60 actually did was to return to law-abiding gun owners many of the rights that had been slowly taken away from them over time, eaten away by government encroachment upon the Second Amendment ever since the ratification of the Bill of Rights in 1791.

O.C.G.A. § 16-11-129, entitled "Weapons Carry License; temporary renewal permit; mandamus; verification of license," contains the law on how Weapons Carry Licenses are administered in Georgia. Throughout this chapter, we will discuss the requirements, the application process, as well as the rights given to WCL holders for carrying a weapon in the State of Georgia. Keep in mind the term "weapon" refers to a handgun, as defined in O.C.G.A. § 16-11-125.1 (previously covered in Chapter 2), or a knife, identified in the same statute as a cutting instrument designed for the purpose of offense and defense, consisting of a blade greater than five inches long and fastened to a handle.

### PRACTICAL LEGAL TIP

A non-Georgia resident may not obtain a WCL in Georgia, but Georgia recognizes and grants "reciprocity" to a number of other states. This means the weapons licenses of other selected states allow those individuals to carry in Georgia, but they must obey Georgia law when doing so. —*Matt*

## II. Qualifications for and steps to obtain a Weapons Carry License

### A. *Persons who are legally qualified to obtain a WCL*

In this section, we will discuss the requirements to apply for a Georgia Weapons Carry License, as well as potential disqualifications to obtaining one. Requirements have been enacted to ensure that only those best suited to responsibly carry may do so. But in order to identify those who may apply for a WCL in Georgia, it may be best to begin with those who may not apply. O.C.G.A. § 16-11-129(b)(2) restricts issuance of Weapons Carry Licenses from:

1. Any person younger than 21 years of age;
2. Any person convicted of a felony, either in Georgia, any other state, or in federal court;
3. Any person with a pending felony charge, no matter the jurisdiction, within the State of Georgia or elsewhere;
4. Fugitives from justice;
5. Any person convicted of a crime of domestic violence, as defined under 18 U.S.C. § 922 (g), and anyone under indictment for a felony under subsection (n) of the same statute;
6. Any person previously convicted for the unlawful manufacture or distribution of controlled substances or dangerous drugs;
7. Any person whose WCL has been revoked within three years of the date of application;
8. Any person convicted of (a) carrying a weapon without a license (under O.C.G.A. § 16-11-126) or (b) carrying a weapon or long gun in an unauthorized location (under O.C.G.A.

§ 16-11-127) and has been free from probation and other arrests for less than five years;

9. Any person convicted of a misdemeanor controlled substance violation who has been free from probation, a second misdemeanor controlled substance violation, or the felony violations listed in 5, 6, and 7 for less than five years;

10. Any person hospitalized as an inpatient in a mental hospital or alcohol or drug treatment center within the five years preceding the application;

11. Any person adjudicated mentally incompetent to stand trial;

12. Any person adjudicated not guilty by reason of insanity under the "Insanity and mental incompetency" guidelines of O.C.G.A. Title 17, Chapter 7, Article 6.

This list defines those who are not eligible for issuance of a Georgia Weapons Carry License. The most common pitfalls to issuance of a license deserve special attention.

1. <u>Persons under 21 years of age restricted from WCL license</u>
One of the restrictions for licensing that must be reviewed in greater detail is the restriction on anyone under the age of 21 obtaining a WCL. Generally, no license may issue to anyone under the age of 21, but there is an exception under O.C.G.A. § 16-11-129(b)(2)(A)(i)-(iii) to grant licenses for those between the ages of 18 and 21 who seek one and qualify. In order to qualify, the individual must be at least 18 years of age and provide to the probate court where he or she applies for a license proof of basic training completion in the U.S. Armed Forces. This training would include weapons handling and safety. Additionally, the applicant must prove he or she is actively serving or has been honorably discharged; this requirement seems to restrict those with any other type of discharge from issuance of a permit only between the ages of 18 to 21, but in reality, any discharge not quantified as an honorable discharge (General, Other Than Honorable, Bad Conduct, or Dishonorable) may restrict an applicant over the age of 21, if the basis of the discharge is a conviction of the type contemplated under subsections (B), (E), (F), or (I).

2. <u>Convicted felons are restricted from being issued a WCL</u>
O.C.G.A. § 16-11-129(b)(2)(B) restricts convicted felons from being issued a Weapons Carry License. This restriction governs not only convictions by a Georgia court, however, but a court of "any other state; by a court of the United States, including its territories, pos-

sessions, and dominions; or by a court of any foreign nation...." A pardon for the felony by the President of the United States or the State Board of Pardons and Paroles would, according to the statute, seem to place the individual back within the good graces of the state so that he or she may apply for a WCL, but in actual practice, a "pardon" is treated separately from a "restoration of rights" in Georgia. A pardon in Georgia does not fully restore the rights a felon loses when suffering a conviction (although the right to vote is immediately restored upon the completion of any felony sentence): the individual affected must apply for a restoration of civil and political rights through the State Board of Pardons and Paroles in order to have his or her civil rights restored. *Even then,* an additional and separate process for restoring the right to possess and transport a firearm must be completed with the State Board of Pardons and Paroles. Only when this separate restoration is granted will the right to apply for and receive a WCL be available. This restoration process is different for convictions for acts that occurred within Georgia, and those that occurred outside Georgia.

### 3. Anyone with a conviction for a misdemeanor crime of domestic violence may not obtain a WCL

As we have seen in Chapter 3, federal law prohibits any individual with a conviction for a misdemeanor crime of domestic violence from possessing or transporting firearms or ammunition. This is a blanket federal disqualification, but it applies to any convictions in the fifty states, Georgia included. Such a conviction will restrict the individual from possessing or shipping "in interstate commerce" not only a firearm, but ammunition as well. 18 U.S.C. § 922(g).

### 4. Drug convictions will disqualify you from a WCL

Pending felony charges and felony convictions will disqualify an otherwise suitable candidate for a Weapons Carry License; similarly, drug manufacture or distribution convictions will disqualify any individual seeking a license. Under O.C.G.A. § 16-11-129(b)(2)(F), convictions for manufacture or distribution of any drug or substance classified as a controlled substance in Schedules I-V of O.C.G.A. § 16-13-25 through § 16-13-29, or in Schedules I-V of 21 C.F.R. Part 1308 (federal law identifying controlled substances) will fit the meaning of a drug conviction. These definitions include convictions for the manufacture or distribution of marijuana, *but not simple possession of marijuana* under O.C.G.A. § 16-13-2. Simple possession of marijuana, referred to as "possession of marijuana less than one ounce," is a misdemeanor: even still, under subsection (b)(2)(I), it will also result in a disqualification for a Weapons Carry License. While a felony conviction of the manufacture or distribution of a controlled substance is a lifetime bar to licensing (subject, of course, to restoration of rights), an individual convicted of a misdemeanor controlled substance violation may be eligible for a license after five years "free of all restraint" from the conviction, so long as no further drug convictions occur. Keep in mind also that O.C.G.A. § 16-11-129(b)(1)(C) emphasizes that a "conviction" is an adjudication of guilt: anyone who receives an order of discharge as a First Offender under O.C.G.A. § 42-8-60 is considered exonerated and without a conviction.

5. <u>Hospitalization in a mental hospital or treatment center disqualifies you</u>

A person is legally disqualified from receiving a WCL if he or she has been hospitalized as an inpatient in a mental hospital or alcohol or drug treatment center within five years prior to applying for a Weapons Carry License. While hospitalization in a mental hospital may seem a rare occurrence in this day, substance abuse treatment is all too common, and an individual who has been treated as an inpatient within the five years immediately preceding the application for a Weapons Carry License is not eligible for the license. Moreover, O.C.G.A. § 16-11-129(b)(2)(J) allows a probate court judge the authority to require any applicant to sign a waiver allowing the court to inquire whether the applicant has been an inpatient in any mental or substance abuse program in the past five years, and to allow the superintendent of the program an opportunity to recommend whether the applicant is a threat to society and ultimately whether the license should be granted. Should such a report be given, it is within the judge's discretion whether to grant the license. The construction of this subsection indicates that—by allowing the judge to ask for a waiver from any applicant, with a recommendation from the program superintendent—a recommendation may be made in the applicant's case by the superintendent of a treatment program *regardless of the length of time elapsed since treatment ended.* This means that the judge may take a recommendation if an applicant has sought treatment as contemplated in the subsection, and base his or her decision to grant the license on any recommendation made, even if the treatment falls outside the five-year disqualification period. There is an appeal process under subsection (b)(1) that will allow anyone disqualified for inpatient treatment under (b)(2)(J), an adjudication of mental incompetency to stand trial under (b)(2)(K), or an adjudication of not guilty by reason of insanity under (b)(2)(L) to petition for relief from a probate court's finding of disqualification. If the judge finds the individual will not pose a danger to the public, the petitioner will be given the opportunity to apply for a license.

When taking into consideration all potential disqualifications under O.C.G.A. § 16-11-129, keep the following in mind: these restrictions may result in a disqualification from obtaining a license, but they do not necessarily constitute a prohibition on possession of a firearm. Any person denied a Weapons Carry License under this subsection who is not prohibited by law from possession (not a felon, juvenile, First Offender probationer, or someone who has been convicted of a misdemeanor crime of domestic violence) will still be able to carry a weapon without a license in his or her home, place of business, and motor vehicle, and will still be eligible to possess and carry a long rifle anywhere.

B. _Am I eligible for a WCL if I received "First Offender Treatment?"_
As we have discussed, a person who has received "First Offender Treatment" as a result of a criminal charge will still be eligible to apply for a Weapons Carry License, so long as First Offender probation has been successfully completed. O.C.G.A. § 42-8-60 provides for First Offender treatment: under this code section, a defendant who has never previously been convicted of a felony may enter a plea (or be found guilty at trial) and, before the judge accepts the plea, be incarcerated or (more commonly) placed on probation. The judge will defer sentencing until the defendant completes the conditions of probation, and—if all conditions are met without violations of probation or new charges being filed—the sentence will be discharged without an adjudication of guilt, and no conviction will be entered. As you recall from Chapter 3, O.C.G.A. § 16-11-131 prohibits First Offender probationers from receiving, transporting, or possessing a firearm. Should First Offender probation be successfully complete, however, the individual is no longer barred from carrying a firearm or from obtaining a Weapons Carry License: O.C.G.A. § 16-11-129(b)(1)(C) defines a conviction as "an adjudication of guilt," and specifically exempts a First Offender discharge from the definition of a conviction, meaning a successful First Offender discharge does not provide on its own grounds a disqualification from obtaining a Weapons Carry License.

C. _Revocation of a Weapons Carry License_
Georgia's probate courts have the authority by law to revoke a

Weapons Carry License. O.C.G.A. § 16-11-129(e), "Revocation, loss, or damage to license," sets out in explicit terms how a probate court can act to revoke a WCL in the county of issuance.

1. "Any reasonable ground"

During any time when a Weapons Carry License is valid, the probate court in the county the license was issued may seek to revoke the WCL if it becomes known to the court there is "any reasonable ground to believe the licensee is not eligible to retain the license." A loss of eligibility most commonly results from a conviction or other change in status that would make the license holder ineligible to apply for the license; those same disqualifications can result in the revocation of a Weapons Carry License if they occur after the license is issued. Pending felony charges and felony convictions; convictions for drug manufacture or distribution; convictions for carrying a weapon without a Weapons Carry License or carrying a firearm or long gun in an unauthorized location; or a misdemeanor conviction for the use or possession of a controlled substance are just a few of the most common scenarios in which a probate court may move to revoke a Weapons Carry License. Depending on the basis of the revocation, an individual who loses his or her Weapons Carry License may suffer the loss for varying periods of time: a general revocation will bring a loss of license with a waiting period of three years until eligible to reapply, while someone convicted of carrying a weapon without a license or carrying in an unauthorized location will be revoked while under sentence (let's say, a twelve month sentence of probation), followed by an additional "waiting period" of five years, in which the individual must be free of sentence and supervision. This means carrying a weapon without a license could mean you will be separated from your Weapons Carry License by up to six years!

2. What happens next?

Should any individual be convicted of a crime that would cause him or her to become ineligible for a WCL, the judge presiding over the case must make an inquiry in court whether the defendant is a Weapons Carry License holder. If so, the judge will then ask in which county the license was issued, notifying the probate court judge in the issuing county of the conviction that could affect the status of the license. It then becomes the probate court's duty to administer a revocation proceeding: upon notice and hearing, the judge may revoke the license based upon an ineligibility factor found in subsection (b). Furthermore, should the probate court find the application for the Weapons Carry License was falsified, the holder is mentally incompetent, or suffers from chronic alcohol or "narcotic use," the Weapons Carry License may be revoked. It will then be a crime to be in possession of a revoked license. O.C.G.A. § 16-11-129(e).

## III.  The WCL application and process

A Georgia Weapons Carry License application containing all required information is necessary to obtain a license. The application must be completed and submitted to the probate court of the county in which the applicant resides, along with a $30.00 application fee, plus additional fees for fingerprinting and associated background check charges. When the application is submitted, the probate court will begin its investigation by submitting the applicant's information and fingerprints to the Federal Bureau of Investigation and the Georgia Criminal Information Center. Both will conduct independent investigations into the applicant's criminal history. Additionally, the court will order a background check from the FBI's National Instant Background Check System, in much the same way an FFL will do when processing the sale of a firearm.

This is the process for all new applications for a Weapons Carry License: there is a further allowance under O.C.G.A. § 16-11-129(d)(1)(B) for license renewals that the individual seeking renewal need only present his or her valid Weapons Carry License to provide evidence of fingerprints on file with the original county of issuance. So long as the renewal of a license is within 90 days before the expiration date of the WCL, or 30 days after the expiration of the license, no new fingerprints shall be required. A Georgia Weapons Carry License is valid in every county in Georgia and in every state that gives reciprocity to Georgia licenses, and allows the licensee to carry in every county in Georgia (as well as states with reciprocity), no matter if the licensee's county of residence changes during the five years the license is valid.

# CHAPTER NINE

## POSSESSING, CARRYING, AND TRANSPORTING FIREARMS WITHOUT A WEAPONS CARRY LICENSE

This chapter deals with when and where a person may possess, carry, or transport a firearm if they are not a Georgia Weapons Carry License Holder or someone with a Georgia-recognized carry permit. One salient fact about Georgia firearms law is that in some respects, Georgia law treats long guns differently from handguns. As a result, in Georgia, the public carrying of a handgun (either openly or concealed) without a Weapons Carry License—and without a recognized exception— is generally unlawful. On the other hand, no Weapons Carry License is required to carry a long gun in public, either openly or concealed, and a long gun must only be carried openly when loaded. More on this distinction will follow in the sections below.

The laws discussed in this chapter are found primarily in Official Code of Georgia Title 16, Chapter 11, Article 4, "Dangerous Instrumentalities and Practices." This chapter of the Georgia Code governs where and when firearms can be possessed and carried in the state, and it also contains various exceptions to any such rules. Because handguns and long guns are treated *somewhat* differently under Georgia law, this chapter will examine each separately when necessary to make the distinctions in the law between the two types of firearms.

## I. Where are firearms (long guns or handguns) and weapons permitted under Georgia law?

| HAVING OR CARRYING HANDGUNS, LONG GUNS, OR OTHER WEAPONS |
|---|

**O.C.G.A. § 16-11-126(a).** Any person who is not prohibited by law from possessing a handgun or long gun may have or carry on his or her person a weapon or long gun on his or her property or inside his or her home, motor vehicle, or place of business without a valid weapons carry license.

**O.C.G.A. § 16-11-126(b).** Any person who is not prohibited by law from possessing a handgun or long gun may have or carry on his or her person a long gun without a valid weapons carry license, provided that if the long gun is loaded, it shall only be carried in an open and fully exposed manner.

**O.C.G.A. § 16-11-126(d).** Any person who is not prohibited by law from possessing a handgun or long gun who is eligible for a weapons carry license may transport a handgun or long gun in any private passenger motor vehicle; provided, however, that private property owners or persons in legal control of private property through a lease, rental agreement, licensing agreement, contract, or any other agreement... shall have the right to exclude or eject a person who is in possession of a weapon or long gun on their private property.

### A. *Permissible carry without a Weapons Carry License*
O.C.G.A. § 16-11-126 governs possession of both handguns and long guns without a Weapons Carry License. The law provides seven locations in Georgia where possession of a handgun or long gun is permissible without a valid Weapons Carry License.

### 1. Personal property and habitation
Under subsection (a), any person "not prohibited by law" from possessing either a handgun or long gun (both rifles and shotguns) may carry a weapon or long gun without a Weapons Carry License on his or her property, as well as in the three locations state law identifies as a "habitation," or place a person "inhabits": the home, place of business, and personal motor vehicle. You will remember these three locations covered in Chapter 7 and the discussion on use of

force in defense of habitation. On your own property, or within these three areas, you may carry without a valid Weapons Carry License.

But who is "not prohibited by law?" Convicted felons, probationers sentenced under Georgia's First Offender Act (allowing a "discharge" and acquittal of felony charges for a first-time felony offender following completed probation), juveniles, and anyone convicted of a misdemeanor crime of domestic violence are prohibited by federal and state law from possessing firearms. Juveniles will "age out" of the prohibition on possession of a handgun at the age of 18 (keep in mind the exceptions that allow a minor to possess a firearm under O.C.G.A. § 16-11-132), but First Offender probationers may only regain the right to possessing firearms after the completion of probation and discharge of their case, while felons and those convicted of domestic violence misdemeanors must petition to have their rights restored to once again possess a firearm.

2.  Long guns: loaded and unloaded

O.C.G.A. § 16-11-126(b) describes the manner in which a long gun (either a rifle or shotgun) may be carried without a valid Weapons Carry License. So long as a citizen is not among those four groups previously discussed who are prohibited from possessing firearms, he or she may carry the firearm in any authorized location without a Weapons Carry License, either openly or concealed, so long as it is unloaded; if the firearm is loaded, it must be carried openly and in a "fully exposed manner."

3.  Enclosed in a case or unloaded

Under subsection (c) of O.C.G.A. § 16-11-126, any person not prohibited from possessing a firearm, as in the previous subsections, may carry a handgun, provided it is unloaded and placed in a protective case.

4.  Private passenger motor vehicle

Georgia House Bill 60, the 2014 change in gun laws known as the "Safe Carry Protection Act," made changes to the then-existing law that both expanded a gun owner's rights to carry, and at the same time protected private property owners who do not wish to have firearms on their property. This specific subsection of the unlicensed carry statute, allowing for carry without a license in any private passenger motor vehicle, was just one of the many areas of firearms laws impacted with the passage of House Bill 60. Under O.C.G.A. § 16-11-126(d), any person not prohibited by law from possessing a firearm—just as in the examples above—but who is also eligible for a Weapons Carry License, may transport a handgun or long gun in any private passenger motor vehicle, either belonging to the individual possessing the firearm, or to any other member of society. The vehicle's owner ("private property owners or persons in legal control of private property," which in this case is the car) has the right to exclude or eject a person from their car who is in possession of a firearm. It is a powerful tool, meant to balance the Second Amendment rights of gun owners with the privacy and control rights of property owners. This rule, however, does not just apply to vehicles: "private property" can be construed to mean real property (real estate, plots of land), residences, and businesses. Should a citizen in possession of a firearm while riding in another's car, or eating in another's restaurant, be asked to leave because of the presence of a weapon, he or she must do so; failure to leave will constitute grounds for arrest under Georgia's criminal trespass statute, O.C.G.A. § 16-7-21.

### 5. Hunting or Fishing

Any person with a valid hunting or fishing license in his or her possession legally hunting, fishing, or sport shooting with permission of the landowner may carry a firearm—handgun, rifle, or shotgun—without a Weapons Carry License. Any person not required by law to obtain a hunting or fishing license may also carry without a Weapons Carry License, so long as he or she falls within a valid exception to the hunting or fishing license requirement.

### 6. Parks, historic sites, or recreational areas

Under O.C.G.A. § 16-11-126(g), any person with a valid Weapons Carry License may carry in "all parks, historic sites, or recreational areas" operated by the Georgia Department of Natural Resources. Buildings in these areas are permissible, as are wildlife management areas and public transportation. This law does not grant permission to carry on land managed by the U.S. Army Corps of Engineers or other federal property, and does not grant the right to carry in any location prohibited by federal law.

Absent one of these six exceptions, no person may carry a weapon without a valid Weapons Carry License; to do so is a misdemeanor, punishable as a first offense by as many as twelve months in custody and a $1000 fine. A second offense within five years (measured from the dates of arrest in cases where convictions were obtained) is a felony, with a minimum sentence of two years in prison, a maximum of five years.

## II. Where are firearms (long guns or handguns) and weapons prohibited under Georgia law?

Under Georgia law, there are certain places where firearms— including long guns and handguns, as well as knives, which are considered weapons under O.C.G.A. § 16-11-125.1—are generally prohibited— often, regardless of whether you possess a Weapons Carry License. O.C.G.A. § 16-11-127 lists six places where a person is prohibited from possessing firearms or weapons, along with exceptions to the prohibition.

### A. *Prohibited places for all weapons: the basics*

Under O.C.G.A. § 16-11-127, "a person shall be guilty of carrying a weapon or long gun in an unauthorized location and punished as for a misdemeanor when he or she carries a weapon or long gun" while in a:

#### Government Building

Using the definitions above, O.C.G.A. § 16-11-127(b)(1) punishes by a misdemeanor those who carry a firearm into a government building, unless the individual is a license holder. While the general rule for those without a Weapons Carry License, then, is that carrying into a government building is a violation of the law, the opposite is true for those who hold a Weapons Carry License: the general rule is that those with a license may carry into a government building when entry into the building is not restricted by a screening process manned by security personnel, one of whom is a certified peace officer (professional law enforcement officer). Other special circumstances apply to this situation, and is dealt with in-depth in our chapter on carry with a Weapons Carry License, and Georgia's recently enacted "right of retreat" for licensed carriers.

#### Courthouse

By virtue of O.C.G.A. § 16-11-127(b)(1), individuals are not permitted to possess firearms or weapons in courthouses, or in any building that is occupied by judicial courts or contains rooms in which court is held. This applies equally to dedicated courthouses, as well as areas of public buildings that are otherwise dedicated to other functions (such as a multi-purpose city council chamber in a municipal court, used as a courtroom on days court is held) but used as a courtroom.

Jail or prison
Georgia law forbids the possession of all firearms and other weapons on the premises of a jail or prison. This would include not only the buildings, but inside the "guard line," that area surrounding a jail or prison meant to separate the public from the confines of the jail: O.C.G.A. § 42-5-15 makes it a felony to "come inside the guard lines established at any state or county correctional institution with a gun, pistol, or other weapon...."

Place of worship
O.C.G.A. § 16-11-127 forbids possession of a firearm in a "place of worship," unless the governing body permits carry by license holders. Permission may be given orally or in writing (with written permission the more clear choice for proof), but may not be given selectively: if any one individual is granted the right to carry in the place of worship, all may exercise the right. License holders who choose to carry without permission may not be arrested if they are found in possession of a firearm on church property, and may only be fined $100.00 for the offense arising from their unlawful carry, but may still be subject to a revocation of their Weapons Carry License. A non-license holder found in possession of a firearm at a place of worship without permission is subject to arrest, and will be punished by a misdemeanor if convicted.

| CARRYING WEAPONS IN UNAUTHORIZED LOCATIONS: DEFINITION OF GOVERNMENT BUILDING |
|---|

**O.C.G.A. § 16-11-127(a)(2)(A)-(C).** (a) As used in this Code section, the term:
  (2) "Government Building" means:
> (A) The building in which a government entity is housed;
> (B) The building where a government entity meets in its official capacity; provided, however, that if such building is not a publicly owned building, such building shall be considered a government building. . . only during the time such government entity is meeting at such building; or
> (C) The portion of any building that is not a publicly owned building that is occupied by a government entity.

| CARRYING WEAPONS IN UNAUTHORIZED LOCATIONS: DEFINITION OF COURTHOUSE |
|---|

**O.C.G.A. § 16-11-127(a)(2)(A)(1).** (a) As used in this Code section, the term:
> (1) "Courthouse" means a building occupied by judicial courts and containing rooms in which judicial proceedings are held....

### State mental health facility

Generally, O.C.G.A. § 16-11-127(b)(5) prohibits anyone from carrying a firearm into a state mental health facility, specifically identifying the facility type as one "which admits individuals on an involuntary basis," ostensibly to differentiate between these types of facilities and those who accept voluntary patients. However, a WCL holder may lawfully keep a weapon or long gun in a motor vehicle, or in a locked rack, container, or compartment in the vehicle while it is parked in the facility's parking area. O.C.G.A. § 16-11-127(d)(3).

### Nuclear power facility

Carry of a firearm onto the premises of a nuclear power facility is strictly prohibited, both to license holders and non-license holders alike. No provision is made for storage within a locked container or rack within a vehicle belonging to a license holder, as such provisions are made for other restricted locations. Authorized security officers protecting a federal nuclear power facility are exempt from the restrictions, under O.C.G.A. § 16-11-127.2, as are certified peace officers, members of the U.S. Armed Services, defense contractors, and any authorized individual exempted under O.C.G.A. § 16-11-130.

## Within 150 feet of any polling place

The possession of firearms and other weapons is prohibited within 150 feet of any place where polling for a primary or an election is taking place. Though there is no direct reference to early voting in the statute, it is reasonable to believe this code section can be applied to any government-operated early voting location. Many polling locations are also often found at places where firearms are not ordinarily prohibited, such as churches (with permission) and government buildings (under exceptions). However, while voting is taking place, those locations become off-limits for firearms and other weapons. Federal, state, county, or municipal peace officers are exempt from the exclusion of firearms at a polling place, as well as certified security guards. O.C.G.A. § 21-2-413.

B. *Exceptions to unauthorized carry in prohibited places*
There are, of course, certain exceptions to possessing firearms and other weapons in the places listed above.

## Exempted individuals

O.C.G.A. § 16-11-130 provides exemptions from the code sections on unlicensed carry, unauthorized carry, and carry in school safety zones and nuclear power facilities to the following individuals:
   a) Peace officers, and certified retired peace officers;
   b) Wardens, superintendents, and keepers of jails and prisons;
   c) Members of the U.S. Armed Forces and State Reserves;
   d) Defense contractors, when necessary to fulfill their obligations under the contract;
   e) Prosecutors;
   f) Specially-Designated State Board of Pardons and Paroles employees;
   g) Georgia's Attorney General and authorized staff;
   h) Department of Corrections-employed probation officers;
   i) City Public Safety Directors;
   j) Explosive ordinance disposal technicians and certified explosives-detection animal handlers;
   k) Current and former judges;

l)   U.S. Attorneys and Assistant U.S. Attorneys;

m)  Coroners and medical examiners;

n)   Clerks of superior courts;

o)   Magistrate court constables;

p)   Full–time law enforcement chief executives;

q)   Active and retired sheriffs and deputy sheriffs;

r)   Active and retired Georgia State Patrol members; and

s)   Active and retired agents of the Georgia Bureau of Investigation.

While it almost seems the exceptions swallow the rule, it is easy to see the exceptions made in the law reflect the notion that those members of the public who serve in the Armed Forces or in various facets of law enforcement that routinely carry a firearm in the discharge of their daily duties have been vested with the training, knowledge, and (perhaps) public confidence that allows them the exemptions listed.

## III.   Law Concerning Handguns

A.   *When is a vehicle under a person's control so as to allow them to possess a concealed handgun legally?*

A person does not have to be the owner of the vehicle or watercraft to carry a concealed handgun legally. For instance, a rental car is the property of the company that rents the car. However, a person who rents the car from a company and takes possession of the car is the person who has control over the vehicle. Where vehicles are concerned, the person "in control" of a vehicle is generally understood to be the driver, as that is the singular individual who has the ability to move the automobile. For that reason, a person may lawfully possess a handgun in a rental vehicle, the same way they can legally possess a handgun in their own vehicle. The same principles would apply to watercraft: whoever drives the boat is the person that has control of the boat. However, there are no appellate cases directly clarifying this issue.

Similar to our discussion on premises, there are no specific laws on the manner in which the gun must be kept (other than concealed) in the vehicle or watercraft such as in a console, under the seat, in the trunk, and so forth, or is there any statutory law on how the handgun must be stored there—*e.g.,* loaded or unloaded, chambered or unchambered.

## B. *May the handgun be loaded?*

Yes. The law allows the handgun to be loaded and accessible.

---

### PRACTICAL LEGAL TIP

If you carry a handgun in your vehicle, don't allow yourself **to be drawn into a road-rage incident, no matter how minor.** Someone who calls 911 to report that you pointed a gun at them, even though it was really just your middle finger, may get you arrested and charged with a crime. So, if you carry a gun in the car, forget how to flip the bird! —*Matt*

---

## C. *Can a person legally conceal a handgun with their body while in a vehicle?*

Yes, because Georgia has no restriction on where you may keep a handgun in a motor vehicle, just a restriction on who can keep one in a motor vehicle. This means that a person could literally conceal a handgun with their body by sitting on the firearm, though this may prove problematic if the person is required to exit the vehicle (such as during a traffic stop). Of course, in addition to the potential problem of a handgun becoming unconcealed when sitting on it, there's also the matter of safety; just because something is legal, does not mean that it's smart!

## D. *May I keep a handgun in my vehicle if there are children in the car?*

Having children in the car does not change the law on whether a person is able to possess a handgun in the vehicle legally. The law does not require the gun to be either loaded or unloaded, or separated from the driver (*e.g.,* in the trunk). However, it could be considered unlawful if an individual furnishes a pistol to a minor in circumstances that can be considered "reckless" under O.C.G.A. § 16-11-101.1(b). See Chapters 2 and 3 for more information on children and firearms.

## E. *Is it legal for a passenger in a private passenger motor vehicle without a Weapons Carry License to have a handgun?*

Yes! Remember, under O.C.G.A. § 16-11-126(d), it is legal for a passenger to possess a firearm without a license if the passenger is not prohibited by law; is eligible for a Weapons Carry License (even though he or she does not possess one); and the owner of the vehicle allows it.

F. _Is it legal for an owner of a vehicle to possess a handgun when a passenger in the vehicle is a felon or is otherwise disqualified from possessing firearms?_
Yes, so long as the felon (or person disqualified) never possesses the firearm in question.

Example:
> Mark arrives at the McDonald's in Jackson, Georgia, to pick up his brother John who is being released from prison. Mark always keeps a handgun under the driver seat of his vehicle. When John gets in the car, he sits in the front-passenger seat.

Has Mark violated the law? No, Mark still has possession of the handgun. It could conceivably constitute a crime to give a handgun to a disqualified individual—like a felon—but it is not a crime to possess a handgun around such an individual.

## IV. Long guns
### A. _May be carried openly in public_
As previously discussed, Georgia law does not require an individual to have a Weapons Carry License to carry a long gun, nor does the law require that a long gun be concealed when in public. O.C.G.A. § 16-11-126(b) allows "[a]ny person who is not prohibited by law (see our prior discussion on prohibitions on possession in Chapter 3) from possessing a handgun or long gun may have or carry on his or her person a long gun without a valid weapons carry license, **provided that if the long gun is loaded, it shall only be carried in an open and fully exposed manner.**" In other words, so long as you are eligible to carry a handgun or long gun in public, you may carry it openly **or** concealed without a Weapons Carry License, unless it is loaded, in which case it must be openly carried.

Moreover, the law will not allow a police officer to detain you solely to determine if you have a Weapons Carry License. A person carrying a weapon shall not be subject to detention for the sole purpose of investigating whether such person has a weapons carry license.

O.C.G.A. § 16-11-137(b). A resourceful officer may divine some other "reason" for questioning you concerning your firearm or Weapons Carry License, but know your rights! Be polite, but be insistent on your rights.

Example:
> Tim is walking down the street from his home to a shooting range with his loaded AR-15 in a sling pointed down to the ground on his back, coffee in one hand, and range tote bag in the other. Tim is stopped by a police officer and questioned on his rifle. "Do you have a license for that?"

Has Tim committed a crime? No. Tim legally carried his rifle down the street in a safe, non-threatening manner. If the officer requests to see Tim's Weapons Carry License, Tim can politely ask if he is being detained, or if he has committed a crime. Tim can be respectful while standing for his rights: it is permissible for Tim to let the officer know he understands the officer cannot stop him merely to determine whether he has a license to carry. It is also permissible to let the officer know Tim won't answer any questions until he speaks to an attorney, but Tim should be prepared for the situation to escalate.

B. *May I keep a long gun in my vehicle under Georgia law?*
Yes, and the long gun does not have to be concealed or locked in a gun rack. However, openly displaying a long gun in one's vehicle may attract thieves—particularly when it is parked and unattended!

C. *May I possess a long gun while riding in another person's vehicle?*
Yes. Just as with a handgun, so long as you are not prohibited from possessing the long gun, and you are eligible for a Weapons Carry License, you may take the long gun in the car with you, with the caveat that the owner of the vehicle, or the person in legal control of the vehicle, has the right to exclude you if he or she desires.

## V.   Traveling across state lines with firearms
Many people vacation and travel outside of Georgia. Naturally, no Georgian wants to travel unarmed if they can help it, but, unfortunately, not every state shares the same views on gun ownership and gun rights as we do in Georgia. This is especially true in the northeast corner and west coast of the United States. How then does a person pass through states that have restrictive firearms laws or those dif-

ferent from Georgia? For example, how does a person legally pass through a state that prohibits the possession of a handgun without a license from that state? The answer: safe-passage legislation.

A.  *Federal law: qualifying for firearms "Safe Passage"*
Traveling across state lines with a firearm means that a person may need to use the provisions of the federal law known as the "Safe Passage" provision. Federal law allows individuals who are legally in possession of firearms in their state (the starting point of traveling) to travel through states that are not as friendly. This protection is only available under federal law to transport such firearms across state lines for lawful purposes, as long as they comply with the requirements of the Firearm Owners Protection Act, 18 U.S.C. § 926A, nicknamed the "Safe Passage" provision. The first requirement to qualify for the Federal "Safe Passage" provision is that throughout the duration of the trip through the anti-firearm-state, the firearm must be unloaded and locked in the trunk, or locked in a container that is out of reach or not readily accessible from the passenger compartment. The ammunition also must be locked in the trunk or a container. Note that for the storage of both firearms and ammunition, the glove box and center console compartment are specifically not allowed under the statute.

B.  *"Safe Passage" requires legal start to legal finish*
To get protection under federal law, a gun owner's journey must start and end in states where the traveler's possession of the firearm is legal; for instance, a person traveling with their Glock 17 starting in Georgia and ending in Vermont. Even though a person must drive through New York or Massachusetts to get to Vermont, as long as the person qualifies under the "Safe Passage" provision then they may legally pass through. However, if the start point was Georgia and the end point was New York (a place where the handgun would be illegal), there is no protection under the federal law. Safe-passage requires legal start and legal finish.

Although traveling across state lines naturally invokes federal law, it is important to remember that whenever a person finally completes their journey and reaches their destination state, the laws of that state control the possession, carrying, and use of the firearm. Federal law does not make it legal or provide any protection for possession of a firearm that is illegal under the laws of the destination state (*i.e.,* the end state of your travels).

C.  *What is the definition of "traveling" for "Safe Passage"*
    *provisions?*

The final requirement for protection under the federal law is that individuals MUST be "traveling" while in the firearm hostile state. The legal definition of "traveling" is both murky and narrow. The "Safe Passage" provision protection has been held in courts to be limited to situations that strictly relate to traveling and nothing more. Traveling is a term that is not defined in the federal statute; however, it has received treatment in the courts that is indicative of what one can expect. Generally speaking, if a person stops somewhere for too long they cease to be "traveling" and, therefore, lose their protection under the "Safe Passage" provision. How long this time limit is has not been determined either statutorily or by case law with any definitiveness.

While stopping for gas or restroom breaks may not disqualify a person from the "traveling" protection, any stop for an activity not directly related to traveling could be considered a destination and thus you would lose the legal protection. For example, in Chicago anyone in the city for more than 24 hours is not considered to be traveling under local policy. In an actual case, stopping for a brief nap in a bank parking lot in New Jersey caused a Texan driving back home from Maine to lose the "traveling" protection. He received 5 years in prison for possession of weapons that are illegal under New Jersey law. Of course, if the driver would have made it to Hershey, Pennsylvania, he would have been safe. The moral of the story is to travel through these gun-unfriendly states as fast as you can (without breaking the speed limit, of course)!

D.  *Protection under federal law does not mean protection from*
    *prosecution in unfriendly states*

To make matters even worse for firearms travelers, even if a person qualifies for protection under the federal "Safe Passage" provision, New Jersey and New York seem quite proud to treat this protection as an affirmative defense. This means that someone can be arrested even though he or she met all of the requirements of the federal statute. Then, they would have to go to court to assert this defense. In other words, while a person could beat the rap, they will not beat the ride! This becomes even more troublesome in the instance of someone who is legally flying with their firearm, and then due to flight complications, must land in New Jersey or New York, as travelers in this position have been arrested or threatened with arrest.

Once again, the "Safe Passage" provision only applies while a person is traveling; as soon as they arrive at their destination and cease their travels, the laws of that state control a person's actions. Remember: check all applicable state firearms laws before you leave for your destination!

## VI.  Air travel with a firearm

A.  *How do I legally travel with a firearm as a passenger on a commercial airline?*

It is legal to travel with firearms on commercial airlines so long as the firearms transported are unloaded and in a locked, hard-sided container as checked baggage. Under federal law, the container must be completely inaccessible to passengers. Further, under U.S. Homeland Security rules, firearms, ammunition and firearm parts, including firearm frames, receivers, clips, and magazines, are prohibited in carry-on baggage. The Transportation Safety Administration (TSA) also requires that "realistic replicas of firearms are also prohibited in carry-on bags and must be packed in checked baggage. Rifle scopes are permitted in carry-on and checked bags."

B.  *Firearms must be inaccessible*

Federal law makes it a crime subject to fine, imprisonment for up to 10 years, or both, if a person "when on, or attempting to get on, an aircraft in, or intended for operation in, air transportation or intrastate air transportation, has on or about the individual or the property of the individual a concealed dangerous weapon that is or would be accessible to the individual in flight." 49 U.S.C. § 46505(b). Additionally, under 49 U.S.C. § 46303(a) "[a]n individual who, when on, or attempting to board, an aircraft in, or intended for operation in, air transportation or intrastate air transportation, has on or about the individual or the property of the individual a concealed dangerous weapon that is or would be accessible to the individual in flight is liable to the United States Government for a civil penalty of not more than $10,000 for each violation."

Firearms must be checked in baggage

The following guidelines are put out by the TSA for traveling with firearms on airlines:

"To avoid issues that could impact your travel and/or result in law enforcement action, here are some guidelines to assist you in packing your firearms and ammunition:

- All firearms must be declared to the airline during the ticket counter check-in process.
- The term firearm includes: (Please see, for instance, United States Code, Title 18, Part 1, Chapter 44 for information about firearm definitions.)
  - Any weapon (including a starter gun) which will, or is designed to, or may readily be converted to expel a projectile by the action of an explosive.
  - The frame or receiver of any such weapon.
  - Any firearm muffler or firearm silencer.
  - Any destructive device.
- The firearm must be unloaded.
  - As defined by 49 CFR § 1540.5, 'A loaded firearm means a firearm that has a live round of ammunition, or any component thereof, in the chamber or cylinder or in a magazine inserted in the firearm.'
- The firearm must be in a hard-sided container that is locked. A locked container is defined as one that completely secures the firearm from being accessed. Locked cases that can be pulled open with little effort cannot be brought aboard the aircraft.
- If firearms are not properly declared or packaged, TSA will provide the checked bag to law enforcement for resolution with the airline. If the issue is resolved, law enforcement will release the bag to TSA so screening may be completed.
- TSA must resolve all alarms in checked baggage. If a locked container containing a firearm alarms, TSA will contact the airline, who will make a reasonable attempt to contact the owner and advise the passenger to go to the screening location. If contact is not made, the container will not be placed on the aircraft.
- If a locked container alarms during screening and is not marked as containing a declared firearm, TSA will cut the lock in order to resolve the alarm.
- Travelers should remain in the area designated by the air-

craft operator or TSA representative to take the key back after the container is cleared for transportation.

- Travelers must securely pack any ammunition in fiber (such as cardboard), wood or metal boxes or other packaging specifically designed to carry small amounts of ammunition.
- Firearm magazines and ammunition clips, whether loaded or empty, must be securely boxed or included within a hard-sided case containing an unloaded firearm.
- Small arms ammunition, including ammunition not exceeding .75 caliber for a rifle or pistol and shotgun shells of any gauge, may be carried in the same hard-sided case as the firearm, as long as it follows the packing guidelines described above.
- TSA prohibits black powder or percussion caps used with black-powder.
- Rifle scopes are not prohibited in carry-on bags and do not need to be in the hard-sided, locked checked bag."

*See* www.tsa.gov.

C. *May I have a firearm while operating or as a passenger in a private aircraft flying just in Georgia?*

Generally, yes. For purposes of Georgia state law, a private aircraft is treated like any other motorized vehicle. For more information concerning firearms in vehicles, see our earlier discussion in this chapter under Sections II and III.

D. *May I have a firearm in a private aircraft that takes off from Georgia and lands in another state?*

In situations where a private aircraft is taking off from one state and landing in another, the law will simply view this as traveling interstate with firearms. Where no other statutes apply to the person's flight, the person will be subject to the provisions of 18 U.S.C. § 926A regarding the interstate transportation of a firearm: "any person who is not otherwise prohibited by this chapter from transporting, shipping, or receiving firearm shall be entitled to transport a firearm for any lawful purpose from any place where he may lawfully possess and carry such firearm to any other place where he may lawfully possess and carry such firearm if, during such transportation the firearm is unloaded, and neither the firearm nor any ammunition being transported is readily accessible or is directly accessible from the passenger compartment of such transporting vehicle."

This statute allows a person to transport firearms between states subject to the following conditions: that the person can lawfully possess the firearm at his or her points of departure and arrival, and that the firearm remain unloaded and inaccessible during the trip. However, what if the person is a Weapons Carry License holder and wants to carry concealed between states? Fortunately 18 U.S.C. § 927 states that section 926A does not pre-empt applicable state law. Thus, if a person can lawfully carry a concealed weapon in the state in which he or she boards the aircraft and in the state in which he or she lands, the Weapons Carry License holder is not subject to the unloaded and inaccessible restrictions of section 926A.

For operations of private aircraft within one state, a person will only be subject to the laws of the state within which he or she is operating. The person will need to review their state's statutes to determine whether they impose any restrictions on possession of firearms within non-secure areas of airports. The person will also need to be familiar with the airports he or she will be visiting to determine whether each airport has any restrictions (e.g., posting to prohibit concealed carry, etc.).

## VII.  Understanding gun-free school zone laws
The discussion of gun-free school zones is one that covers many different areas of the law and affects both persons who hold a Weapons Carry License as well as those who do not. This is because the "Gun Free School Zone" law and its meaning cause a great deal of confusion. Signs warning about being in a "gun free school zone" are common around schools, but what does this mean to people lawfully in possession of firearms? Georgia does not have a statute specifically detailing "gun free zones," but does have specific laws on carry within "school safety zones." For this reason, we will explain the applicable rules to individuals who possess and do not possess a Weapons Carry License in this chapter, although the chapter has been dedicated to possessing or carrying a firearm without a license.

### A.   *Carrying weapons within school safety zones*
O.C.G.A. § 16-11-127.1 codifies carrying weapons within a school safety zone in Georgia. "School functions" are also protected by the law, and encompass any school function or activity outside the school safety zone. The school safety zone itself refers to any property owned or leased by any public or private elementary, secondary, technical, or vocational school, as well as colleges and universities. The statute makes it a misdemeanor for a Georgia Weapons Carry

License holder to possess or control any weapon or explosive (other than fireworks) within a school safety zone or at a school function; for a non-license holder, the crime is punished as a felony, with a minimum term of imprisonment of two years, and not more than ten years, with a possible fine of up to $10,000.

The statute goes further to allow for entry by a license holder when in possession of a firearm: among other exceptions, it allows a Weapons Carry License holder who "carries or picks up a student within a school safety zone, at a school function, or on a bus or other transportation furnished by the school" to possess a firearm when doing so, and to keep a legally possessed weapon "within a vehicle" when the vehicle is parked within the safety zone or traveling through it. The law also allows a Weapons Carry License holder to keep a firearm in a locked compartment of the vehicle when the vehicle is on the campus.

B. _Federal "Gun Free School Zone" law: 18 U.S.C. § 922(q)_

The text of the federal "Gun Free School Zone" law is found in 18 U.S.C. § 922(q), and creates its own independent criminal offense. This law states that it is a federal crime for a person to possess a firearm that has moved through interstate commerce (this includes virtually all firearms), on the grounds of or within 1,000 feet of a public, parochial, or private school. As surprising as it may seem, under this federal law, the mere possession of a firearm by the occupant of a motor vehicle while driving past a school or dropping off a child, is a federal crime.

However, federal law provides seven exceptions:

1. Exception one: if the possession is on private property which is not part of the school grounds. This means that a person living within 1,000 feet of a school can keep a firearm in their house.
2. Exception two: if the individual possessing the firearm is licensed to do so by the state in which the school zone is located or a political subdivision of the state, and the law of the state or political subdivision requires that, before an individual obtains such a license, the law enforcement authorities of the state or political subdivision verify that the individual is qualified under law to receive the license. This means that a Weapons Carry License holder may legally carry a concealed firearm into a "gun free school zone." However, there is one important note about the statute: a person can only lawfully carry in a school zone located in the state

that issued the firearms license. Therefore, if a person has a Weapons Carry License they can only carry through Georgia school zones. If that Georgia Weapons Carry License holder is traveling through another state, the exception under federal law does not apply to them, and they are in violation of this law. It also means that a Georgia resident, who holds a non-resident non-Georgia concealed carry license or permit, does not benefit from this exception and is in violation of the law if they take a firearm into a school zone.

3. Exception three: if the firearm is not loaded, and is in a locked container, or a locked firearms rack that is on a motor vehicle. This means that if a firearm is unloaded and carried in a locked case, or other type of locked container, such as a glove box or trunk, there is no violation of the federal law.

4. Exception four: if the firearm is carried by an individual for use in a program approved by a school in the school zone. This exception covers school-sponsored shooting activities, such as an ROTC program.

5. Exception five: if the firearm is carried by an individual in accordance with a contract entered into between a school in the school zone and the individual or an employer of the individual. This means that school security guards can carry firearms while on the job.

6. Exception six: if the firearm is carried by a law enforcement officer acting in his or her official capacity. This exception covers police officers while on-duty only. It does not appear to cover them while they are off-duty, even if they are required by state law to carry while off-duty.

7. Exception seven: if the firearm is unloaded and is in the possession of an individual while traversing school property for the purpose of gaining access to public or private lands open to hunting, if the entry on school premises is authorized by school authorities. This means that if a hunter must cross school property to get to a lawful hunting ground, they must have the permission of the school, and the firearm must be unloaded.

C. *Is a person legally permitted to possess a firearm in their vehicle in the parking lot of a college or university?*

Yes, an individual may possess a firearm in a vehicle the person owns or is under their control in a college or university parking lot, subject to the rules under O.C.G.A. § 16-11-127.1: remember, the individual must be a Weapons Carry License holder.

# Chapter Ten

LAW OF CONCEALED CARRY: PART II.
WHAT, HOW, AND WHERE YOU CAN
LEGALLY CARRY WITH A WCL

## I.  To conceal or not to conceal: that is the question!

In this chapter, we will discuss the second aspect of lawful carry: how and where you may lawfully carry with a Weapons Carry License (WCL). The first and most obvious question: must you carry concealed? NO! In Georgia with a Weapons Carry License, you may carry openly or concealed. Georgia law makes no distinction between "open carry" or "concealed carry". So long as you have a valid license (remember also, it's a license, not a permit!), you may carry openly or concealed, in any of the locations we shall discuss. Remember also, these rules for the most part involve handguns; as we found out in the last chapter, so long as you're not prohibited from possessing a firearm, a Weapons Carry License is never required for long guns.

## II.  Where can a WCL holder legally carry a handgun?

A person in possession of a WCL may legally carry a handgun openly or concealed in any place where it is not illegal for them to possess a handgun under state or federal law. Sounds simple enough, right? The places both permitted and prohibited under Georgia law can be found in O.C.G.A. § 16-11-126 and § 16-11-127, among other scattered laws and regulations. In addition, because a WCL is issued by the State of Georgia and not the federal government, a WCL holder may not legally carry their concealed handgun on federal property unless specifically authorized by law. We will touch on this again when we discuss parks.

### A.  *Permissible Carry for WCL holders*
#### 1.  Separating licensed carry from unlicensed carry

In any discussion of permissible carry, it is vitally important to realize the distinction between lawful carry pursuant to a license, and lawful carry without a license. As we discussed in Chapter 9, lawful carry without a license is permitted in Georgia, subject to specific guidelines found in O.C.G.A. § 16-11-126. What we must focus on now, however, is the breadth of permissive carry with a license in Georgia, and how—ultimately—carry with a WCL may be your best bet to protect yourself and the ones you love.

2. Lawful carry with a WCL

Begin with the notion that Georgia grants wide latitude to any resident (or visitor claiming reciprocity with a recognized license or permit from another state) for lawful carry when the individual possesses a WCL. O.C.G.A. § 16-11-127(c) allows any license holder or individual from another state with reciprocal rights to carry "in every location in this state."

| HAVING OR CARRYING HANDGUNS, LONG GUNS, OR OTHER WEAPONS |
| --- |
| **O.C.G.A. § 16-11-127(c).** A license holder or person recognized under subsection (e) of Code Section 16-11-126 shall be authorized to carry a weapon as provided in Code Section 16-11-135 and in every location in this state not listed in subsection (b) or prohibited by subsection (e) of this Code section. |

There are, of course, a number of places under Georgia law where persons are prohibited from carrying a firearm or illegal knife or club, whether or not that person is a WCL holder. We discussed these places in detail in Chapter 9. We also discussed "Gun Free School Zones" in Chapter 9 to explain the limits of carrying or possessing a firearm at or near a school. Specific to our discussion on prohibited locations, however, an individual may not legally carry a firearm in the following places:

1. a government building as a non-license holder;
2. a courthouse;
3. a jail or prison;
4. a place of worship (without permission);
5. a state mental health facility;
6. a nuclear power facility;
7. within 150 feet of a polling place during polling.

These are the "subsection (b)" prohibitions mentioned in O.C.G.A. § 16-11-127: no matter your license status, the law restricts entry to anyone with a weapon, because these locations are considered sensitive.

As with any such restrictive rule, however, there are exceptions, and this rule is not different. Generally, the law allows an exception first for a license holder who enters any of these restricted locations and makes it clear he or she is in possession of a firearm: the restrictions on carry found in subsection (b) do not apply to a license holder who approaches security or management, informs them of the possession of the weapon or long gun, "and explicitly follows the security or management personnel's direction for removing, securing, storing, or temporarily surrendering such weapon or long gun." O.C.G.A. § 16-11-127(d)(2). Additionally, any license holder who possesses his or her weapon or long gun in a motor vehicle or stores it in a "locked compartment of a motor vehicle" or other locked container or firearms rack in a parking facility is excepted from the provisions of the statute. O.C.G.A. § 16-11-127(d)(3).

Other individual locations have rules that benefit WCL holders specifically: in at least two of these locations, having a weapons carry license may mean the difference between your arrest and freedom, and in one, having the license will actually *protect you from a conviction.*

a. Government buildings

| HAVING OR CARRYING HANDGUNS, LONG GUNS, OR OTHER WEAPONS |
|---|
| **O.C.G.A. § 16-11-127(e)(1).** A license holder shall be authorized to carry a weapon in a government building when the government building is open for business and where ingress into such building is not restricted or screened by security personnel. A license holder who enters or attempts to enter a government building carrying a weapon where ingress is restricted or screened by security personnel shall be guilty of a misdemeanor if at least one member of such security personnel is certified as a peace officer pursuant to Chapter 8 of Title 35; provided, however, that a license holder who immediately exits such building or immediately leaves such location upon notification of his or her failure to clear security due to the carrying of a weapon shall not be guilty of violating this subsection or paragraph (1) of subsection (b) of this Code section. A person who is not a license holder and who attempts to enter a government building carrying a weapon shall be guilty of a misdemeanor. |

An important exception to the general rule of universal carry found in O.C.G.A. § 16-11-127 is the government-building rule (those "subsection (e)" prohibitions). As a general rule, governments discourage (and where possible, criminalize) firearms possession in a government building. But is it against the law? Recall the rule we learned in Chapter 9: those individuals with a WCL **may** carry into a government building when entry into the building is not restricted by a screening process manned by security personnel, at least one of whom is a certified peace officer (professional law enforcement officer). As a Weapons Carry License holder, Georgia law allows you to enter a government building carrying a weapon—concealed or openly— when there is no "law enforcement screening" conducted in the building. "Law enforcement screening" is exactly what it sounds like: magnetometers, x-ray machines, and certified peace officers searching you for weapons as you enter. At least one of the members of the screening team must be certified as a peace officer by the State of Georgia, meaning deputy sheriff, police officer, county marshal, *etc.*: while well-trained and well-intentioned, private security personnel are not as a rule certified as peace officers, which means if there is no certified officer present, it is not considered "law enforcement screening."

But what of the WCL holder who enters a government building with law enforcement screening? According to the statute, "[a] license holder who enters or attempts to enter a government building carrying a weapon where ingress is restricted or screened by security personnel shall be guilty of a misdemeanor," if one of the security personnel is a certified peace officer. O.C.G.A. § 16-11-127(e)(1). There exists, however, a very powerful exception for WCL holders caught in the predicament of entering a government building and being found in possession of a firearm. This exception takes the form of a "right of retreat," a right woven into the law that exists *only for Weapons Carry License holders* and gives a WCL holder stopped at a security checkpoint the right to leave the checkpoint after attempting to enter with a firearm:

> "...provided, however, that a license holder who immediately exits such building or immediately leaves such location upon notification of his or her failure to clear security due to the carrying of a weapon **shall not be guilty** of violating this subsection or paragraph (1) of subsection (b) of this Code section."

"This subsection" is O.C.G.A. § 16-11-127(e)(1), where entry to a government building monitored by "security personnel" is a misdemeanor; "paragraph (1) or subsection (b) of this Code section" is O.C.G.A. § 16-11-127(b)(1), which makes it a misdemeanor to carry a weapon or long gun "[i]n a government building as a non-license holder." What the Georgia General Assembly has crafted is what is known as an absolute defense: any WCL holder who attempts entry to a government building with security personnel, who then exits the building or leaves the location after he or she is notified of the firearm, shall not be guilty of violating the law. An individual who attempts entry with a firearm who is not a WCL holder will be guilty of a misdemeanor.

But be forewarned: "shall not be guilty" does not mean "shall not be arrested." This defense to a conviction does not bar law enforcement officers (particularly those unaware of the right of retreat) from arresting someone lawfully carrying: such an unfortunate circumstance reinforces the old saying, "You can beat the rap, but you can't beat the ride." If you find yourself facing arrest by an officer who doesn't know the law, be polite, but insist upon your rights. And call your lawyer!

Example:

> Steve decides to take thirty minutes of his lunch break from a jobsite close to the courthouse to research a few names in the courthouse for a family genealogy project. Steve is in a hurry, so he parks in a metered spot, drops a few coins in the meter, and makes a mental note to be back outside before his time runs out. In the rush to beat the clock, Steve forgets to take out of his pocket the .380 he keeps with him on the jobsite. As he walks through the courthouse metal detector, a siren blares, and sheriff's deputies advance upon him, announcing Steve has a gun, and commanding him to put his hands up.

What should Steve's next step be? The deputies know Steve has a gun, and now Steve remembers the tiny pistol in his pocket. According to the statute, he has a right to retreat, but in this scenario, is it wise to just walk away? Steve's goal—as anyone's goal should be in this situation— should be to leave with his life and liberty intact, but not at the risk of the deputies misinterpreting his actions. Perhaps the best course of action would be one where Steve allows the deputies to secure the scene, then calmly discusses with them the fact he is a WCL holder who simply jumped out of his car too quickly to remember the pistol, and that he would like to exit and properly store the pistol, as is his right. If the deputies allow Steve to do so, it's a victory for everyone, since the law has worked as intended. If, however, Steve is arrested (despite his statutory defense), the arrest must run its course, even though the law says Steve shall not be found guilty of the violation. Steve's use of an attorney who understands the use of the statutory right of retreat will be key in the resolution of the case.

### b. Places of worship

In terms of prohibitions, O.C.G.A. § 16-11-127(b)(4) restricts weapons carry "[i]n a place of worship, unless the governing body or authority of the place of worship permits the carrying of weapons or long guns by license holders...." This is yet another "subsection (b)" restriction with a decidedly different outcome, however, for Weapons Carry License holders. Section 16-11-127(e)(2) paints a different picture for a WCL holder:

> *Any license holder who violates subsection (b) of this Code section in a place of worship shall not be arrested but shall be fined not more than $100.00. Any person who is not a license holder who violates subsection (b) of this Code section in a place of worship shall be punished as for a misdemeanor.*

If you are a WCL holder who carries in church without permission and are caught doing so, you cannot be arrested. No arrest is to take place; that will not deter police officers from handing you a citation and summoning you to face a judge for carrying a firearm in an unauthorized location. Should you be found guilty, the judge can only fine you $100 for a violation of O.C.G.A. § 16-11-127, but there is a significant unintended consequence: by virtue of O.C.G.A. § 16-11-129(H)(ii), the probate court who issued the offender's Weapons Carry License will revoke his or her WCL for a period of five years:

> Any person who has been convicted of... [c]arrying a weapon or long gun in an unauthorized location in violation of Code Section 16-11-127... and has not been free of all restraint or supervision in connection therewith and free of any other conviction for at least five years immediately preceding the date of the application. O.C.G.A. § 16-11-129(H)(ii)

### 3. What is the rule on carry on private property?

As we know, a WCL holder or individual granted reciprocity is authorized to carry "in every location in this state" so long as carry is not specifically prohibited through state or federal law. This is how Georgia chooses to recognize and honor the Second Amendment rights of its citizens, and this recognition extends to private property: with a Weapons Carry License, an individual may lawfully carry either openly or concealed on the private property of another person.

The General Assembly must, however, balance the Second Amendment rights of an individual lawfully carrying a firearm with the rights of a property owner to freely associate with whom they wish, and also to restrict access to their property in a manner of their choosing. Accordingly, Georgia legislators have struck a balance between the rights of an individual carrying a firearm onto private property and the rights of the property owner: while a WCL holder or individual granted reciprocity may carry onto private property,

> private property owners or persons in legal control of private property through a lease, rental agreement, licensing agreement, contract, or any other agreement to control access to such private property shall have the right to exclude or eject a person who is in possession of a weapon or long gun on their private property.... O.C.G.A. § 16-11-127(c)

This means the owner of the property; the lessee; the manager (of a restaurant, for instance); or security hired by the owner or management *can restrict* a lawful WCL holder from entering the owner's property with a weapon ("exclude"), or can remove a WCL holder carrying a weapon from the property ("eject").

4.   Is a "No Weapons" sign enough to keep me out of a business? The legal issues created with the notice requirement in Georgia law lead to interesting factual questions, usually centered around signs: is it enough for a business to post a sign that simply says "No Weapons Allowed"? Can that keep a WCL holder out of the business with a firearm? As is the case with most questions in the law, two lawyers may give two completely different answers, but it is the authors' opinion that signage is **not** enough to restrict a WCL holder from entering a building with a weapon.

This opinion is based on the statute itself: the Code section authorizing private property owners to exclude Weapons Carry License holders only allows them to do so in accordance with the procedures found in O.C.G.A. § 16-7-21(b)(3), the criminal trespass statute. The statute makes it a crime when an individual "knowingly and without authority... [r]emains upon the land or premises of another person... after receiving notice from the owner, rightful occupant, or, upon proper identification, an authorized representative of the owner or rightful occupant to depart." O.C.G.A. § 16-7-21(b)(3). The criminal trespass statute requires the notice actually be given by the owner, rightful occupant, or authorized representative, *to the individual*. There is nothing in the statute or case law that contemplates a posted sign to be sufficient notice from the proper party that entry to any specific individual is prohibited; on the contrary, cases in Georgia have specifically found notice to be an essential element of the crime of criminal trespass, and that the notice not to enter the premises must be given to the accused by the owner, rightful occupant, or by an authorized representative of the owner or rightful occupant. *Sheehan v. State,* 314 Ga. App. 325 (Ga. Ct. App. 2012)(*see also Jackson v. State,* 242 Ga. App. 113 (Ga. Ct. App. 2000)).

### 5. Places of employment: barred or not?

Places of employment are yet another location where the rules can be confusing. Under O.C.G.A. § 16-11-135, employers may restrict weapons carried into a place of employment: employers are treated as property owners or "persons in legal control of property" and therefore can forbid entry to the building with a firearm. License holders are allowed to conceal their handgun within their locked, privately-owned motor vehicle in an employee parking lot, garage, or other parking area provided by an employer, however, if the following conditions are met:

1. the firearm or ammunition is in an employee's privately owned motor vehicle;
2. the firearm is locked out of sight "within the trunk, glove box, or other enclosed compartment or area"; and
3. the employee possesses a Weapons Carry License.

If these conditions are present, employers may not restrict the possession of firearms within the parking lot, and furthermore may not condition employment "upon any agreement by a prospective employee that prohibits an employee from entering the parking lot and access thereto" with a firearm in the car, so long as the conditions for entering above are met. O.C.G.A. § 16-11-135.

Employers still have a great deal of authority, however, in the application of these rules. Subsection (e) states that at-will employees continue to be at-will employees, which means they may still be terminated at the employer's discretion for any reason. Furthermore, the rules allowing employee's to keep firearms in their vehicles do not allow for *company* vehicles; company vehicles are by definition the employer's property, and subject to the employer's rules on weapons carry. Moreover, while O.C.G.A. § 16-11-135(a) generally restricts employer's from enforcing "any policy or rule that has the effect of allowing such employer or its agents to search the locked privately owned vehicles of evmployees or invited guests on the employer's parking lot and access thereto", law enforcement officers may still search the vehicle when conducting a valid legal search, with or without a warrant, and employers may search an employee's private vehicle in "any situation in which a reasonable person would believe that accessing a locked vehicle of an employee is necessary to prevent an immediate threat to human health, life, or safety"(O.C.G.A. § 16-11-135(c)(3)), and also in any situation where there is probable cause to believe the employee is unlawfully in possession of the employer's property (theft), but only with the employee's permission. O.C.G.A. § 16-11-135(c)(4).

Perhaps the most important exception to the firearm carry and search rule, however, is this: if an employer provides a "secure parking area" (one that "restricts general public access through the use of a gate, security station, security officers, or other similar means which limit public access into the parking area"), employers (this includes both private and public employers) **may** restrict entry to the parking facility while in possession of a firearm, and **may** search every car that enters the secure parking area, so long as the searches are conducted frequently and uniformly upon all entrants. O.C.G.A. § 16-11-135 (d)(1). The Code section does not require employers to take any additional security measures to protect employees (subsection (h)), and employers (and property owners and agents) are protected from criminal and civil liability in relation to any action brought based on a firearm brought in an employee's personal vehicle (subsection (g)). The statute is a confusing but nevertheless important part of personal protection in Georgia.

## B. *Automobiles, watercraft, and other places*

1. <u>May a person carry a concealed handgun in an automobile?</u>
Yes. A WCL holder in Georgia can legally carry a concealed handgun in their vehicle. As the reader will recall, however, a person does not need a WCL to possess a handgun in their vehicle or a vehicle under their control. O.C.G.A. § 16-11-126 allows an individual to carry in

his or her motor vehicle without a license so long as he or she is not prohibited from possessing a firearm, and further allows unlicensed carry in any private vehicle, so long as the individual is not prohibited from possessing a weapon and is eligible for a Weapons Carry License, subject to the owner's permission. A Weapons Carry License protects your right to carry legally in both your vehicle, and another's private vehicle. For non-WCL holders, see Chapter 9.

2. May a person legally carry a concealed handgun in a commercial vehicle?

Yes. One question that is often asked is whether a person who operates a commercial shipping vehicle is entitled to follow the same rules and regulations governing ordinary WCL holders in Georgia. The answer to this question is simple: YES! There are no specific Georgia or federal regulations regarding carry in a commercial shipping vehicle beyond those regulations that may be imposed by the commercial employer. This may be a breach of company policy, but not the law and is not a crime. Remember the owner of the commercial vehicle, as any private property owner, may lawfully restrict carry inside the vehicle.

3. May a person carry a concealed handgun on a boat or watercraft?

Yes. A boat does not fit the definition of "vehicle" in Georgia, so the rules on weapons carry *without* a license for automobiles do not necessarily apply. Consequently, unless your boat is of a type that may be considered a "habitation" or home for purposes of carrying without a license, you must have a Weapons Carry License to possess a firearm in a boat (should the boat be of a type that would be considered a home or habitation, an individual may be covered for carry without a license under O.C.G.A. § 16-11-126(a)). Inasmuch as O.C.G.A. § 16-11-127 allows for carry with a Weapons Carry License "in every location in this state" not prohibited by state or federal law, however, a WCL holder should feel free to carry a firearm in a boat in the same manner he or she would on dry land: on any public or private property, so long as not prohibited or excluded by the property owner.

The one caveat to this rule is carrying on land administered by the United States Corps of Engineers. Federal regulations restrict possession of firearms on Corps lands. 36 CFR § 327.13 prohibits "the possession of loaded firearms, ammunition. . . or other weapons" on

Corps-managed property, unless carried by law enforcement, carried for hunting or trapping (note: self-defense is not a listed exception), at authorized shooting ranges, or by permission of the District Commander. This is a potentially serious exception for boaters, since much of Georgia's leisure boating and fishing takes place on property managed by the Corps of Engineers: Lake Sydney Lanier, Lake Allatoona, and West Point Lake, to name a few, all are managed by the Corps of Engineers. All property managed by the U.S. Army Corps of Engineers nationwide falls under this general ban on weapons carry.

4.   Can a WCL holder carry in the airport?

### CARRYING A WEAPON OR LONG GUN AT A COMMERCIAL SERVICE AIRPORT

**O.C.G.A. § 16-11-130.2 (a)-(b).** (a) No person shall enter the restricted access area of a commercial service airport, in or beyond the airport security screening checkpoint, knowingly possessing or knowingly having under his or her control a weapon or long gun. Such area shall not include an airport drive, general parking area, walkway, or shops and areas of the terminal that are outside the screening checkpoint and that are normally open to unscreened passengers or visitors to the airport. Any restricted access area shall be clearly indicated by prominent signs indicating that weapons are prohibited in such area.

(b) A person who is not a license holder and who violates this Code section shall be guilty of a misdemeanor. A license holder who violates this Code section shall be guilty of a misdemeanor; provided, however, that a license holder who is notified at the screening checkpoint for the restricted access area that he or she is in possession of a weapon or long gun and who immediately leaves the restricted access area following such notification and completion of federally required transportation security screening procedures shall not be guilty of violating this Code section.

Everyone is aware that airports have "restricted access areas" for boarding, departure, and arrival where only ticketed passengers and other authorized personnel may enter; non-travelers or anyone without authorization are restricted from entry. These areas are separated from the non-secure, general public areas of the airport (parking, main terminals, ticket desks, baggage claim, *etc.*); anything outside the screening checkpoints manned by full-time employees or contractors of the federal Transportation Safety Administration is in the non-secure portion of the airport.

In Georgia a Weapons Carry License holder may carry, openly or concealed, in the general public, non-secure sections of the airport. This includes the "airport drive, general parking area, walkway, or shops and areas of the terminal that are outside the screening checkpoint and that are normally open to unscreened passengers or visitors to the airport." O.C.G.A. § 16-11-130.2. The law criminalizes weapons carry within the restricted access areas of the airport. By specifically identifying those areas not included in the restriction, the law permits carry within those non-secure areas, but only by an individual possessing a valid Weapons Carry License.

A non-license holder who violates the law by knowingly carrying a weapon or long gun through the restricted access area is guilty of a misdemeanor. A WCL holder is likewise guilty of a misdemeanor, but holds a statutory right of retreat, like that contemplated by O.C.G.A. § 16-11-127.

This statutory right of retreat is meant to provide a defense to a state-law crime for those WCL holders who unwittingly carry a firearm through the secured access portions of an airport in Georgia, and for almost two years after Georgia's Governor Nathan Deal signed it into law in 2014, it did just that. In May, 2016, however, the U.S. Attorney's Office for the Northern District of Georgia issued a press release decrying the frequent carry of firearms through the security checkpoint at Atlanta's Hartsfield-Jackson International Airport, consistently one of the world's busiest airports. Because carry of a firearm past an airport security checkpoint is still a federal crime, the U.S. Attorney's Office announced that, henceforth, individuals possessing a valid WCL who carried a firearm (or attempted to do so) through the security checkpoint in the Atlanta airport would receive a citation to appear in federal court, while an individual without a WCL who attempted the same act would be charged in state court. The effect of this policy change is to strip valid Georgia Weapons Carry License holders of their statutory right of retreat and the legal defense that comes from it. At the time of publication, this policy change was still in effect.

O.C.G.A. § 16-11-130.2(c) classifies as a separate felony any attempt to bring a firearm into an airport to commit a felony, with maximum possible imprisonment of fifteen years. Subsection (d) preempts any county or municipal ordinance in conflict with this statute.

### 5. Can a WCL holder carry in a restaurant?

Restaurants are establishments that are subject to the same rules discussed earlier in the section governing the rights of private property owners. Restaurant owners, operators, managers, and security may exclude or eject those who are in possession of a weapon or long gun, but that notice must be given to the individual possessing the weapon. The authors believe a posted sign is not enough to restrict entry on the basis of possessing a firearm for personal protection, but ask yourself this: if you know a business doesn't want you to protect yourself, are you willing to spend your money there?

### 6. Can an individual carry a firearm in a hotel?

Yes. If an individual is staying overnight in a hotel, consider the hotel a "home" in which a firearm may be carried with a license or without, so long as the individual is not prohibited from possession otherwise. Certainly, then, lawful carry with a WCL would also be permitted. If an individual is visiting a hotel but not dwelling there temporarily, consider the hotel "private property" as you would any other establishment. Consequently, a Weapons Carry License holder may carry there unless excluded or ejected based on possession of a firearm. In either instance—staying overnight in the hotel, or visiting as anyone might visit any other type of private property—a WCL holder will be able to carry a firearm in a hotel.

### 7. Can an individual with a WCL carry a concealed handgun in public transit?

Yes. By virtue of O.C.G.A. § 16-12-123, any person "who boards or attempts to board an aircraft, bus, or rail vehicle with. . . a firearm **for which such person does not have on his or her person a valid weapons carry license**" shall be guilty of a felony. The language of the statute provides entry (1) to a WCL holder; (2) who has his or her license in their possession. The second element is important, as opposed to someone who has a license but does not carry it; make sure you carry it with you! The prohibition on carry does not apply to anyone "transporting weapons contained in baggage which is not accessible to passengers if the presence of such weapons has been declared to the transportation company" and the weapons are secured in compliance with the law, but a notification requirement does not seem to exist for WCL holders. O.C.G.A. § 16-12-123(b). The owners of private aircraft, bus, and rail vehicles may permit carry in the vehicle by express permission.

C. *Government properties*
A Weapons Carry License and the rights attached are a product of state law and convey no rights to the WCL holder that have been recognized under federal law. However, in certain instances, the federal government recognizes these state rights on certain federal property, which means it is important to know how the state and federal laws interact.

1. Are firearms permitted in federal buildings?

| FIREARMS PROHIBITED IN FEDERAL FACILITIES |
|---|
| **18 U.S.C. § 930(a).** ...whoever knowingly possesses or causes to be present a firearm or other dangerous weapon in a Federal facility (other than a Federal court facility), or attempts to do so, shall be fined under this title or imprisoned not more than 1 year, or both. |

No: under this statute, a "federal facility" refers to any building or part of a building that is owned or leased by the federal government and is a place where federal employees are regularly present for the purpose of performing their official duties. *See* 18 U.S.C. § 930(g)(1). However, this statute does not apply to "the lawful performance of official duties by an officer, agent, or employee of the United States, a State, or a political subdivision thereof, who is authorized by law to engage in or supervise the prevention, detection, investigation, or prosecution of any violation of law," nor does it apply to federal officials or members of the armed forces who are permitted to possess such a firearm by law, or the lawful carrying of a firearm incident to hunting or "other lawful purposes." 18 U.S.C. § 930(d). This statute does not govern the possession of a firearm in a federal court facility.

2. May a person with a WCL carry a concealed handgun in a state or municipal park?
The answer is: Yes. O.C.G.A. § 16-11-126 (g) and (h) specifically allow WCL holders to carry handguns in state parks. Furthermore, a local municipality is preempted by state law from prohibiting the carrying of a concealed handgun by a license holder and is, therefore, not authorized to prevent the legal carry of a firearm in a city park.

| HAVING OR CARRYING HANDGUNS, LONG GUNS, OR OTHER WEAPONS |
| --- |
| **O.C.G.A. § 16-11-126(g-h).** ...[A]ny person with a valid weapons carry license may carry a weapon in all parks, historic sites, or recreational areas... including all publicly owned buildings located in such parks, historic sites, and recreational areas, in wildlife management areas, and on public transportation; provided, however, that a person shall not carry a handgun into a place where it is prohibited by federal law. |
| (h) (1) No person shall carry a weapon without a valid weapons carry license unless he or she meets one of the exceptions to having such license as provided in subsections (a) through (g) of this Code section. |

3.  <u>May a person with a WCL carry a concealed handgun in a national park?</u>
WCL holders are permitted to carry in National Parks located in Georgia, but not buildings within the park, such as ranger stations and visitor centers, because these are federal buildings. Under federal law, for firearms purposes, all federal parks are subject to the state law of the state in which the park is located. *See* 16 U.S.C. § 1a-7b.

4.  <u>VA Hospitals: firearms prohibited</u>

| FIREARMS PROHIBITED AT VETERANS AFFAIRS HOSPITALS |
| --- |
| **38 CFR § 1.218(a)(13).** No person while on property shall carry firearms, other dangerous or deadly weapons, or explosives, either openly or concealed, except for official purposes. |

One place where many law-abiding WCL holders fall victim is at the VA Hospital. While hospitals are not generally prohibited locations for carry under Georgia law, the VA Hospital system is governed by federal laws that prohibit the carrying of any firearm while on VA property. This includes the parking lot, sidewalk, and any other area that is the property of the VA.

Under federal law, 38 CFR § 1.218(a)(13) states that "no person while on property shall carry firearms, other dangerous or deadly weapons, or explosives, either openly or concealed, except for official purposes." The "official purposes" specified refer specifically to the VA Hospital Police. The area where this specific law gets good people in trouble is that the Department of Veterans Affairs has its own set of laws and guidelines and is not controlled strictly by the Gun Control Act and the general provisions regarding the prohibition of firearms on federal property. The VA law is much more restrictive, and many veterans have found themselves in trouble when they valet-park their vehicle and the valet discovers a concealed handgun in the console or concealed in the door storage area. How rigidly this law is enforced is determined by the individual hospital administrators as described in 38 CFR § 1.218(a), however, regardless of how strictly the law is enforced firearms are still prohibited under the law and the VA police are very aggressive in enforcing them.

### 5. United States Post Offices: firearms prohibited

| FIREARMS PROHIBITED AT POST OFFICES |
| --- |
| **39 CFR § 232.1(l).** Notwithstanding the provisions of any other law, rule or regulation, no person while on postal property may carry firearms, other dangerous or deadly weapons, or explosives, either openly or concealed, or store the same on postal property, except for official purposes. |

Under this regulation, firearms or other deadly weapons are prohibited on postal property, which includes not only the building, but all property surrounding the building where a post office is located. This includes the parking lot (*e.g.,* a person's vehicle where a firearm may be stored), as well as the sidewalks and walkways. Earlier in this chapter, we mentioned that parking lots, sidewalks and walkways, and other related areas are generally not included when discussing the premises of a location where the carrying of a weapon is prohibited by law. Like the VA Hospital, United States Post Offices are another exception to the rule. In 2013, there was a decision by a United States District Court addressing this issue in Colorado which allowed a license holder to bring his firearm into the parking lot of the Avon, Colorado Post Office. However, in 2015, that case was reversed on appeal by the U.S. Tenth Circuit Court of Appeals. In 2016, the U.S. Supreme Court refused to review the Tenth Circuit's reversal. It should be noted that the U.S. Tenth Circuit does not include Georgia, and therefore had no legal bearing on the prohibition against possessing firearms on United States Post Office property in Georgia.

6. <u>Military bases and installations: firearms generally prohibited</u>

Military bases and installations are treated much like the VA Hospital and US Post Offices in that they have, and are governed by, a separate set of rules and regulations with respect to firearms on the premises of an installation or base and are generally prohibited. Military installations are governed by the federal law under Title 32 of the Code of Federal Regulations. Moreover, the sections covering the laws governing and relating to military bases and installations are exceedingly numerous. There are, in fact, sections which are dedicated to only certain bases such as 32 CFR § 552.98 which only governs the possessing, carrying, concealing, and transporting of firearms on Fort Stewart/Hunter Army Airfield.

D. *Can municipalities restrict firearms rights?*
<u>Can cities or other governmental agencies enact firearms laws or regulations regarding the carrying of a concealed handgun by WCL holders that are more restrictive than state laws?</u>

No, because municipalities are restricted by Georgia law from passing ordinances further restricting the concealed carry of a handgun by a WCL holder. By law, municipalities can neither regulate "the possession, ownership, transport, carrying, transfer, sale, purchase, licensing, or registration of firearms or other weapons or components of firearms or other weapons", nor can they impose local ordinance regulations on gun shows or local weapons dealers. O.C.G.A. § 16-11-173.

E. *What size handgun may a WCL holder legally carry?*

As we mentioned in Chapter 2, federal law dictates that any firearm which has any barrel with a bore of more than one-half inch in diameter (.50 caliber) is a "destructive device" and is subject to the National Firearms Act (except for certain shotguns).

Possession of any such firearm without the proper paperwork associated with NFA firearms is illegal whether a person is a WCL holder or not. For more information on destructive devices and the NFA, see Chapter 14.

### III. <u>WCL holders dealing with law enforcement</u>

A. *Do I legally have to present my WCL to a police officer if they ask for my identification and I am carrying my gun?*

O.C.G.A. § 16-11-137(b) is very clear with respect to this issue: "A person carrying a weapon shall not be subject to detention for the sole purpose of investigating whether such person has a weapons carry license." Put simply, an officer may not stop anyone carrying openly just to determine whether the individual has a Weapons Carry License. The same rule applies to those who carry concealed, although it is somewhat less likely the officer will have knowledge of the firearm.

Yet again, forewarned is forearmed: even though you may know an officer can't stop you just to check your Weapons Carry License, the officer may not! Be respectful, show the officer he or she has nothing to fear from you, but insist upon your rights. Remember also, O.C.G.A. § 16-11-137(a) requires a WCL holder to carry his or her license when carrying a weapon. Failure to do so will be "*prima facie*" evidence (evidence "on its face") the individual has violated the law.

B.  *Can a police officer legally take a WCL holder's handgun away?*
A police officer should disarm a WCL holder only if the Weapons Carry License holder consents, or if the officer obtains the firearm through a legally valid search, whether that search is a warrantless search based upon exigent circumstances, a search based upon a warrant issued by a neutral magistrate, or a search incident to the valid arrest of the license holder. The law does not authorize officers to freely disarm every civilian with a weapon without cause.

C.  *Is a WCL holder required to inform an officer during a traffic stop he or she has a firearm?*
No, Georgia law does not require that a license holder (or a non-licensed holder legally carrying a firearm, for that matter) inform a law enforcement officer of a firearm in the car. There is no legal obligation to make an officer aware of any weapon in the vehicle whatsoever; the decision to do so is one based solely on personal preference and common sense. If there is no reason to reveal the presence of the firearm, drivers should use their own best judgment.

D.  *What are passengers with a WCL in a vehicle legally obligated to do when the driver is stopped by law enforcement?*
Sometimes, police will ask passengers in a vehicle for identification to run a check for outstanding warrants—or for a Weapons Carry License—when the driver has been stopped for a traffic infraction. The same rules for weapons carry apply to passengers as to drivers: passengers in Georgia are not obligated to inform officers of a WCL or firearm in the car, but may use their best judgment in de-

termining how to answer. As with any other individual, an officer may not detain a vehicle's passenger solely to determine if he or she has a Weapons Carry License. More generally, officers may freely ask questions of passengers, or for consent to search, but have no authority to do so unless consent has been granted, a warrant has been issued, or the officer has a reasonable suspicion to believe the passenger has committed or is about to commit a crime.

## IV.  Reciprocity

A.  *Can I carry a concealed handgun in other states if I have a Georgia WCL?*

Yes, in the following states that recognize a Georgia Weapons Carry License:

| | | |
|---|---|---|
| Alabama | Louisiana | Pennsylvania |
| Alaska | Maine | South Carolina |
| Arkansas | Michigan | South Dakota |
| Arizona | Mississippi | Tennessee |
| Colorado | Missouri | Texas |
| Florida | Montana | Utah |
| Idaho | New Hampshire | West Virginia |
| Indiana | North Carolina | Wisconsin |
| Iowa | North Dakota | Wyoming |
| Kansas | Ohio | |
| Kentucky | Oklahoma | |

Reciprocity either exists between Georgia and these states, or they have unilaterally decided to recognize Georgia WCLs. Every state has the authority to determine whether or not their state will recognize a carry license or permit issued by another state. Reciprocity occurs when states recognize one another's carry licenses, either by enabling statutes that provide reciprocity to the residents of any state that recognizes the home state's weapons license or permit, or by directly entering into an agreement with each other to do so.

States are neither required to have reciprocity with one another, nor  to recognize another state's carry license. As an example, while Virginia officially recognized the Weapons Carry Licenses of all other states, Georgia has not granted reciprocity for Virginia permit holders, ostensibly because Virginia currently will not recognize weapons permits issued to individuals with current or prior military service between the ages of 18 and 21, who are individuals eligible for a Georgia license. This situation leaves the recognition of Georgia Weapons Carry Licenses in dispute, meaning Georgia residents should travel with caution in this state, or any state that refuses to recognize a Georgia WCL.

### B. *What state's laws apply to me when using my Georgia WCL in another state?*

Anytime a WCL holder is in another state, even if that state recognizes a Georgia WCL, the law of the state where the person is currently located will be the law that governs the individual's firearms possession and use. If a person is traveling to another state, he or she must abide by that state's laws. A Georgian visiting Texas may carry a handgun, but must comply with Texas law; the same requirement exists for a Texan in Georgia. The most common laws Georgians should be aware of are a state's requirement to present a license to law enforcement upon request, and the places that are off-limits to Weapons Carry License holders, as much of the time these laws vary from state to state. For example, while a Georgia officer may not stop an individual who is carrying openly just to determine whether he or she has a WCL, in Texas a police officer has the authority to do just that!

### C. *Can persons who are not Georgia residents obtain a Georgia WCL?*

No. Remember, in order to be eligible for a Georgia Weapons Carry License, you must be an individual "whose domicile is in that county [where you seek the license] or who is on active duty with the United States armed forces" in that county. O.C.G.A. § 16-11-129(a). You must be able to claim a residence in Georgia in order to obtain a WCL in Georgia.

# CHAPTER ELEVEN

## RESTORATION OF FIREARMS RIGHTS: THE LAW OF PARDONS, EXPUNGEMENT, AND RESTRICTION

## I. Is it possible to restore a person's right to bear arms?

What happens after a conviction for a crime? Is it possible to later clear your name and your criminal record? If it's possible, what is the process for removing a conviction and restoring your right to purchase and possess firearms? This chapter will explain how an individual—under very limited circumstances—can have arrest records, criminal charges, and even criminal convictions removed or restricted. But be forewarned: success in this endeavor can be tricky. Each state has different rules concerning restrictions and restoration of rights, as well as a completely different set of rules under federal law. Before we begin a meaningful discussion, it is important to explain two terms and concepts: clemency and "restriction."

### A. *What is clemency?*

Clemency is the action the government, usually the chief executive (*e.g.,* the President on the federal level or a governor on the state level), takes in forgiving or pardoning a crime or canceling the penalty of a crime, either wholly or in part. Clemency can include full pardons after a conviction; full pardons after completion of pretrial diversion; conditional pardons; pardons based on innocence; commutations of sentence; emergency medical reprieves; and family medical reprieves. Clemency can be granted at both the federal and state level.

### B. *What is a records restriction?*

Records restriction (formerly known in Georgia, and still known in many states, as "expungement") is the physical act of restricting access to arrests and convictions on your criminal record. If properly restricted, only law enforcement and judicial agencies can see a restricted arrest and sentence on your record. Under certain circumstances, a person may have their criminal record restricted, or in the case of what is known as a First Offender plea, sealed.

> **PRACTICAL LEGAL TIP**
> While our intention is to provide you with as much information as possible as to how you can have your firearms rights restored if you are convicted of a crime, it's also important to make sure you are aware of how rarely pardons, restrictions, and restorations of firearms rights are granted. While it's certainly worth the effort to apply for a pardon in the event you receive one, be careful not to get your hopes up, because they are seldom granted. —*Matt*

## II.   Federal law

### A.  *Presidential Pardon*

Under Article II, Section 2 of the United States Constitution, the President of the United States has the power "to grant reprieves and pardons for offenses against the United States, except in cases of impeachment." The President's power to pardon offenses has also been interpreted to include the power to grant conditional pardons, commutations of sentence, conditional commutations of sentence, remission of fines and forfeitures, respite, and amnesty. The President's clemency authority only extends, however, to federal offenses; the President cannot grant clemency for a **state crime.**

#### 1.  How does a person petition for federal clemency or a pardon?

Under federal law, a person requesting executive clemency must petition the President of the United States by submitting the petition to the United States Department of Justice, Office of the Pardon Attorney. The Office of the Pardon Attorney can provide petitions and other required forms necessary to complete the application for clemency. *See* 28 CFR § 1.1. Petition forms for commutation of sentence may also be obtained from the wardens of federal penal institutions. In addition, a petitioner applying for executive clemency with respect to military offenses should submit his or her petition directly to the Secretary of the military branch that had original jurisdiction over the court-martial trial and conviction of the petitioner.

The Code of Federal Regulations requires an applicant to wait five years after the date of the release of the petitioner from confinement, or in a case where no prison sentence was imposed, five years after the date of conviction, prior to submitting a petition for clemency. The regulation further states that "generally, no petition should be submitted by a person who is on probation, parole, or supervised release." 28 CFR § 1.2. Notwithstanding this rule, however, the President can grant clemency at any time, whether an individual has made a formal petition or not. For example, President Gerald Ford granted a full and unconditional pardon to former President Richard Nixon prior to any indictment or charges being filed related to his involvement in Watergate.

2. What should a petition for clemency include?

Petitions for executive clemency should include the information required in the form prescribed by the United States Attorney General. This includes information:

1. that the person requesting clemency must state specifically the purpose for which clemency is sought, as well as attach any and all relevant documentary evidence that will support how clemency will support that purpose;
2. that discloses any arrests or convictions subsequent to the federal crime for which clemency is sought;
3. that discloses all delinquent credit obligations (whether disputed or not), all civil lawsuits to which the applicant is a party (whether plaintiff or defendant), and all unpaid tax obligations (whether local, state, or federal);
4. that includes three character affidavits from persons not related to the applicant by blood or marriage.

In addition, acceptance of a Presidential pardon generally carries with it an admission of guilt. For that reason, a petitioner should include in his or her petition a statement of the petitioner's acceptance of responsibility, an expression of remorse, and atonement for the offense. All of the requirements are contained in 28 CFR §§ 1.1-1.11.

3. What happens after a petition for executive clemency is submitted?

All petitions for federal clemency are reviewed by the Office of the Pardon Attorney. A non-binding recommendation on an application is then made to the President. Federal regulations also provide for guidelines and requirements to notify victims of the crimes, if any, for which clemency is sought. The President will then either grant or deny a pardon. There are no hearings held on the petition, and there is no appeal of the President's decision.

### 4. What is the effect of a Presidential pardon?

A pardon is the forgiveness of a crime and the cancelation of the penalty associated with that crime. While a Presidential pardon will restore various rights lost as a result of the pardoned offense, it will not expunge the record of your conviction. Should an individual be pardoned, he or she must still disclose the conviction on any form where such information is required, although the individual may also disclose the fact that the offense for which they were convicted was pardoned.

### B. *Expungement of federal convictions*
#### 1. No law exists for general federal expungement

Expungement is the act of wiping an arrest or conviction from a criminal history, and it can be a powerful tool to correct an indis- cretion. Unfortunately, Congress has not provided federal legislation that offers any comprehensive authority or procedure for expung- ing criminal offenses. There exist statutes that allow expungement only in certain cases for possession of small amounts of controlled substances (see below) and—interestingly—a procedure to expunge DNA samples of certain members of the military wrongfully convict- ed. Because there is no statutory guidance, federal courts have liter- ally made up the rules and procedures themselves, often coming to different conclusions. Some federal court circuits have stated they have no power to expunge records. On the other hand, other circuits have indicated that they do have the power to expunge. The Elev- enth Circuit Court of Appeals, which includes Georgia, has held that the court does not have ancillary jurisdiction to determine the issue of expungement. *See Hall v. Alabama,* 2010 U.S. Dist. LEXIS 14082 (M.D. Ala. Jan. 19, 2010). The Supreme Court has passed on hearing cases that would have resolved the split between the circuits. This issue remains legally murky.

#### 2. Possible procedure for federal expungement

While there are no statutory guidelines for how to seek an expunge- ment under federal law, the best place to start would be to file a motion with the federal court that issued the conviction. As a rule, federal judges very rarely grant these types of motions. Some cir- cuits have adopted a balancing test to determine whether a record held by the court may be expunged: "if the dangers of unwarranted adverse consequences to the individual outweigh the public inter- est in maintenance of the records, then expunction is appropriate." Further, these same courts have freely stated that this balancing test "rarely tips in favor of expungement," and that expungement should be granted in only the most extreme cases. *United States v. Flowers,* 389 F.3d 737 (7th Cir. 2004). Some of the areas where expungement has worked are in incidents of extreme police misconduct, or where the conviction is being misused against the person. But unless there exist compelling reasons, a federal judge is highly unlikely to grant expungement.

### 3. Expungement for drug possession: statutory authority

Under a federal law entitled "special probation and expungement procedures for drug possessors," certain persons are allowed to request a federal court to issue an expungement order from all public records. 18 U.S.C. § 3607. Congress intended this order to restore the person to the status he or she "occupied before such arrest or institution of criminal proceedings." 18 U.S.C. § 3607(c).

In order to qualify for the expungement, you must have been under the age of 21 when you were convicted, you must have no prior drug offenses, and your conviction must have been for simple possession of a small amount of a controlled substance.

### 4. How does a person have firearms rights restored under federal law?

Under the Gun Control Act of 1968, a person who has received a Presidential pardon is not considered convicted of a crime preventing the purchase and possession of firearms subject to all other federal laws. *See* 18 U.S.C. §§ 921(a)(20) and (a)(33). In addition, persons who had a conviction expunged or set aside, or who have had their civil rights restored are not considered to have been convicted for purposes of the GCA "unless the pardon, expungement, or restoration of civil rights expressly provides the person may not ship, transport, possess, or receive firearms." 18 U.S.C. §§ 921(a)(20) and (a)(33).

The GCA also provides the United States Attorney General with the authority to grant relief from firearms disabilities where the Attorney General determines that the person is not likely to act in a manner dangerous to the public safety and where granting relief would not be contrary to the public interest. 18 U.S.C. § 925(c). The Attorney General has delegated this authority to the ATF. Unfortunately, the ATF reports that it has been prohibited from spending any funds in order to investigate or act upon applications from individuals seeking relief from federal firearms disabilities. This means that until the ATF's prohibition has been lifted, a person's best—and most likely—option to have their firearms rights restored is through a Presidential pardon. *See* www.atf.gov.

## III.  Georgia law

### A.  *The Georgia State Board of Pardons and Paroles*

In Georgia, the Governor has no power to grant clemency: that power resides solely with the State Board of Pardons and Paroles. Unlike federal clemency, where the President (as chief executive) is free to pardon whomever the President chooses, the five members of the Governor-appointed, executive-branch Board have sole authority to grant parole (early release from a period of confinement following conviction of a crime) and—the topics we are particularly concerned with—restoration of rights and pardons.

### 1.  Restorations: basic restoration and regaining "most" of your rights

When any individual is convicted of a felony in Georgia, he or she will lose several significant civil rights: the right to vote; the right to hold public office; the right to serve on a jury; the right to serve as a Notary Public; and the right to possess a firearm. While the right to vote will automatically be restored to a probationer as soon as his or her sentence is complete, keep in mind, it is a felony violation of the law to possess a firearm after being convicted of a felony, even if you are no longer under court supervision. This is a right (among the others that are listed) that is not automatically restored, but the processes of restoration and pardon assist in returning the full rights of citizenship to any individual.

The simplest method for regaining those rights is to petition the Board of Pardons and Paroles for a "Restoration of Civil and Political Rights." This process will restore any civil rights lost to a convicted felon at the time of conviction except the right to vote and possess firearms (remember, the right to vote is immediately restored upon completion of the sentence). That means a restoration will assist in returning the right to serve on a jury, either run for or hold public office, and to serve as a Notary Public, to the felon. In order to qualify for a restoration, the applicant must have completed his or her sentence at least two years prior to applying (this rule establishes a two-year "waiting period" to apply for a restoration), and must have lived a "law-abiding life" during that two-year waiting period.

2. Restorations: restoring your firearms rights

If an applicant has successfully completed his or her sentence, waited the two years prior to applying, and lived without additional criminal trouble during that time, a restoration will be granted that gives all legal rights back except the right to possess a firearm. Additional steps must be taken to regain that right in Georgia.

At a minimum, and as a greater hurdle than simply restoring your rights, you must wait five years past the completion of any sentence imposed by the court (including probation), and during that five-year period, must live a "law-abiding life," just as with a restoration. You must also be qualified for either a pardon or a restoration (qualification for the restoration seems to be the two-year mark as noted above); anyone who has waited five years to restore his or her firearms rights and otherwise qualified would also meet the minimum requirements for a restoration.

This is the rule for in-state offenses: for offenses committed out-of-state, the right to possess firearms in Georgia will be restored alongside all other rights in the two-year restoration described in subsection one. In addition:

1. All fines, as well as any restitution ordered in the criminal case, must be paid in full. In short, it appears nothing may be left over from the criminal case in order to consider a restoration of firearms rights.
2. Three notarized letters of reference must be submitted by non-family U.S. citizens "of unquestionable integrity." These letters must include biographical data of the reference; how the reference knows the applicant; and why the reference feels the applicant deserves a restoration of firearms rights.
3. A personal interview will be conducted by the Board to determine eligibility to restore the firearms rights. This step is required of any applicant, including those who live out-of-state.

3. Pardons

A pardon is an official declaration of forgiveness for a conviction of a crime, and in Georgia is only given to those who have maintained a crime-free lifestyle and exemplary reputation. A pardon does not wipe a conviction from an arrest record: the record will note that a pardon has been granted, but the pardoned individual must still acknowledge the arrest and conviction within his or her criminal record, because it's still listed there. And while any individual convicted of a crime may petition the Board for a pardon, the following restrictions apply:

1. The applicant must complete all requirements of his or her sentence and be free from supervision for at least five years, just as with a restoration of firearms rights. During this time the applicant must live a "law-abiding life," as with the other forms of clemency discussed above.
2. No pending charges are allowed at the time of application.
3. As with restoration, all fines, as well as any restitution ordered in the criminal case, must be paid in full.

There is an exception for an accelerated request for a restoration or pardon: the two and five-year waiting periods may be waived by the Board if the applicant can show the waiting period has caused a delay in qualification for employment. This is judged on a case-by-case basis. Interestingly, a pardon will restore all civil and political rights. It should be noted the rules referenced above are for pardons for offenses other than sex offenses: there are much more stringent requirements for obtaining a pardon for sex offenses, including—among other requirements—a ten-year waiting period, a psychosexual evaluation, and a disclosure polygraph.

4. How does a person seek clemency in Georgia?

A person seeking clemency in Georgia is required to complete an application made available from the State Board of Pardons and Paroles. Once properly submitted, the file of any applicant eligible for clemency will be reviewed by the Board.

The Board will review the application and vote whether a pardon is granted: according to O.C.G.A. § 42-9-42, an applicant must obtain a majority number of votes of the Board before the pardon will be granted. For more information on the process, please visit the official website for the Georgia State Board of Pardons and Paroles, www.pap.georgia.gov.

5. What is the effect of executive clemency in Georgia?

Similar to federal clemency, the records of the original conviction continue to exist. While a person granted clemency must still disclose the conviction on any relevant form seeking such information, the individual may also state the nature of the clemency received.

Georgia law does not appear to allow pardoned offenses to be restricted (expunged) from a criminal record.

## B.   *Georgia records restriction*

O.C.G.A. § 35-3-37 controls records restriction under Georgia law. This chapter provides for instances when a person is entitled to having information regarding an arrest and conviction for certain offenses on his or her record restricted for viewing only to "judicial officials and criminal justice agencies," meaning judges and law enforcement. If a record is restricted, it shall not be disclosed or "otherwise made available to any private persons or businesses." O.C.G.A. § 35-3-34. Note that the technical term under Georgia law is restriction, but that many individuals use the term "expungement." This was the legal term for the process of restricting an arrest or conviction from a record until July 1, 2013, when the new term (and changes in the law supporting and expanding its use) went into effect. The chapter allows restriction for a number of different types of situations: persons who were acquitted; those who had charges dead-docketed, dismissed, or whose charges were no-billed by a grand jury; individuals who were sentenced under the conditional discharge provisions of O.C.G.A. § 16-13-2 for a minor drug offense, and those who successfully completed a court treatment program of several different types, just to name a few. *See* O.C.G.A. § 35-3-37.

Records restrictions can become adversarial proceedings involving one or more parties, including the State, which may object to the court granting the restriction. In fact, there are circumstances, such as in the case of acquittals where the prosecutor was barred from presenting evidence by the granting of a motion to suppress, where the State may object to a restriction. Furthermore, no restriction shall be granted where the charges were dismissed because of an agreement to plead to another charge arising from the same occurrence, or the charges were dismissed because the prosecutor was barred from presenting evidence, just as in the acquittal above. There does not appear to be an avenue under Georgia law to request a records restriction for pardoned offenses.

# CHAPTER TWELVE

## I'M BEING SUED FOR WHAT?
## CIVIL LIABILITY IF YOU HAVE USED YOUR GUN

### I.    What does it mean to be sued?

The term "lawsuit" refers to one party's assertion in a written filing with a court that another party has violated the law. In the context of firearms, typically the party suing has been injured and wants a ruling or judgment from the court to that effect; a ruling that will entitle the person suing to recover monetary damages.

### A.    *What is a civil claim or lawsuit?*

A civil "lawsuit" or "suit" refers to the actual filing of written paperwork with a court (1) asserting that another party violated the law, and (2) seeking some type of redress. A "claim" can exist without the filing of a lawsuit. A claim is simply the belief or assertion that another party has violated the law. Many parties have claims they never assert, or sometimes parties informally assert the claim in hopes of resolving the disputes without the filing of a lawsuit. Also, another term commonly used is "tort" or "tort claim." A tort is a civil claim arising out of a wrongful act, not including a breach of contract or trust, that results in injury to another's person, property, reputation, or the like. The claims described below are all tort claims.

### B.    *Difference between "civil claims" and "criminal charges"*

There are two different aspects of the legal system gun owners may face after the use of a firearm: criminal and civil. There are several names and descriptive terms used for each (*e.g.,* civil lawsuit, criminal actions, civil claims, criminal proceedings, *etc.*), but regardless of the terms, the same breakdown applies; most cases are either criminal or civil. There is another subgroup of proceedings called administrative actions. Those actions are not covered by this chapter but can sometimes impact WCL holders. For example, appealing the denial of a WCL is an administrative act. See Chapters 8 and 9 for more information.

With that said, the three primary differences between a criminal action and a civil proceeding are: (1) who or what is bringing the action or lawsuit, (2) what are they seeking, and (3) what is the burden of proof? These differences are fairly straightforward.

1.  State versus individual bringing claims

In a criminal case, the party bringing the action is the "sovereign," meaning the United States, state, municipality, county, *etc.* that believes that a person violated their laws. Even if an individual calls the police, fills out a criminal complaint, or even asks the district attorney to file charges, the party that actually brings a criminal action is the state, county, *etc.*, not the individual.

However, a civil action may be filed by any individual, business or other entity (partnership, LLC, trust, *etc.*). The entity bringing the claim is called the "plaintiff." Even governmental entities can bring civil claims; *i.e.,* if you negligently shoot a county propane tank causing a fire, the county can sue you civilly for those damages. The typical gun case, though, will involve an individual filing a lawsuit against another individual for damages caused by the firearm. If the incident occurs at a place of business, the plaintiff may also sue the business claiming that it is in some way at fault for the incident. The party being sued is typically called the "defendant."

2.  Relief sought/awarded

In a criminal case, the entity prosecuting the case is usually seeking to imprison or fine you. Most crimes are punishable by "X" number of days/months/years in prison or jail, and a fine not to exceed "X" dollars. By contrast, the plaintiff in the civil case is almost always seeking a monetary award. Several other types of relief are available (declaratory, injunctive, specific performance), but for the most part, gun cases will involve the plaintiff seeking monetary damages.

3.  Burden of proof

In a criminal case, the standard is "beyond a reasonable doubt." In civil cases, however, a plaintiff must prove a person is liable for damages by a "preponderance of the evidence" standard. A preponderance of the evidence is a much lower standard than the criminal standard of beyond a reasonable doubt. It generally means that the party with the greater weight of credible evidence wins that issue. The preponderance of the evidence has been described as "more than half;" that is, if the evidence demonstrates that something "more likely occurred than not," this meets the burden of proof. Whereas in a criminal case, if there exists any "reasonable doubt," the burden of proof is not met. It does not mean the party with the most exhibits or greater number of witnesses will prevail. One highly credible witness can prevail over the testimony of a dozen biased, shady witnesses.

Example:

> *John mistakes a utility meter reader for a burglar due to his disheveled appearance, tool bag, and because he looks to be snooping around John's house. John fires a shot without warning and injures the meter reader.*

Possible criminal liability: the State of Georgia could bring criminal charges against John for a number of crimes (aggravated assault, criminal attempt to commit murder, reckless conduct, discharge of a firearm inside the city limits, *etc.*). The State would be seeking to imprison or fine John for his conduct, and it would be required to prove that John committed the crime at issue "beyond a reasonable doubt."

Possible civil liability: the meter reader could also file a civil lawsuit against John alleging that John was negligent or committed the tort of assault. The meter reader would seek monetary damages and be required to prove his claims by a "preponderance of the evidence."

C.  *Impact of result in one court upon the other*
    1.  Can a result in a criminal trial be used in a civil trial?
Yes, because of the legal doctrines of *res judicata* and collateral estoppel. These two legal doctrines govern the impact of a ruling or judgment in one case, upon a separate case involving the same set of facts and circumstances. For the present discussion, if a person is found guilty of a crime in a criminal proceeding, because that court uses a higher standard of "beyond a reasonable doubt" than the civil requirement of "preponderance of the evidence," the finding of the criminal court may be used for purposes of establishing civil liability. Entire chapters in law books have been written on these topics, so, suffice to say, this section is a brief overview of these laws.

The criminal concept of *nolo contendere*—or "no contest"—often generates confusion in this area. In a criminal case, a plea of *nolo contendere,* or "no contest", means that the defendant does not admit guilt, but rather does not contest the allegations. Should the judge allow the plea (and the decision whether to accept such a plea is the judge's alone), the defendant will be sentenced just as if he or she pled guilty, with the same range of sentencing available to the judge, *but the plea shall not constitute an admission of guilt.*

Except as otherwise provided by law, a plea of nolo contendere shall not be used against the defendant in any other
court or proceedings as an admission of guilt or otherwise
or for any purpose; and the plea shall not be deemed a
plea of guilty for the purpose of effecting any civil disqualification... to hold public office, to vote, to serve upon any
jury, or any other civil disqualification imposed upon a person convicted of any offense under the laws of this state.
O.C.G.A. § 17-7-95

Such a plea may prove critical to a defendant who wishes to resolve
a criminal case under potentially favorable circumstances—consider an offer of probation without jail time by the prosecutor, conditioned upon a "nolo" plea to certain offenses—who still wishes to
protect against civil liability: a *nolo contendere* plea in such a circumstance will assist in resolving a criminal case without an admission
of guilt that could be used against the same defendant in a civil case
arising from the incident.

Example:
*Phil and Jeremy become involved in a road rage incident,
and an altercation follows. Phil shoots Jeremy, wounding
him. When all is sorted out, Phil is found guilty of aggravated assault and receives punishment from the court
(remember, criminal trials use the "beyond a reasonable
doubt" standard).*

If Jeremy later sues Phil from the injuries he received when Phil shot
him, Jeremy, in his civil action, will very likely be allowed to use the
finding of guilt in the criminal case (because it used the higher standard of reasonable doubt) to establish his burden in the civil case
(the lower preponderance of the evidence standard) that he is owed
damages or money in the civil case. This is an example of "collateral
estoppel": once Phil has been found guilty (or pled guilty) he will not
be permitted to re-litigate his guilt in the civil case. This doctrine is
based on the concept that a party to a legal proceeding should not
be able to endlessly litigate issues that have already been decided
by the legal system. At its most basic level, it means that a party to a
legal proceeding who receives a final ruling on a particular issue, win
or lose, cannot attempt to have another trial court or even the same
court decide the same issue. If, however, Phil were to complete the

criminal case by entering a plea of *nolo contendere*, he could potentially insulate himself from an admission of guilt in the criminal case that may prove beneficial to him if he is then sued for the same occurrence.

A note about appeals and what are known as post-conviction proceedings: collateral estoppel is a different concept than the right to appeal, or asking the court in the first proceeding to reconsider its ruling, or grant a new trial. An appeal is a request to a higher court to review the decision of a lower court. Likewise, in any given case, the parties will have numerous opportunities to ask the current court to reconsider its rulings, or even ask for a new trial after a trial is completed. Collateral estoppel and the related legal concept of *res judicata* ("the thing has been judged," referring to the notion that a case that has been completed may not then be re-litigated) come into play after a final judgment that is no longer subject to appeal or revision by the trial court.

Example:
> *Michele is sued for accidentally shooting Nancy. Nancy wins a judgment of $350 against Michele, much less than Nancy believed she was damaged.*

In that case, Nancy can appeal the decision, or even ask that trial court for a new trial. However, Nancy cannot file another, or new, lawsuit regarding the same incident and attempt to recover more in the second case: this is the concept of *res judicata*. In order for the doctrine to apply, the facts, circumstances and issues must be the same.

Example:
> *Justin fires his hunting rifle from his deer blind, hitting Peter with one round. Peter files a civil suit against Justin and loses at trial. The court awards Peter no damages. Peter appeals and loses the appeal also.*

Peter is legally barred from recovering in another lawsuit against Justin involving the same incident. However, Peter is not barred from filing suit against Justin for damages arising out of another set of facts and circumstances; for example, if the two are involved in a car wreck on a different day, Peter would not be barred from seeking damages in that case.

## 2. Civil case result impact on criminal case

Suppose you lose a civil suit arising out of a shooting incident, and a judgment is entered against you. Can that judgment be used to establish that you committed a crime? No. The burden of proof is much higher in the criminal context than the civil case. The plaintiff proved his civil case by a lower standard of proof, called a "preponderance of the evidence." This does not mean that he proved his case "beyond a reasonable doubt," the highest level of proof in our judicial system, meaning a separate criminal trial is required to make that determination.

The one area where a civil case can impact a criminal case is the potential overlapping use of evidence and testimony. Your admission in one case can almost always be used against you in another case. Meaning, your sworn testimony in the civil case ("yes, I shot the guy") can almost always be used against you in the criminal case, and vice versa.

## II. What might you be sued for? Gun-related claims in civil courts

### A. *Liability for negligent discharge*

This section deals with an accidental or negligent discharge of your firearm. Common negligent discharges are associated with hunting and cleaning accidents or the mishandling of a weapon. Intentional shootings are addressed in the following section.

With that said, the following are the types of civil claims that may be asserted in connection with an unintentional discharge:

### 1. Negligence/gross negligence

Most civil cases for damages resulting from an accidental discharge will include a negligence or gross negligence claim. What does this mean and what does a plaintiff have to prove before he or she can win? Under Georgia law, negligence is defined as the absence of ordinary diligence, where ordinary diligence is "that degree of care which is exercised by ordinarily prudent persons." The failure to exercise the degree of care common to an ordinary person in a given situation that results in injury to another party is called "ordinary negligence," or simply negligence. The determination of negligence is based on an "objective standard," meaning, the test is not whether you believed you acted prudently, but whether the judge or jury believes you acted (or failed to act) as a person of ordinary prudence would have acted.

What, then, is gross negligence and how is it different than "regular" negligence? Many gun cases will include a claim for "gross negligence" by the plaintiff. The primary reason for this is that if a plaintiff establishes gross negligence by a defendant, the plaintiff may be entitled to additional types or amounts of money than are legally available if mere negligence is established. Georgia law and interpreting decisions have defined gross negligence as the absence of "slight diligence," which is "that degree of care which every man of common sense, however inattentive he may be, exercises under the same or similar circumstances." O.C.G.A. § 51-1-4. The absence of even the smallest amount of diligence to either act, or refrain from acting in a given situation, is the concept of gross negligence. The examples that follow help to define the difference between negligence and gross negligence.

Example:

> *Jessica has practiced her shooting at a private range on her country property for 20 years, without incident. Jessica shoots towards an area where she has never seen another person, and she believes the range of her guns cannot reach her property line. One day, a neighbor is hit by a shot as he is strolling through the woods just behind Jessica's property.*

Result: Jessica may be liable for negligence if a jury determines, for example, that an ordinarily prudent person would have acted differently, tested the range of her guns, or built a different type of back stop or berm, *etc.* The precedent Jessica has set over the past 20 years of shooting on her property, however, will support her argument that she exercised ordinary diligence in the present circumstance. Change Jessica's awareness level, however, and it changes the result, and potentially the level of liability.

Example:

> *Jessica has received several complaints over the years about bullets leaving her property and hitting her neighbor's property. Nevertheless, Jessica ignores the complaints and continues practicing in the direction that she typically shoots. One day while practicing, her bullet leaves her property and hits her neighbor. She is later sued by the neighbor for gross negligence.*

Result: Jessica may very well be liable for gross negligence because she was aware that her shots were reaching the neighbor's property and that there were people in the same area (*i.e.*, the folks who reported the shots), and despite that knowledge, she continued to shoot without changing direction or building a back stop or berm and someone was injured as a result. If "every man of common sense" would understand the complaints as a real danger of injury to passersby, Jessica's actions could rise to the level of gross negligence. It should be noted that Georgia has a "slight negligence" standard as well, but this standard is not commonly alleged in scenarios dealing with personal injury.

2.   Negligent entrustment of a firearm

A claim may be pursued by a Georgia plaintiff against a defendant for negligently entrusting (*e.g.*, giving, lending, transferring) a firearm to another person. Plaintiffs will often allege the more general count of negligence against the individual who harms them with a firearm, while simultaneously filing against the individual who entrusted the firearm to the shooter. To prevail on a claim of negligent entrustment of a firearm, a party must show the defendant has *entrusted* someone with a firearm "with actual knowledge that the person to whom he has entrusted the instrumentality is incompetent by reason of his age or inexperience, or his physical or mental condition, or his known habit of recklessness." *Parker v. Silviano,* 284 Ga. App. 278 (Ga. Ct. App. 2007).

Example:

> Shaun lets his adult grandson Gordon borrow a shotgun to take on a fishing trip because he knows there are water moccasins in the spot where they plan to fish. Gordon has never been in trouble with the law, has repeatedly been trained in firearms safety, and has never had an incident with a gun. However, while on the trip, Gordon accidentally shoots a fellow fishing buddy with Shaun's shotgun. The fishing buddy, now turned plaintiff, sues Gordon for negligence and Shaun for negligent entrustment of a firearm.

Can the plaintiff win his claim for negligent entrustment? This one will be difficult for the plaintiff. Shaun may get sued for giving the shotgun to his grandson, but the facts described do not meet the elements necessary to establish negligent entrustment, and Shaun should prevail in any lawsuit. First, there are no facts that suggest Gordon was incompetent or reckless. Further, there are no facts showing *actual knowledge* by Shaun that Gordon was either incompetent or reckless. Thus, the negligent entrustment claim should legally fail.

Many plaintiffs have urged Georgia appellate courts to adopt a "strict liability" standard when looking at gun cases. In other words, if you give someone your gun, you are automatically liable for whatever happens. At the time of this writing, Georgia has no strict liability standard.

### 3. "Am I liable if someone steals my gun?"

A question commonly asked by gun owners is "if someone steals my gun, am I liable if they shoot someone?" In other words, if I store my gun and a criminal or another less-than-responsible person gets the gun, am I liable if they shoot someone? As of the date of this publication, the answer in Georgia is "probably not." Georgia law neither criminalizes the improper storage of a firearm, nor recognizes a separate civil action for negligent storage that results in injury or death. What does this mean? If someone accesses your gun and you did not intend for them to access your gun, Georgia does not currently recognize this claim, and a plaintiff should not be able to recover if the person who accesses your gun injures himself or others.

Several caveats to this exist: (1) many other states do recognize this claim; (2) even though this cause of action may not exist, it does not preclude a party from seeking damages under general negligence and gross negligence standards; and (3) there are still criminal consequences for recklessly furnishing a pistol or revolver to a minor, and the specific facts of a "theft" could conceivably support a criminal charge (at least in the eyes of an over-zealous prosecutor) if the actions in securing the firearm were of such a nature as to be deemed "reckless." *See* O.C.G.A. § 16-11-101.1, discussed in Chapter 3.

As a result, while no civil liability exists in Georgia today for the theft of a firearm, it remains extraordinarily important to exercise care in the storage of your firearms. Always maintain proper control and storage of your firearms, and keep a log of serial numbers. Finally, report any theft to law enforcement immediately. Protect yourself!

B. _Intentional discharge: a person intended to shoot_
   1.  Negligence/gross negligence

Just because you intend to shoot someone, or otherwise "use" your firearm (or knife, baseball bat, metal pipe, folding chair, or car) as a weapon, does not necessarily mean the plaintiff **won't** assert negligence or gross negligence claims. In other words, you may have fully intended to pull the trigger, but the plaintiff may claim that you were negligent for any number of reasons; for example, you mistook the mailman for a burglar, or the criminal was retreating and you were negligent in using deadly force. The negligence and gross negligence claims, as defined above, can be brought even if you intended to pull the trigger.

   2.  Assault and battery

If a person has shot at (and possibly injured) someone, and is then sued, the suit may include a claim for assault, or for battery, or both. Each are intentional acts, not an accident or a claim based on a deviation from a standard of care. An assault (O.C.G.A. § 16-5-20) occurs if a person:

(1) attempts to commit a violent injury to the person of another; or
(2) commits an act which places another in reasonable apprehension of immediately receiving a violent injury.

Example:

> Bill is startled while driving. Martha is standing next to his passenger window at a light screaming that he cut her off in traffic, but taking no action to indicate she intends to harm Bill or do anything besides verbally lodge her complaints. In response, Bill points his gun at Martha and says "You're dead!" He fires his gun but misses. Martha escapes to her vehicle to call police.

Apart from potential criminal elements of the example, Bill has committed a civil assault. He attempted a violent injury to Martha without legal justification, and committed an act that placed Martha in reasonable apprehension of receiving an injury. Therefore, a civil jury would likely find Bill liable and award damages to Martha.

3. <u>False imprisonment/false arrest: being sued for detaining people</u>

What if a gun owner detains someone at gunpoint? If the individual detained later decides to sue, the complaint will likely include a claim for "false imprisonment" or "false arrest," or both. Georgia recognizes a civil claim for both false imprisonment and false arrest. False imprisonment is the unlawful detention of the person of another, for any length of time, whereby such person is deprived of his personal liberty. O.C.G.A. § 51-7-20. To arrest one illegally and detain him for any length of time is a criminal offense, and is likewise a tort for which an action for damages will lie. *Livingston v. Schneer's Atlanta, Inc.,* 61 Ga. App. 637 (Ga. Ct. App. 1940); *Duchess Chenilles, Inc. v. Masters,* 84 Ga. App. 822 (Ga. Ct. App. 1951). False imprisonment is also considered an "intentional tort," not a tort of negligence. *Williams v. Smith,* 179 Ga. App. 712 (Ga. Ct. App. 1986). This claim can arise when someone detains persons waiting for police, *e.g.* homeowners detaining burglars, *etc.* However, it arises frequently in shoplifting cases (see Chapter 7).

Similarly, false arrest is defined by statute as an arrest under process of law, without probable cause. O.C.G.A. § 51-7-1. The law also warns that, when made maliciously, a false arrest "shall give a right of action to the party arrested." In this context, an arrest is effected by seizing or detaining an individual, "either by touching or putting hands on him, or by any act indicating an intention to take such person into custody," and then subjecting him or her to your control; "it is sufficient if the arrested person understands that he is in the power of the one arresting and submits in consequence thereof." *Conoly v. Imperial Tobacco Co.,* 63 Ga. App. 880 (Ga. Ct. App. 1940). Such an arrest, particularly without a warrant, unless allowed by law, is illegal and tortious. *Standard Sur. & Cas. Co. v. Johnson,* 74 Ga. App. 823 (Ga. Ct. App. 1947).

Example:

*Emily fears she is about to be attacked in a grocery store parking lot by Randall. Randall follows her step-by-step through the parking lot and stops right next to Emily's car. Emily draws her .380 and tells Randall to "stay right there while I call the police." Randall complies, and Emily holds him at gunpoint until the police arrive. When the police arrive, they determine that Randall was an out-of-uniform store employee tasked with rounding up the grocery carts in the parking lot and was no threat to Emily.*

If a jury determines that Emily acted without justification (*i.e.,* she was not reasonably in fear of death or bodily injury), Emily could be civilly liable for falsely imprisoning or arresting Randall—or both!—and owe him damages, if any.

4. Wrongful death

If a person is in the unfortunate position of having shot and killed another individual, and a civil suit occurs because of the shooting, it likely will include a claim for wrongful death. In Georgia, a surviving spouse may recover for the homicide of a deceased spouse in a wrongful death action; a child may recover for the homicide of a parent, if there is no other surviving parent; a parent may be able to recover for the homicide of a child; and the estate of a homicide victim may even have standing to recover when there is no spouse or children. *See* O.C.G.A. § 51-4-2; O.C.G.A. § 19-7-1; and O.C.G.A. § 51-4-5.

The death in each of the scenarios listed above must be classified as a homicide, which is a death that results from a crime, from criminal or other negligence, or from property which has been defectively manufactured. O.C.G.A. § 51-4-1. Establishing a death as a result of a crime (after a plea by a defendant, or a trial resulting in a conviction), or that one of the other claims described in this chapter—negligence or gross negligence, for instance—caused the death of another person could lay the basis for a successful wrongful death action. In other words, the act needed to establish a wrongful death claim can be established by proving that the defendant committed a crime or was liable for a tort (such as battery) or negligence and that the tort caused the death of a person.

Bear in mind, however, that in a wrongful death action, justification is an affirmative defense, but the defendant bears the burden of proving his or her actions meet the requirements to satisfy the defense. *Bell v. Smith,* 227 Ga. App. 17 (Ga. Ct. App. 1997). Doing so will result in the plaintiff's inability to recover, just as a successful justification defense will provide immunity from criminal prosecution and immunity from civil suit by the aggressor, or the aggressor's accomplices.

### III.  What can the plaintiff recover?

If a person is sued in civil court and the plaintiff convinces a jury that the defendant was liable for damages, what and how much can a plaintiff get? There are scores of cases discussing the details of each category of damages that a plaintiff can recover in a civil lawsuit. The following is a brief description of two very important concepts: (1) "proximate cause," which is essential to recover damages in most circumstances, and (2) the basic types of damages that a plaintiff may typically seek in a gun case.

#### A.  *Proximate cause*

One basic concept that is important to most civil claims, and is usually required to recover damages, is "proximate cause." Virtually every tort claim will require the plaintiff to prove that his damages were proximately caused by the defendant. "Proximate cause" is defined as cause that was a substantial factor in bringing about an event and without which the event would not have occurred. This concept has few bright-line tests.

For a gun owner, the most obvious cases of proximate cause are pulling the trigger on a firearm and hitting the person or thing you aimed at. The law will hold that your action proximately caused whatever physical damage the bullet did to persons or property. But what about those circumstances where the use of the gun is so far removed from the damages claimed? This is where the doctrine of proximate cause will cut off liability. If the damage is too far removed from the act, then the act cannot be a proximate cause of that damage.

Example:

> *Anthony is cleaning his AR-15 one night in his apartment and is negligent in his handling of the rifle. He has a negligent discharge: the bullet goes through the wall of his apartment and strikes his neighbor, Ray, in the leg. Ray, although in massive pain, received prompt medical care from his wife, Gail, and made a speedy recovery.*

If Anthony is later sued by Ray and his wife Gail, Anthony's negligence undoubtedly "proximately caused" damages for things like Ray's medical bills, hospital stay, and perhaps even lost wages. But what if Gail claims that because of her having to treat Ray's wounds she missed a big job interview and lost out on a big raise in pay and that she wants Anthony to pay that as a component of damages? The law would hold that Gail likely could not recover damages for her lost raise in pay because the loss would not be "proximately caused" by the act being sued for. To put it another way, it is reasonably foreseeable that the negligent discharge of a firearm will cause medical bills, *etc.* for someone struck by a bullet. Therefore, this is recoverable. However, the law would say that the loss of a possible job opportunity for the wife who treated the person who was actually shot is not a reasonably foreseeable consequence of negligently discharging a firearm and, therefore, was not proximately caused by the act of negligence. In that case, there will be no recovery for the plaintiff, Gail. Proximate cause must be established in every case and may appear to be arbitrary legal line drawing because it is.

As discussed below, Georgia law also recognizes a doctrine that unforeseen criminal conduct breaks the causal link between an action and a third-party's injuries.

B.   *What types of damages can a plaintiff recover?*
The following is merely a brief snapshot of the types of damages recoverable in a firearms case. To recover any of the damages below, the plaintiff must first prove his or her claim by a preponderance of the evidence. For example, if the jury determines a defendant was not negligent, a plaintiff cannot recover his or her medical costs, no matter how severe the plaintiff's injuries. Some of the damages a plaintiff can try to recover include:

- Lost Wages
- Medical Costs
- Disability
- Pain & Suffering (Physical, Mental & Emotional)
- Funeral and Burial Costs
- Loss of Consortium
- Punitive or exemplary damages (Note, the standard of proof for punitive/exemplary damages is "clear and convincing evidence," which is higher than a "preponderance of the evidence." Punitive damages are also only available in cases of intentional or reckless conduct, or gross negligence.)

A court can find the defendant 100% at fault, but award no damages because the plaintiff failed to prove damages by a preponderance of the evidence. For example, a plaintiff who seeks reimbursement for medical expenses but has no evidence of a visit to a doctor or hospital, will very unlikely be able to recover those medical expenses.

## IV.   Do Georgia civil immunity laws protect gun owners?

### A.   *Immunity from liability does not mean immunity from lawsuits*

A common misunderstanding exists with respect to lawsuits and immunity, in that many people (wrongly) believe if you are legally justified in using your gun, you can't be sued. This is just not the case. If a person has the filing fee, anyone can sue anyone else in the State of Georgia. There is no one stopping anyone else from filing a lawsuit. Prevailing in a lawsuit, however, is a different issue entirely. As we will soon discuss, an individual who is justified in the use of deadly force to prevent death or great bodily injury is immune from civil liability in Georgia. If the thwarted perpetrator files a lawsuit, though, no matter how frivolous, it still must be dealt with, and it still must be shown to the court the lawsuit is barred by civil immunity, or some other similar preclusion or defense. This process can take significant time, money, and legal energy even for the most frivolous cases. In short, lawyers get paid and even if you beat the "rap," you still have to take the civil "ride." So, if there is no immunity to lawsuits for gun owners, what protection is there?

### B.   *Civil immunity for the use of deadly force*

Most important for gun owners if they find themselves included in a civil suit after a justified use of deadly force will be O.C.G.A. § 51-11-9, "Immunity from civil liability for threat or use of force in defense of habitation."

| IMMUNITY FROM CIVIL LIABILITY FOR THREAT OR USE OF FORCE IN DEFENSE OF HABITATION |
|---|
| **O.C.G.A. § 51-11-9.** A person who is justified in threatening or using force against another under the provisions of Code Section 16-3-21, relating to the use of force in defense of self or others, Code Section 16-3-23, relating to the use of force in defense of a habitation, or Code Section 16-3-24, relating to the use of force in defense of property other than a habitation, has no duty to retreat from the use of such force and shall not be held liable to the person against whom the use of force was justified or to any person acting as an accomplice or assistant to such person in any civil action brought as a result of the threat or use of such force. |

As a careful reading makes clear, an individual who uses or threatens force or deadly force that is justified under Georgia law is immune from civil liability for personal injury or death that results from the defendant's use of threats of force or deadly force, as applicable. And while the statute's title invokes immunity "in defense of habitation," the language of the law protects and immunizes those who threaten or use force in defense of self or others; in defense of habitation; and in defense of real property. Bear in mind: this statute does not prevent lawsuits. It makes suits filed against individuals justified in protecting themselves harder to win. Immunity from liability is a statutory, affirmative defense, and, as such, this defense will be considered after a plaintiff has sued a defendant. The statute provides immunity from liability if the use of force is justified; it does not provide immunity from being sued.

Also, note the language in the statute that one who uses force "shall not be held liable to the person against whom the use of force was justified or to any person acting as an accomplice or assistant to such person in any civil action brought as a result of the threat or use of such force." While Georgia appellate courts have not interpreted it, this language could mean injury to a third party (not involved as a perpetrator or victim) is not covered. What could that mean?

Example:
> John is the victim of a home invasion. He fires several shots at the intruder. The intruder is hit and stopped. One shot, however, misses the intruder and hits a propane tank at the house across the street. The propane tank explodes and burns down the neighbor's home.

The resulting damage occurred, not to the victim or any perpetrator, but to an otherwise uninvolved third party, the neighbor. It is unlikely that the immunity statute will provide John with any protection from a civil suit by the neighbor for the damages to the house.

## C.   *Justification*
The justifications of defense of self or others, defense of habitation, and defense of real property may all be asserted as affirmative defenses in a civil action. This means, for example, if you shoot someone in defense of yourself, others, your home, or your property and are sued as a result, you may assert the applicable sections of Georgia law as a defense to the civil claims. If the judge or jury agrees that your actions

were justified, you will be immune from liability, and the plaintiff will be barred from recovery. See Chapters 4 through 7.

## D. *Statute of limitations for civil claims*

The statute of limitations is a doctrine in Georgia (and almost every other jurisdiction) that requires civil claims to be brought within a certain period of time after the incident. If the claim is not brought within the statute of limitations period, it is barred. There are a number of issues relating to when the statute of limitations starts to run in many cases, but for the most part in the scenarios we are concerned with, limitations will start to run immediately after a shooting incident. The statute of limitations can vary depending on the type of claim involved. In Georgia, the limitation periods most likely to apply to gun cases are two years for personal injury and four years for injury to property. Assault, battery, negligence, wrongful death, and false imprisonment claims all provide two-year limitations periods.

What does this mean for gun owners? If you "use" your gun, the plaintiff must bring a civil suit against within two years of the incident in cases of personal injury, and four years in cases of injury to personal property, or else the claim will be barred.

## E. *Superseding or intervening criminal conduct*

Georgia law recognizes a doctrine that absolves someone from responsibility for conduct that might otherwise be a tort (*e.g.,* negligence) if a criminal act breaks the causal connection between the tort and the injury.

Generally, a third party's criminal conduct is a superseding cause that relieves the negligent actor from liability. However, the intervening wrongful act does not insulate the defendant from liability if the defendant had reasonable grounds for apprehending that such wrongful act would be committed. *Mayor & City Council of Richmond Hill v. Maia,* 336 Ga. App. 555 (Ga. Ct. App. 2016).

Example:

> *Justin allows his nephew Randall to use his handgun for protection. Justin knows Randall has been in trouble with the law repeatedly and has been accused of armed robbery. While Randall has the handgun, his apartment is burglarized, and the gun is stolen and used in a crime spree. During the crime spree, Melanie is shot and injured.*

Melanie would not be able to recover from Justin, even though Justin may have been negligent in giving his gun to Randall, because the criminal act of burglarizing Randall's apartment and subsequent crime spree were superseding causes that broke the link between Justin's actions and the resulting injuries.

## F.  *Comparative negligence and the apportionment rule*

In assessing responsibility for damages and making awards to a plaintiff, Georgia first applies the doctrine of comparative negligence. What must first be determined is: could the plaintiff, by the exercise of ordinary care, have avoided any injury caused by defendant's negligence? If so, the plaintiff's recovery of damages is reduced by his or her portion of responsibility for those damages. And while the law states a plaintiff is not entitled to recover damages where they could have been avoided by the exercise of "ordinary care," even if the defendant is negligent, courts have found "the comparative negligence rule does not defeat recovery by a negligent plaintiff unless it is made to appear that his negligence was the sole. . . proximate cause of the injury." *United States v. Fleming,* 115 F.2d 314 (5th Cir. 1940). In a scenario in which damages are to be awarded, either the judge or the jury will be asked to determine the percentage of fault or responsibility of the parties involved in the incident. The damages are then apportioned based upon the percentages assigned by the judge or jury: this is the apportionment rule, found in O.C.G.A. § 51-12-33.

Example:

> *Richard is a young adult trick-or-treater. He uses a fake gun as a part of his costume and knocks loudly on Nancy's door at 11:30 p.m. on October 31. Nancy, having forgotten about Halloween, is frightened by the knock, the fake gun, and the late hour of Richard's arrival. She fires through the door, injuring Richard.*

In the civil suit that follows by Richard against Nancy, the jury will be permitted to consider whether Richard's negligence, if any, contributed to cause the resulting injuries. The jury could determine that Richard was 0% at fault, 100%, or anything in between. By way of example only, if the jury awarded Richard $100,000 in damages, but found he was 30% at fault, and Nancy 70%, Richard would only be able to recover $70,000 of his damages.

## V.   What about third-parties?

Should you find yourself in a life-or-death situation, protect yourself, of course. Keep mind, however, that should you defend yourself, others, or your property, and in doing so create an unreasonable risk to others, you may be liable if one of those third-parties is injured. Example:

> Mel fires her rifle at Anthony as he unlawfully breaks into Mel's occupied home at night. She fires a single shot with her .22 that narrowly misses Anthony but hits a man washing his car down the street.

Mel is most likely not liable to the man down the street, because her conduct did not unreasonably place third-parties at risk.

Example:

> Ben shoots at Anthony as he unlawfully breaks into Ben's occupied home at night. Ben fires 30 shots with his fully-automatic M-16, missing with the initial burst. Anthony turns and runs. Ben continues to fire haphazardly at Anthony as he runs down the street. One shot hits a man washing his car four houses away.

Ben could very likely be liable to the man washing his car because he unreasonably placed third-parties at risk by firing a fully-automatic weapon down a neighborhood street. It is important to note that whether liability attaches could be a question of degree, and because these questions of degree can be razor-thin, the decisions on liability, given the same facts, made by two different juries (different jurisdictions, different judges and lawyers, even different days of the week!) could be entirely different.

## VI.   Will insurance cover it if I shoot someone?

### A.   *Homeowners' insurance*

With few exceptions, almost every homeowner's insurance policy excludes coverage for intentional acts. The act of using your firearm in self-defense is almost always an intentional act. You intended to stop the threat. Plaintiffs' attorneys will very likely assert a negligence claim against a homeowner in an attempt to fall within the coverage, but at the end of the day, if the only evidence is that you intentionally shot the plaintiff because you intended to stop a threat, it is likely that any policy with an intentional act exclusion will not provide coverage for any damages awarded.

B. _Auto insurance_

Scores of cases around the country exist where the parties allege that a gun incident is covered by automobile insurance merely because the use of the firearm occurs in the auto or involves an auto. Almost universally, courts have held that these incidents are not covered merely because the discharge occurs in a car or involves a car.

Example:
> _Justin is cleaning his 9mm handgun in the car. It accidentally discharges causing his passenger Edwin severe injuries._

This event will almost certainly not be covered by auto insurance.

Example:
> _Justin discharges his 9mm handgun in the car at Edwin during an attempted carjacking, causing Edwin severe injuries and also hitting a bystander._

This event will almost certainly not be covered by auto insurance. For an injury to fall within the "use" coverage of an automobile policy (1) the accident must have arisen out of the inherent nature of the automobile, as such, (2) the accident must have arisen within the natural territorial limits of an automobile, and the actual use must not have terminated, (3) the automobile must not merely contribute to cause the condition which produces the injury, but must itself produce injury.

### VII. What civil liability does a person face if a child accesses a firearm?

A. _Parents are not responsible for minor children's actions merely because they are parents, but...._

As a general rule, minors are liable for their own tortious conduct (that is, their wrongful actions such as negligence, gross negligence, assault, _etc._). The mere fact of paternity or maternity does not generally make a parent liable to third parties for the torts of his or her minor children. Under this general rule, parents are not responsible for their minor children's tortious actions when the minor child commits a tort and the parent had no direct relationship to the child's action, such as providing a firearm in a negligent manner, failing to supervise the child, or allowing the child to engage in behavior the parent knows is dangerous or risky.

Georgia law does attach liability in certain parent-child situations where an agency relationship may be seen to exist (*i.e.,* where the child is acting at the command of the parent, as an "agent"). O.C.G.A. § 51-2-2 assigns liability for tortious conduct committed by an individual's "wife, his child, or his servant by his command or in the prosecution and within the scope of his business, whether the same are committed by negligence or voluntarily." While the language of the statute may be antiquated (it does seem to address the notion that only males may hold this agency relationship with others), the rule still holds true: an act committed at the parent's request that results in an injury, whether intentional or accidental, could result in liability for the parent.

What is the scope or limit of agency liability? Courts in Georgia have ruled parents are not liable in damages for the torts of their minor children merely because of the parent-child relationship, as discussed above. Liability exists, however, in "a principal-agent or a master-servant relationship where the negligence of the child is imputed to the parent, or it is based on the negligence of the parent in some factual situation such as allowing the child to have unsupervised control of a dangerous instrumentality." *Hill v. Morrison,* 160 Ga. App. 151 (Ga. Ct. App. 1981). Recovery has also been permitted where negligence was found on the part of the parent "in furnishing or permitting a child access to an instrumentality with which the child likely would injure a third party." *Muse v. Ozment,* 152 Ga. App. 896 (Ga. Ct. App. 1980). The scenarios contemplated by these Georgia judicial decisions could very easily encompass the negligent entrustment of a firearm to a child by a parent, or in the more basic negligent act of ignoring a substantial risk that a child could obtain a firearm that is improperly stored. What, then, does this teach us?

B.   *Parents who fail to "parent" may become responsible for minor children's actions*

While a parent who has no direct relationship to a minor child's tortious actions is generally not liable for that child's actions, if the parent negligently allows his child to act in a manner likely to harm another, if he gives his child a dangerous instrumentality, or if he does not restrain a child known to have dangerous tendencies, the parent may be liable. And while there is no direct Georgia law prescribing liability to a parent who negligently stores a firearm that then winds up in the hands of a child who uses it, an action for negligent entrustment against the parents may still be viable, if the parents had reason to believe the child could somehow obtain the firearm. But remember: the absence of any direct statute imposing liability does not mean you cannot be sued!

Example:

*Your 17-year-old son Jon has been hunting since he was 11 and has taken several firearms training courses.*

If you take Jon hunting, and for some reason Jon accidentally discharges his shotgun, injuring another person, it is highly unlikely that you, the parent, will be civilly liable for an accident that occurs while hunting.

Example:

*Your 12-year-old son Gordon has never handled a gun or taken a firearms training course. You decide to take him to the range for the first time, but you are both asked to leave the range after Gordon repeatedly fires into the ceiling and the floor. Fed up, you take Gordon to another range with no additional instruction or training.*

If Gordon shoots and injures someone at the second range, it is likely that you will be liable, because you allowed him to act in a manner likely to harm another, and you did not restrain him despite his dangerous conduct.

# CHAPTER THIRTEEN

### BEYOND FIREARMS:
### KNIVES, ELECTRONIC CONTROL DEVICES, IMPACT
### WEAPONS, AND CHEMICAL SPRAYS

In addition to Georgia's firearms laws, state laws exist governing the possession and use of other objects that are commonly referred to as weapons. This includes any object that is not a firearm, but could be used as (or is designed to be) a weapon. This chapter will briefly discuss the laws governing these other objects, including those that are absolutely illegal under the law, those that are illegal to carry, and exceptions to the laws prohibiting the carrying of illegal weapons.

## I.   Knife Laws

Georgia's past is filled with varying attitudes concerning weapons law, and knives are no exception. As long as a century ago, there were restrictions on how and where knives could be carried. At various times restrictions were placed on different types of knives, including spring-assisted knives, "switchblades," and devices such as butterfly knives. Georgia's current statutory scheme is much more clear and easy to understand: examiners of knife law across the country have gone so far as to declare Georgia "knife friendly."

### A.   *Knife ordinances and state pre-emption*

In 2012, groundbreaking legislation governing knives was passed in Georgia. O.C.G.A. § 16-11-136, "Restrictions on possession, manufacture, sale, or transfer of knives" now restricts local government bodies from enacting or enforcing any laws other than state laws (and applicable federal laws) that restrict edged instruments, except in courthouses or government buildings; it does not restrict citizens in any way.

It is important to note, however, that there are still municipalities and counties that list ordinances that are in violation of this statute. It is wise to check for ordinances that may still be active in areas you frequent. When in doubt, carrying a copy of this code section in the event that you encounter a law enforcement officer who has not been kept up to date of changes to Georgia statutes may keep you out of harm's way.

## B. *Knives: the definitions vary!*

Georgia law frequently defines a word or phrase such as "knife" in more than one code section, with overlapping (and confusing) results. Take, for instance, O.C.G.A. § 16-11-125.1 and the definition for knife found there. The definitions in this section apply to the carrying and possession of weapons. A knife is defined therein as "a cutting instrument designed for the purpose of offense and defense consisting of a blade that is greater than five inches in length which is fastened to a handle." These are the defining aspects of a knife that requires a Weapons Carry License to possess and carry. When exploring the question whether a license is required to carry a knife, any object that meets the elements of the definition in O.C.G.A. § 16-11-125.1 requires it: first, the knife must be designed for the purpose of offense and defense; second, the object must have a blade greater than five inches in length which is fastened to a handle.

This definition differs from the definition of knife found in O.C.G.A. § 16-11-136, which restricts local governments from enacting knife ordinances. Here a knife is "any cutting instrument with a blade" including any implement that fits the definition of O.C.G.A. § 16-11-125.1 above. The definition of "knife" contained within O.C.G.A. § 16-11-136 only applies to this specific code section. In contrast, O.C.G.A. § 16-11-173—which restricts counties from enacting local laws and ordinances on more than just knives, to include other weapons, gun shows, and firearms dealers— defines a "weapon" in a manner that also includes knives, as "any device designed or intended to be used, or capable of being used, for offense or defense, including but not limited to firearms, bladed devices, clubs, electric stun devices, and defense sprays." This is yet another example of how differently individual statutes construe definitions for purposes of legislation.

Keep in mind, any object designed, even if not used, for the purpose of offense or defense meets the definition of a knife requiring a license. To examine the incredible list of edged objects found worldwide would be beyond the scope of this book, and several could be arguable. For example, the KA-BAR is a branded knife issued to the United States Marine Corps as a fighting/utility knife since 1942. It appears this knife was not only designed as a fighting object, but also a tool for everyday cutting, other than for purposes of offense and defense. It would be much easier to look at iconic instruments that have been used for centuries to cut human adversaries. Any sword or dagger with a blade over five inches would automatically be encompassed by this definition. But what about a machete? The machete is sold in hardware stores in the same aisle (and often the same rack) as shovels and rakes and is used the world over for harvesting crops and clearing brush. Clearly, it is not designed to be a weapon, even though it could be used as one.

The regulation of weapons in school safety zones gives us yet another permutation of the definition of knife. O.C.G.A. § 16-11-127.1 (a)(4) does not specifically define "knife": instead, this law pertaining to weapons in school safety zones defines the word "weapon" to mean "...any pistol, revolver, or any weapon designed or intended to propel a missile of any kind, or any dirk, bowie knife, switchblade knife, ballistic knife, [or] any other knife having a blade of two or more inches...." This definition restricts the size of a blade in a school zone, making a blade of two or more inches unlawful, as opposed to the definition in O.C.G.A. § 16-11-125.1, that requires a WCL for any blade five inches or more in length. To add even more confusion, O.C.G.A. § 16-11-106, which criminalizes the possession of weapons during the commission of a crime, limits prosecution under this statute to knives with a blade of three or more inches.

C.   _When is a license required for a knife?_
Licenses are required to carry a knife—defined in O.C.G.A. § 16-12-125.1 as having a five-inch blade (or longer), affixed to a handle, and designed for the purpose of offense or defense— any time the possessor is outside of those places described in O.C.G.A. § 16-11-126 as exceptions: the home, place of business, personal vehicle, or property owned or leased by the possessor (previously discussed in Chapter 9 as "the habitation"). As currently written, the exceptions for license requirement do not include carrying a knife that is enclosed in a case. If an individual buys a handgun in a store and does not have a Weapons Carry License, he or she may keep the gun unloaded in a case from the checkout counter to the car. A person who buys a knife that fits the requirements for a license, however, would immediately need a license to possess that knife (or sword, dirk, _etc._) unless possession was taken in the home, vehicle, place of business, or property owned or leased by the possessor.

This is also an important issue for those persons who carry functional weapons to such events as renaissance festivals and historical re-enactments: even if the knife or sword is secured, a license would still be required to be in possession of it.

D. *Are knives prohibited in schools?*

Yes. Georgia's prohibition on knives in school safety zones has been partially explained in the definition section above: it is unlawful for a person to enter the "school safety zone" with any object that fits into the definition of weapon pertaining to that code section.

The definition for schools is a very important departure from other definitions. In the school law here, the term "weapon" includes any knife with a blade of two or more inches, instead of the five inches required in the law describing when a license would be required to carry a knife. This broad definition could conceivably include a plastic knife that is included in a pre-packaged lunch, intended to spread peanut butter on bread.

Does this mean that a student commits a felony by being in possession of this object? No. A 2015 change in legislation excepts this scenario from criminal action. O.C.G.A. § 20-2-1184(a)(3), which details teacher's responsibilities to report certain acts on a school campus, only requires teachers to report possession of a weapon (as defined in O.C.G.A. § 16-11-127.1) when it is combined with an assault. While an individual in authority could certainly confiscate anything declared to be contraband from a student, it will not be reported to the police and the superintendent of schools unless it was combined with some type of assault. Generally, a Weapons Carry License holder may be prosecuted for a misdemeanor if found in possession of a knife in a school safety zone; an individual who does not possess a Georgia Weapons Carry License may be prosecuted for a felony in that same situation.

E. *Switchblades, butterfly knives, Oriental stars, and caltrops*

Other than prohibitions on school carry, there are no restrictions found in Georgia law relating to any particular design of edged weapon. Switchblades and knives with similar mechanisms are legal for purchase and carry in Georgia, with the license requirements only applying to those knives designed for offense/defense that have a blade longer than five inches. As mentioned before, many counties and cities had ordinances pertaining to these devices in effect prior to 2012, and law enforcement officers who encounter these objects today may not be aware that these laws have changed.

### F. *Knives in prohibited places*

Knives are considered weapons, according to their definition in O.C.G.A. § 16-11-125.1. This means there are prohibited places where a knife may not be possessed, locations shared with firearms as we discussed in Chapter Nine. As with firearms, the prohibited places are:

1. in a government building as a non-licensed carrier;
2. in a courthouse;
3. in a jail or prison;
4. in a "house of worship," unless the governing authority permits the carry by licensed individuals;
5. in a state mental health facility;
6. on the premises of a nuclear power plant; and
7. within 150 feet of a polling place, when voting is under way.

Refer to Chapter 9 for a detailed review of these prohibited locations.

### G. *Transportation restrictions on knives*

As we have seen with firearms in Chapter 9, there are important restrictions on the carry of knives and hand-held weapons on public and commercial transportation. Two Georgia statutes specifically address edged weapons. The word "knife" is not defined in either of them, leaving the courts to identify a common definition to apply to the word.

First, recalling O.C.G.A. § 16-12-123, "Bus or rail hijacking; boarding with concealed weapon" from our discussion on firearms carry, you will remember the statute concerns concealed weapons carried on buses or rail vehicles, and includes a "knife or other device designed or modified for the purpose of offense and defense." Anyone who attempts to board an aircraft, bus, or rail vehicle (including public transportation) with a knife "concealed on or about his or her person or property which is or would be accessible to such person while on the aircraft, bus, or rail vehicle" is guilty of a felony.

A close reading of the statute reveals a crime is only committed when the knife is concealed upon the person and accessible to the person while within the method of transportation. The prohibition on carry does not apply to those who transport a knife but disclose to the transportation company and store the knife in "baggage not accessible to passengers." There also appears to be no exception for individuals who have a Weapons Carry License, as the language of this statute only applies this exception to firearms, not knives.

The second law restricting transport of knives applies specifically to airport terminals in addition to buses, rail vehicles, and other transportation; these restrictions have been previously reviewed with respect to firearms. O.C.G.A. § 16-12-123 makes it illegal for a person to introduce into a terminal an explosive, firearm (for which the individual possesses no valid WCL), hazardous substance, or knife by having it in his or her possession; placing it in a container or freight of a transportation company; putting it into the baggage of another without knowledge or authorization, or placing it aboard an aircraft, bus, or rail vehicle.

No mention is made in the statute about concealing the knife or its accessibility. It is VERY important to point out both of these statutes are felonies. If at all possible, when carrying knives avoid travel by bus, rail, or plane, unless you fit one of the exceptions to carry. As with the exceptions to various firearms statutes, law enforcement officers, members of the Armed Forces, and other government agents are not required to have a license in order to carry knives.

## II.   Other weapons: knuckles, tasers, and sprays

No examination of knives and their legal carry would be complete without a discussion of how some of the more "exotic" weapons are treated by statute in Georgia. These include knuckles, stun guns, batons, and chemical sprays.

### A.   _Furnishing knuckles or a knife to a person under the age of 18 years_

O.C.G.A. § 16-11-101 defines the offense of furnishing knuckles or a knife to anyone under the age of 18:

> A person is guilty of a misdemeanor of a high and aggravated nature when he or she knowingly sells to or furnishes to a person under the age of 18 years knuckles, whether made from metal, thermoplastic, wood, or other similar material, or a knife designed for the purpose of offense and defense.

This statute is the only mention of brass or metal knuckles in any state law; it would seem to be the only prohibition on the possession or carry of any form of knuckles in state law. One could assume, then, that because knuckles are specifically adopted under state licensing statutes and requiring a Weapons Carry License, their possession or use does not require a WCL.

Additionally, the word "knife" is undefined in this statute, except that it must be "designed for the purpose of offense and defense." The definition found in O.C.G.A. § 16-11-125.1 does not apply to this particular law. Consider, then, this scenario: a juvenile (remember, under the age of 18) may possess a knife outside of school grounds provided that it does not meet the elements where a license would be required (having a blade less than five inches affixed to a handle and designed for offense or defense). But, if someone provides a knife designed for offense or defense to a juvenile, the one providing the knife could be prosecuted for a high and aggravated misdemeanor.

### B.  *Stun guns and tasers*
No license is required to carry a stun gun or taser: these items are not included in the definition of "weapon" under O.C.G.A. § 16-11-125.1, and consequently fall outside the license requirement.

Tasers and stun guns are prohibited in schools (O.C.G.A. § 16-11-127.1) unless the possessor meets the exceptions in O.C.G.A. §§ 16-11-127.1 or 16-11-130. Local ordinances may not be constructed to restrict stun guns and tasers. They are protected by the state pre-emption doctrine found within O.C.G.A. § 16-11-173(f).

### C.  *Nightsticks, saps, and batons*
Impact weapons such as nightsticks, "saps", and batons are not included in the definition of weapons for which a license would be required before lawful carry. They may be prohibited by the school safety zone law, but are not considered weapons by definition in O.C.G.A. § 16-11-125.1 if carried in the unauthorized locations listed in O.C.G.A. § 16-11-127. Impact weapons are included in the state pre-emption doctrine codified in O.C.G.A. § 16-11-173(f). No local jurisdiction may enact ordinances regulating them.

### D.  *Statute of limitations for civil claims*
Chemical sprays are included in the state pre-emption doctrine found in O.C.G.A. § 16-11-173(f). As with impact weapons, no local jurisdiction may enact ordinances regulating or restricting them. Furthermore, they are not included in the definition of the word "weapon" in

the school carry law. No license is required to carry any type of chemical spray, since these are not included in the definition of weapon in O.C.G.A. § 16-11-125.1. If, however, the spray is designed to be flammable or produce any other effect than being a chemical irritant, it could be included in the term "poison gas" as defined in O.C.G.A. § 16-7-80 ("any toxic chemical or its precursors that... causes death or permanent injury to human beings).

# CHAPTER FOURTEEN

SILENCERS, SAWED-OFF WEAPONS, AND MACHINE GUNS:
THE NATIONAL FIREARMS ACT

Can an individual in Georgia legally own a silencer or suppressor, sawed-off shotgun, sawed-off rifle, machine gun, or "destructive device?" Yes, if all NFA regulations are satisfied. This chapter deals with the laws regarding the possession and use of firearms that are subject to the provisions of the National Firearms Act (NFA) codified in 26 U.S.C. Chapter 53: specifically, silencers, short-barreled firearms, machine guns, and firearms that are otherwise illegal. These firearms are illegal to purchase or possess without possessing the proper paperwork and a "tax stamp." In this chapter, we will discuss the purpose behind the NFA, what firearms are regulated by the Act, as well as the process and procedure for legally possessing weapons that are subject to the Act's provisions.

## I.   What is the National Firearms Act?

The National Firearms Act was enacted in 1934 in response to gangster crimes. Prior to the Act's passage, any person could go to the local hardware store and purchase a Thompson submachine gun or shorten the barrel on their rifle or shotgun. President Roosevelt pushed for the passage of the NFA in an attempt to diminish a gangster's ability to possess and carry dangerous and/or easily concealable firearms, such as machine guns, and short-barreled rifles and shotguns.

*NFA is a firearms regulation using a registration and tax requirement*
The NFA requires both the registration of and tax on the manufacture and transfer of certain firearms. The law created a tax of $200 on the transfer of the following firearms: short-barreled shotguns, short-barreled rifles, machine guns, silencers, and destructive devices. The tax is only $5 for firearms that are classified as "Any Other Weapons" or AOWs. Back in 1934, a $200 tax was the approximate equivalent to about $3,500 today!

Five years after the NFA's passage, the Supreme Court held in *United States v. Miller* that the right to bear arms can be subject to federal regulation. Miller defended himself against the government, stating that the NFA infringed upon his Constitutional right to bear arms under the Second Amendment. While the Court agreed that the Constitution does guarantee a right to bear arms, it held that the right does not extend to every firearm. *See United States v. Miller,* 307 U.S. 174 (1939).

## II.   What firearms does the NFA regulate?
### A.   *Short-barreled rifles and shotguns*
In order to be legal, short-barreled shotguns and rifles must be registered, and a tax paid on the firearm. What is a short-barreled shotgun? Under both federal and Georgia law, short-barreled shotguns (known as "sawed-off shotguns" in Georgia statutes) have one or more barrels less than 18 inches in length and the overall length of the shotgun is less than 26 inches. What is a short-barreled rifle? It is any rifle with one or more barrels less than 16 inches in length, and the overall length of the rifle is less than 26 inches. *See* 27 CFR § 478.11. Georgia law identifies short-barreled rifles as "sawed-off rifles", with the same size parameters. *See* O.C.G.A. § 16-11-121.

Short-barreled shotguns and rifles may be purchased from an FFL that deals in NFA items. Also, short-barreled firearms are very popular for individuals to build and/or modify on their own. This is legal if the person has properly registered the firearm to be modified into a short-barreled firearm with the ATF and paid the tax before it is modified. Once approved, a person may alter or produce a short-barreled firearm and must engrave legally required information on the receiver of the firearm such as manufacturer, location, *etc.* See discussion later in this chapter for detailed requirements.

### B.   *Machine guns*
Machine guns are illegal under federal and state law. However, if the requirements of the NFA are satisfied, individuals may legally own machine guns. First, what is a machine gun? Federal law defines a machine gun as "any weapon which shoots, is designed to shoot, or can be readily restored to shoot, automatically more than one shot, without manual reloading, by a single function of the trigger. The term shall also include the frame or receiver of any such weapon, any part designed and intended solely and exclusively, or combination of parts designed and intended, for use in converting a weapon into a machine gun, and any combination of parts from which a machine gun can be assembled if such parts are in the possession or under the control of a person." 27 CFR § 478.11. As a result of this definition, the individual metal components that make up a whole

machine gun, such as a full-auto sear, individually meet the federal definition of machine gun. The parts for the machine gun do not have to be assembled.

Similarly, under Georgia law, a machine gun is defined as "any weapon which shoots or is designed to shoot, automatically, more than six shots, without manual reloading, by a single function of the trigger." O.C.G.A. § 16-11-121. Georgia law identifies machine guns as prohibited weapons under O.C.G.A. § 16-11-122 unless, among other exceptions listed, the possessor holds the proper paperwork under the NFA. In other words, if more than six bullets discharge from a firearm with only one pull of the trigger, the firearm is a machine gun under Georgia's definition.

*No new manufacturing of machine guns for private ownership*
Because of a federal law that effectively disallows private ownership (not military, police department, *etc.*) of any machine gun manufactured after May 19, 1986, machine guns available for private ownership are limited to the legally registered machine guns that existed prior to May 19, 1986. Thus, the private market is very limited and prices, as a result, are very high.

C.   *Firearm suppressors*
What is a suppressor? It is just a muffler for a firearm and is legal if all NFA requirements are met. In legal terms, a firearm suppressor is defined in 27 CFR § 478.11 as "any device for silencing, muffling, or diminishing the report of a portable firearm, including any combination of parts, designed or redesigned, and intended for use in assembling or fabricating a firearm silencer or firearm muffler, and any part intended only for use in such assembly or fabrication." The Georgia definition, closely related to the federal one, identifies "any device for silencing or diminishing the report of any portable weapon such as a rifle, carbine, pistol, revolver, machine gun, shotgun, fowling piece, or other device from which a shot, bullet, or projectile may be discharged by an explosive." O.C.G.A. § 16-11-121.

The Georgia definition goes further by specifically identifying types of devices that fall within the definition, but stops short of the inclusion of "any combination of parts" that makes the federal definition more expansive.

Firearm suppressors are very practical instruments. They are great for hunting and recreational shooting not only because it suppresses gunshots in a way so as to not alarm other animals being hunted nearby, but also because it lessens the impact on the shooter's ears. However, firearms owners should be carefully aware that the definition of a suppressor is very broad whether under federal or Georgia law. Suppressors do not need to be items manufactured specifically for use as a suppressor. There are some ordinary, every-day items that could be easily converted into a suppressor such as a water bottle or an automotive oil filter. Possession of otherwise legal items when used or modified to be used as a suppressor is illegal.

## DESTRUCTIVE DEVICES

**27 C.F.R. § 478.11.**
**Part A.** Any explosive, incendiary, or poison gas (1) bomb, (2) grenade, (3) rocket having a propellant charge of more than 4 ounces, (4) missile having an explosive or incendiary charge of more than one-quarter ounce, (5) mine, or (6) device similar to any of the devices described in the preceding paragraphs of this definition.

**Part B.** Any type of weapon (other than a shotgun or shotgun shell which the Director finds is generally recognized as particularly suitable for sporting purposes) by whatever name known which will, or which may be readily converted to, expel a projectile by the action of an explosive or other propellant, and which has any barrel with a bore of more than one-half inch in diameter.

**Part C.** Any combination of parts either designed or intended for use in converting any destructive device described in [part] (A) and (B) of this section and from which a destructive device may be readily assembled.

## D. *Destructive devices*

The term "destructive device" is a legal term given to certain firearms, objects, and munitions that are illegal under the NFA. The "destructive devices" as defined in the statute are effectively broken down into three categories: explosive devices, large caliber weapons, and parts easily convertible into a destructive device.

Initially, the definition of a destructive device deals with explosive, incendiary and poison gas munitions. The definition specifies that any explosive, incendiary, or poison gas bomb, grenade, mine or similar device is a destructive device. In addition, the definition includes a rocket having a propellant charge of more than four ounces and a missile (projectile) having an explosive or incendiary charge of more than one-quarter ounce. These topics and the regulations thereof are beyond the scope of this book's discussion.

The second section of the definition addresses large caliber weapons and states that any type of weapon that has a bore diameter of more than one-half inch is a destructive device with the exception of shotguns (and shotgun shells) that are suitable for sporting purposes. Thus, any caliber in a rifle or handgun more than .5 inches or fifty caliber is classified as a destructive device. Shotguns are exempt from this prohibition on size unless the ATF rules it is not for "sporting purposes." How do you know if a shotgun is suitable for sporting purposes? The ATF keeps a list, and has issued rulings classifying specific shotguns as destructive devices because they are not considered to be particularly "suitable for sporting purposes" including the USAS-12, Striker-12, Streetsweeper, and 37/38mm Beanbags. The ATF does not provide any specific definition of what constitutes being "suitable for sporting purposes" nor does it specify the methodology in which it determines what makes a particular shotgun suitable for sporting purposes. Ultimately, one will have to check with the ATF lists to see whether a particular shotgun with a larger bore-diameter is classified as a destructive device or not.

Finally, a destructive device does not need to be a completed and assembled product to fall under the federal definition and regulation under the NFA. Much like machine guns, if a person possesses parts that can be readily assembled into a destructive device, then whether or not the device has actually been constructed is irrelevant—by law it's already a destructive device.

Although these firearms, munitions, and devices are prohibited by the law on its face pursuant to the National Firearms Act, a person may nevertheless receive permission to possess them so long as they possess the correct legal authorization.

E. *"Any Other Weapons" or AOWs*

The AOW category under the NFA pertains to firearms and weapons that may not fit the traditional definition of some of the firearms discussed elsewhere in this book due to the way in which they are manufactured or modified. Under federal law, an AOW is "any weapon or device capable of being concealed on the person from which a shot can be discharged through the energy of an explosive, a pistol or revolver having a barrel with a smooth bore designed or redesigned to fire a fixed shotgun shell, weapons with combination shotgun and rifle barrels 12 inches or more, less than 18 inches in length, from which only a single discharge can be made from either barrel without manual reloading, and shall include any such weapon which may be readily restored to fire. Such term shall not include a pistol or a revolver having a rifled bore, or rifled bores, or weapons designed, made, or intended to be fired from the shoulder and not capable of firing fixed ammunition." 26 U.S.C. § 5845(e).

1. Concealable weapons and devices

Weapons which are capable of being concealed from which one shot can be discharged are AOWs. This includes such weapons as a pen-gun, knife gun, or umbrella gun. Georgia law does not use the term AOW.

**Some concealable devices include, from left, the pen-gun, umbrella gun, knife gun, and wallet gun.**

2. Pistols and revolvers having a smooth-bore barrel for firing shotgun shells

Pistols and revolvers that have a smooth bore (no rifling) that are designed to shoot shotgun ammunition are defined as an AOW. The ATF cites firearms such as the H&R Handy Gun or the Ithaca Auto

& Burglar Gun as firearms that fall under the AOW category. Note: handguns with partially rifled barrels such as The Judge from Taurus or Smith & Wesson's Governor do not fall under this category due to the rifling of the barrel.

**Above left, the H&R Handy Gun;
above right, the Ithaca Auto & Burglar Gun.**

3. <u>Weapons with barrels 12 inches or longer and lengths 18 inches or shorter</u>

The definition of Any Other Weapon also includes any weapon which has a shotgun or rifle barrel of 12 inches or more but is 18 inches or less in overall length from which only a single discharge can be made from either barrel without manual reloading. The ATF identifies the "Marble Game Getter" as the firearm most commonly associated with this definition (excluding the model with an 18" barrel and folding shoulder stock).

4. <u>Pistols and revolvers with vertical handgrips</u>

If a pistol is modified with a vertical grip on the front, it will now be legally classified as an AOW and require registration and a paid tax.

Note, vertical grips are readily available and are legal to own as long as they are not placed on a handgun.

The definition of a handgun is a weapon which is intended to be fired by one hand, the addition of the vertical foregrip makes it so the weapon now is intended to be used with two hands to fire. This modification changes the weapon from a handgun to what is known as an "AOW" and is now a prohibited weapon without the proper documentation.

F.  *Antique firearms*

Firearms that are defined by the NFA as "antique firearms" are not regulated by the NFA. The NFA definition of antique firearm is found in 26 U.S.C. § 5845(g) as "any firearm not designed or redesigned for using rim fire or conventional center fire ignition with fixed ammunition and manufactured in or before 1898 (including any matchlock, flintlock, percussion cap, or similar type of ignition system or replica thereof, whether actually manufactured before or after the year 1898) and also any firearm using fixed ammunition manufactured in or before 1898, for which ammunition is no longer manufactured in the United States and is not readily available in the ordinary channels of commercial trade."

Under this statute and for NFA purposes, the only firearms that are antiques are firearms which were both actually manufactured in or before 1898 and ones for which fixed ammunition is no longer manufactured in the United States and is not readily available in the ordinary channels of commercial trade.

With this in mind, the ATF states in its NFA guidebook that "it is important to note that a specific type of fixed ammunition that has been out of production for many years may again become available due to increasing interest in older firearms. Therefore, the classification of a specific NFA firearm as an antique can change if ammunition for the weapon becomes readily available in the ordinary channels of commerce."

G.  *NFA curio firearms and relics*
Under federal law, curios or relics are defined in 27 CFR § 478.11 as "firearms which are of special interest to collectors by reason of some quality other than is associated with firearms intended for sporting use or as offensive or defensive weapons." Persons who collect curios or relics may do so with a special collector's license although one is not required.

The impact of an NFA item being classified as a curio or relic, however, is that it allows the item to be transferred interstate to persons possessing a collector's license. The collector's license does not allow the individual to deal in curios or relics, nor does it allow the collector to obtain other firearms interstate as those transactions still require an FFL.

To be classified as a curio or relic, federal law states that the firearm must fall into one of the following three categories:

1.  Firearms which were manufactured at least 50 years prior to the current date, but not including replicas thereof;
2.  Firearms which are certified by the curator of a municipal, state, or federal museum which exhibits firearms to be curi-

ous or relics of museum interest; or

3. Any other firearms which derive a substantial part of their monetary value from the fact that they are novel, rare, bizarre, or because of their association with some historical figure, period, or event.

The ATF maintains a list of firearms that are classified as curios or relics. *See* 27 CFR § 478.11.

H. *How can some after-market gun parts make your firearm illegal?*
A number of companies manufacture and sell gun products or parts that alter the appearance or utility of a firearm (*i.e.* shoulder stocks, forward hand grips, *etc.*).

However, some of these after-market products can actually change the firearm you possess from one type of a weapon to another type of weapon for legal purposes whether you realize it or not. As a result, many individuals make the modifications to their firearms thinking that because there was no special process for purchasing the accessory, any modification would be in compliance with the law. Unfortunately, this is not always the case.

> ### PRACTICAL LEGAL TIP
>
> Some of the items regulated by the NFA simply don't make as much sense as the other things it regulates. Suppressors are really nothing more than mufflers for your firearm—they aren't really firearms themselves (notwithstanding the legal definition). Thinking about the utility of the suppressor, if the firearm was invented today, you can be sure that not only would the government not prohibit them, OSHA would probably require them for safety purposes! — *Matt*

Consider the example of short-barreled uppers for AR-15s: selling, buying, or possessing AR-15 "uppers" with barrels less than 16 inches is legal. However, it is illegal to put the upper on a receiver of an AR-15 because this would be the act of manufacturing a short-barreled rifle and is legally prohibited. This is equally true of vertical forward grips on a handgun. Vertical foregrips are legal to buy or possess, however, if you actually install one on a handgun, you have manufactured an AOW, and it is illegal, unless registered and a tax paid. Note: there are other types of braces that are permissible in their proper application and illegal in any application or adaptation that would alter the classification of the weapon. For example, the Sig Arm Brace is legal to attach to an AR Pistol when used as an arm brace, but illegal when used as a shoulder stock.

### III. Process and procedure for obtaining NFA firearms
#### A. *Who can own and possess an NFA firearm?*
Any person may own and possess an NFA firearm as long as they are legally not disqualified to own or possess firearms and live in a state that allows possession of NFA items. See Chapters 2 and 3. The ATF also allows for a non-person legal entity to own these items, such as corporations, partnerships, and trusts, *etc.*

---

### PRACTICAL LEGAL TIP

Even if you don't own a machine gun today, that doesn't mean you won't be the intended owner of one later. A person could always leave you their NFA items in a will. If this happens, you must file the appropriate paperwork with the ATF as soon as possible, or at least before probate is closed. —*Matt*

---

#### B. *What are the usual steps for buying or manufacturing NFA items?*
Whether a person is buying or making (manufacturing) an NFA firearm, there are several steps in the process. The transfer or manufacture of an NFA firearm requires the filing of an appropriate transfer form with the ATF, payment of any federally-mandated transfer tax, approval of the transfer by the ATF, and registration of the firearm to the transferee. Only after these steps have occurred may a buyer legally take possession of the NFA item, or may a person legally assemble or manufacture the NFA item. In this section, we will walk through the process, step-by-step, of (1) purchasing an NFA item that already exists, and (2) manufacturing an NFA firearm.

*Steps for buying an existing NFA item (for example, a suppressor)*

1. Select and purchase the item (suppressor) from a transferor who is usually an FFL dealer who is authorized to sell NFA weapons;

2. Assemble appropriate paperwork: ATF Form 4 (see Appendix B), fingerprints on an FBI Form FD-258, a passport size photograph, and a payment for the tax ($200);
   (a) If the buyer is an individual they must notify the Chief Law Enforcement Officer of their city or county of residence by serving the CLEO a copy of ATF Form 4;
   (b) If the buyer is a corporation or trust, each "responsible person" of the corporation or trust must complete an ATF Form 5320.23 (see Appendix B), including fingerprints and passport photograph, and must notify the Chief Law Enforcement Officer of their city or county by delivering to them the CLEO copy of ATF Form 5320.23;

3. Submit paperwork, fingerprints, and tax to the ATF for review and approval;

4. ATF sends approval (tax stamp affixed to Form 4) to the dealer;

5. FFL dealer notifies the buyer to pick up suppressor.

*Steps for manufacturing an NFA item (for example, a short-barreled AR-15 from an 80% lower)*

1. Select the item to manufacture or modify (short-barreled AR-15);

2. Assemble appropriate paperwork: ATF Form 1 (see Appendix B), fingerprints on an FBI Form FD-258, a passport size photograph, and a payment for the tax ($200);
   (a) If the buyer is an individual they must notify the Chief Law Enforcement Officer of the city or county of their residence by delivering the CLEO copy of ATF Form 1;
   (b) If the buyer is a corporation or trust, each "responsible person" of the corporation or trust must complete an ATF Form 5320.23 (see Appendix B), including fingerprints and passport photograph, and must notify the Chief Law Enforcement Officer of their city or county of residence by delivering to them the CLEO copy of ATF Form 5320.23;

3. As "Applicant" you submit paperwork and tax to the ATF for review and approval;

4. ATF sends you the approval (tax stamp affixed to Form 1);

5. You may then legally assemble the AR-15, *i.e.,* put upper

with a barrel length of less than 16 inches on a lower receiver, etc. The item must now be engraved and identified.

When purchasing an NFA firearm from a dealer, the dealer is required to have the purchaser fill out ATF Form 4473 when the purchaser goes to pick up the item from the dealer.

C. *How must an NFA item be engraved and identified if I make it myself?*

Once you receive ATF approval to manufacture your own NFA item (such as the short-barreled AR-15 in the previous section), federal law requires that you engrave, cast, stamp, or otherwise conspicuously place or cause to be engraved, cast, stamped, or placed on the frame, receiver, or barrel of the NFA item the following information:

1. The item's serial number;
2. The item's model (if so designated);
3. Caliber or gauge;
4. The name of the owner whether individual, corporation, or trust; and
5. The city and state where the item was made.

This information must be placed on the item with a minimum depth of .003 inch and in a print size no smaller than 1/16 inch. *See* 27 CFR § 479.102.

D. *Which way should I own my NFA item? Paperwork requirements for individuals, trusts, or business entities to own NFA items*

   1. Form 4 and Form 1

The appropriate paperwork that must be assembled and submitted to the ATF under the NFA varies depending on whether an individual or a legal entity, such as a trust, corporation, or partnership, is purchasing or manufacturing the NFA item. The paperwork generally starts either with an ATF Form 4 (used for purchasing an existing item), or an ATF Form 1 which is used if a person wishes to manufacture a new NFA item. All relevant portions of the Form must be completed. Both Form 4 and Form 1 have a requirement that a Chief Law Enforcement Officer's must be notified. Therefore, unlike in the past, a Chief Law Enforcement Officer signature is not necessary.

   2. Who is a Chief Law Enforcement Officer who must be notified?

For the purposes of ATF Forms 1 and 4, and the responsible person questionnaire, Form 5320.23, a CLEO is considered to be a chief law enforcement officer who has jurisdiction where the transferor, the applicant, and any "responsible persons" are located. These persons include "the Chief of Police; the Sheriff; the Head of the State Police; or a State or local district attorney or prosecutor."

3. Photograph and fingerprints are required for individual applicants and "responsible persons"

If an individual is purchasing or manufacturing an NFA item, the applicant must submit an appropriate photograph and their fingerprints. An entity such as a trust or corporation must designate "responsible persons" who are allowed to have access to use and possess an NFA weapon. As of July 13, 2016, corporations and trusts must submit the appropriate documents showing its existence, such as the trust or corporate formation documents, the ATF responsible person questionnaire, and fingerprints and passport photographs of these persons.

"Responsible persons" of trusts, partnerships, associations, companies, or corporations, are defined as "any individual who possesses, directly or indirectly, the power or authority to direct the management and policies of the trust or entity to receive, possess, ship, transport, deliver, transfer or otherwise dispose of a firearm for, or on behalf of, the trust or legal entity." The ATF Form 5320.23 provides examples of "responsible persons," including, "settlors/ grantors, trustees, partners, members, officers, directors, board members, or owners." Persons who are not "responsible persons" are "the beneficiary of a trust, if the beneficiary does not have the capability to exercise the enumerated powers or authorities."

E. *Why are trusts so popular to own NFA items?*
There are several major reasons trusts are very popular to own NFA items: paperwork, control, and ease of ownership. A trust is a legal entity that can hold property for the benefit of a third party.

A major reason for having a trust own an NFA item is that it makes owning and using the NFA item easier if more than one person wishes to possess and use the item. If an individual owns the item, then only the registered individual can ever "possess" it. On the other hand, if the item is owned by a trust, all trustees, including co-trustees, are able to possess and use the items contained in the trust. Therefore, co-trustees may be added or removed.

Further, unlike other entities such as corporations, LLCs, etc., a trust requires no filings with the government to create, which saves expenses. Further, these expense savings continue because there are no continuing government fees or compliance requirements. Thus, trusts are one of the best ways currently to own an NFA item.

F.  *The Tax Stamp*

Once the ATF has an applicant's materials in hand, they will be reviewed and checked by NFA researchers and an examiner. The application will then either be approved or denied. A denial will be accompanied by an explanation of why the application was denied and how to remedy it, if possible. If the application is approved, the examiner will affix a tax stamp to the submitted Form 1 or Form 4 and send the newly-stamped Form to the  applicant. This tax stamp on the appropriate form is a person's evidence of compliance with the NFA's requirements and is a very important document. A copy of the stamp should always be kept with the NFA item.

G.  *What documents should I have with me when I am in actual possession of my suppressor, short-barreled firearm, or other NFA item?*

If you have an NFA item, always have the proper documentation with you to prove that you legally possess the item. Again, if you are in possession of your suppressor, short-barreled firearm, destructive device, or if you are lucky enough, your machine gun—always have your paperwork showing you are legal, or it may be a long day with law enforcement. To show you are legal, always keep a copy of your ATF Form 4 or Form 1 (whichever is applicable) with the tax stamp affixed for every NFA item in your possession, personal identification, and if the item is held in a trust or corporation, a copy of the trust or articles of incorporation, and the authorization for possession. Care should be given to make sure these documents name the individual so as to show legal ownership, *i.e.,* trust and/or amendments showing the person is a co-trustee or an officer of the corporation.

Practically, individuals should not carry around the original documents as they could be destroyed by wear and tear, rain, or be misplaced, effectively destroying the required evidence of compliance. Photocopies of the stamp and any other pertinent documents are generally enough to satisfy inquisitive law enforcement officials. You may choose to take pictures on your phone or other mobile device, or even upload them to a cloud database. Keep in mind that if the phone dies or the cloud cannot be reached, and you have no way to access the documents, your proof is gone and you may have a very bad day ahead of you! We recommend keeping photocopies of the ATF form with the tax stamp affixed and appropriate documents to avoid any problems with technology.

### H.  *Why is the paperwork necessary?*

According to O.C.G.A. § 16-11-122, "sawed-off" shotguns (short-barreled shotguns), "sawed-off" rifles (short-barreled rifles), machine guns, dangerous weapons, and silencers are illegal to possess. It is a defense to criminal prosecution, however, that possession was pursuant to the National Firearms Act, which provides an exemption under O.C.G.A. § 16-11-124 (which lists other exemptions, such as possession by peace officers or members of the Armed Forces). In other words, even though possession of such articles arguably meets the elements of committing a crime (possessing the listed items), the law provides a lawful possessor an exemption from the restrictions on possession (proving possession pursuant to the NFA). In theory, law enforcement officers could arrest individuals, who would then be forced to show up to court to prove this exemption; practically, however, showing the proper paperwork to a law enforcement officer when necessary is likely sufficient to avoid any further entanglement in the legal system.

# APPENDIX A

## SELECTED GEORGIA STATUTES

**O.C.G.A. § 1-2-6**
**Rights of citizens generally**
(a) The rights of citizens include, without limitation, the following:
   (1) The right of personal security;
   (2) The right of personal liberty;
   (3) The right of private property and the disposition thereof;
   (4) The right of the elective franchise;
   (5) The right to hold office, unless disqualified by the
       Constitution and laws of this state;
   (6) The right to appeal to the courts;
   (7) The right to testify as a witness;
   (8) The right to perform any civil function; and
   (9) The right to keep and bear arms.
(b) All citizens are entitled to exercise all their rights as citizens unless specially prohibited by law.

**O.C.G.A. § 10-1-100**
**Out of state purchase of rifles and shotguns by residents**
Residents of the State of Georgia may purchase rifles and shotguns in any state of the United States, provided such residents conform to applicable provisions of statutes and regulations of the United States, of the State of Georgia, and of the state in which the purchase is made.

**O.C.G.A. § 10-1-101**
**Nonresidents may purchase rifles and shotguns in Georgia**
Residents of any state of the United States may purchase rifles and shotguns in the State of Georgia, provided such residents conform to applicable provisions of statutes and regulations of the United States, of the State of Georgia, and of the state in which such persons reside.

**O.C.G.A. § 16-1-3**
**General Provisions: Definitions**
As used in this title, the term:
(1) "Affirmative defense" means, with respect to any affirmative defense authorized in this title, unless the state's evidence raises

the issue invoking the alleged defense, the defendant must present evidence thereon to raise the issue. The enumeration in this title of some affirmative defenses shall not be construed as excluding the existence of others.

(2) "Agency" means:

(A) When used with respect to the state government, any department, commission, committee, authority, board, or bureau thereof; and

(B) When used with respect to any political subdivision of the state government, any department, commission, committee, authority, board, or bureau thereof.

(3) "Another" means a person or persons other than the accused.

(4) "Conviction" includes a final judgment of conviction entered upon a verdict or finding of guilty of a crime or upon a plea of guilty.

(5) "Felony" means a crime punishable by death, by imprisonment for life, or by imprisonment for more than 12 months.

(6) "Forcible felony" means any felony which involves the use or threat of physical force or violence against any person.

(7) "Forcible misdemeanor" means any misdemeanor which involves the use or threat of physical force or violence against any person.

(8) "Government" means the United States, the state, any political subdivision thereof, or any agency of the foregoing.

(9) "Misdemeanor" and "misdemeanor of a high and aggravated nature" mean any crime other than a felony.

(10) "Owner" means a person who has a right to possession of property which is superior to that of a person who takes, uses, obtains, or withholds it from him and which the person taking, using, obtaining, or withholding is not privileged to infringe.

(11) "Peace officer" means any person who by virtue of his office or public employment is vested by law with a duty to maintain public

order or to make arrests for offenses, whether that duty extends to all crimes or is limited to specific offenses.

(12) "Person" means an individual, a public or private corporation, an incorporated association, government, government agency, partnership, or unincorporated association.

(13) "Property" means anything of value, including but not limited to real estate, tangible and intangible personal property, contract rights, services, choses in action, and other interests in or claims to wealth, admission or transportation tickets, captured or domestic animals, food and drink, and electric or other power.

(14) "Prosecution" means all legal proceedings by which a person's liability for a crime is determined, commencing with the return of the indictment or the filing of the accusation, and including the final disposition of the case upon appeal.

(15) "Public place" means any place where the conduct involved may reasonably be expected to be viewed by people other than members of the actor's family or household.

(16) "Reasonable belief" means that the person concerned, acting as a reasonable man, believes that the described facts exist.

(17) "State" means the State of Georgia, all land and water in respect to which this state has either exclusive or concurrent jurisdiction, and the airspace above such land and water.

(18) "Without authority" means without legal right or privilege or without permission of a person legally entitled to withhold the right.

(19) "Without his consent" means that a person whose concurrence is required has not, with knowledge of the essential facts, voluntarily yielded to the proposal of the accused or of another.

## O.C.G.A. § 16-3-21
**Use of force in defense of self or others; evidence of belief that force was necessary in murder or manslaughter prosecution**
(a) A person is justified in threatening or using force against anoth-

er when and to the extent that he or she reasonably believes that such threat or force is necessary to defend himself or herself or a third person against such other's imminent use of unlawful force; however, except as provided in Code Section 16-3-23, a person is justified in using force which is intended or likely to cause death or great bodily harm only if he or she reasonably believes that such force is necessary to prevent death or great bodily injury to himself or herself or a third person or to prevent the commission of a forcible felony.

(b) A person is not justified in using force under the circumstances specified in subsection (a) of this Code section if he:

(1) Initially provokes the use of force against himself with the intent to use such force as an excuse to inflict bodily harm upon the assailant;
(2) Is attempting to commit, committing, or fleeing after the commission or attempted commission of a felony; or
(3) Was the aggressor or was engaged in a combat by agreement unless he withdraws from the encounter and effectively communicates to such other person his intent to do so and the other, notwithstanding, continues or threatens to continue the use of unlawful force.

(c) Any rule, regulation, or policy of any agency of the state or any ordinance, resolution, rule, regulation, or policy of any county, municipality, or other political subdivision of the state which is in conflict with this Code section shall be null, void, and of no force and effect.

(d) In a prosecution for murder or manslaughter, if a defendant raises as a defense a justification provided by subsection (a) of this Code section, the defendant, in order to establish the defendant's reasonable belief that the use of force or deadly force was immediately necessary, may be permitted to offer:

(1) Relevant evidence that the defendant had been the victim of acts of family violence or child abuse committed by the deceased, as such acts are described in Code Sections 19-13-1 and 19-15-1, respectively; and
(2) Relevant expert testimony regarding the condition of the

mind of the defendant at the time of the offense, including those relevant facts and circumstances relating to the family violence or child abuse that are the bases of the expert's opinion.

## O.C.G.A. § 16-3-22
## Immunity from criminal liability of persons rendering assistance to law enforcement officers

(a) Any person who renders assistance reasonably and in good faith to any law enforcement officer who is being hindered in the performance of his official duties or whose life is being endangered by the conduct of any other person or persons while performing his official duties shall be immune to the same extent as the law enforcement officer from any criminal liability that might otherwise be incurred or imposed as a result of rendering assistance to the law enforcement officer.

(b) The official report of the law enforcement agency shall create a rebuttable presumption of good faith and reasonableness on the part of the person who assists the law enforcement officer.

(c) The purpose of this Code section is to provide for those persons who act in good faith to assist law enforcement officers whose health and safety is being adversely affected and threatened by the conduct of any other person or persons. This Code section shall be liberally construed so as to carry out the purposes thereof.

## O.C.G.A. § 16-3-23
## Use of force in defense of habitation

A person is justified in threatening or using force against another when and to the extent that he or she reasonably believes that such threat or force is necessary to prevent or terminate such other's unlawful entry into or attack upon a habitation; however, such person is justified in the use of force which is intended or likely to cause death or great bodily harm only if:

(1) The entry is made or attempted in a violent and tumultuous manner and he or she reasonably believes that the entry is attempted or made for the purpose of assaulting or offering personal violence to any person dwelling or being therein and

that such force is necessary to prevent the assault or offer of personal violence;

(2) That force is used against another person who is not a member of the family or household and who unlawfully and forcibly enters or has unlawfully and forcibly entered the residence and the person using such force knew or had reason to believe that an unlawful and forcible entry occurred; or

(3) The person using such force reasonably believes that the entry is made or attempted for the purpose of committing a felony therein and that such force is necessary to prevent the commission of the felony.

## O.C.G.A. § 16-3-23.1
### No duty to retreat prior to use of force in self-defense
A person who uses threats or force in accordance with Code Section 16-3-21, relating to the use of force in defense of self or others, Code Section 16-3-23, relating to the use of force in defense of a habitation, or Code Section 16-3-24, relating to the use of force in defense of property other than a habitation, has no duty to retreat and has the right to stand his or her ground and use force as provided in said Code sections, including deadly force.

## O.C.G.A. § 16-3-24
### Use of force in defense of property other than a habitation
(a) A person is justified in threatening or using force against another when and to the extent that he reasonably believes that such threat or force is necessary to prevent or terminate such other's trespass on or other tortious or criminal interference with real property other than a habitation or personal property:
  (1) Lawfully in his possession;
  (2) Lawfully in the possession of a member of his immediate family; or
  (3) Belonging to a person whose property he has a legal duty to protect.

(b) The use of force which is intended or likely to cause death or great bodily harm to prevent trespass on or other tortious or criminal interference with real property other than a habitation or personal property is not justified unless the person using such force reasonably believes that it is necessary to prevent the commission of a forcible felony.

## O.C.G.A. § 16-3-24.1
### Habitation and personal property defined

As used in Code Sections 16-3-23 and 16-3-24, the term "habitation" means any dwelling, motor vehicle, or place of business, and "personal property" means personal property other than a motor vehicle.

## O.C.G.A. § 16-3-24.2
### Immunity from prosecution; exception

A person who uses threats or force in accordance with Code Section 16-3-21, 16-3-23, 16-3-23.1, or 16-3-24 shall be immune from criminal prosecution therefor unless in the use of deadly force, such person utilizes a weapon the carrying or possession of which is unlawful by such person under Part 2 of Article 4 of Chapter 11 of this title.

## O.C.G.A. § 16-7-21
### Criminal trespass

(a) A person commits the offense of criminal trespass when he or she intentionally damages any property of another without consent of that other person and the damage thereto is $500.00 or less or knowingly and maliciously interferes with the possession or use of the property of another person without consent of that person.

(b) A person commits the offense of criminal trespass when he or she knowingly and without authority:

(1) Enters upon the land or premises of another person or into any part of any vehicle, railroad car, aircraft, or watercraft of another person for an unlawful purpose;
(2) Enters upon the land or premises of another person or into any part of any vehicle, railroad car, aircraft, or watercraft of another person after receiving, prior to such entry, notice from the owner, rightful occupant, or, upon proper identification, an authorized representative of the owner or rightful occupant that such entry is forbidden; or
(3) Remains upon the land or premises of another person or within the vehicle, railroad car, aircraft, or watercraft of

another person after receiving notice from the owner, rightful occupant, or, upon proper identification, an authorized representative of the owner or rightful occupant to depart.

(c) For the purposes of subsection (b) of this Code section, permission to enter or invitation to enter given by a minor who is or is not present on or in the property of the minor's parent or guardian is not sufficient to allow lawful entry of another person upon the land, premises, vehicle, railroad car, aircraft, or watercraft owned or rightfully occupied by such minor's parent or guardian if such parent or guardian has previously given notice that such entry is forbidden or notice to depart.

(d) A person who commits the offense of criminal trespass shall be guilty of a misdemeanor.

(e) A person commits the offense of criminal trespass when he or she intentionally defaces, mutilates, or defiles any grave marker, monument, or memorial to one or more deceased persons who served in the military service of this state, the United States of America or any of the states thereof, or the Confederate States of America or any of the states thereof, or a monument, plaque, marker, or memorial which is dedicated to, honors, or recounts the military service of any past or present military personnel of this state, the United States of America or any of the states thereof, or the Confederate States of America or any of the states thereof if such grave marker, monument, memorial, plaque, or marker is privately owned or located on land which is privately owned.

## O.C.G.A. § 16-11-101
**Furnishing metal knuckles or a knife to person under the age of 18 years**
A person is guilty of a misdemeanor of a high and aggravated nature when he or she knowingly sells to or furnishes to a person under the age of 18 years knuckles, whether made from metal, thermoplastic, wood, or other similar material, or a knife designed for the purpose of offense and defense.

## O.C.G.A. § 16-11-101.1
## Furnishing pistol or revolver to person under the age of 18 years

(a) For the purposes of this Code section, the term:

    (1) "Minor" means any person under the age of 18 years.

    (2) "Pistol or revolver" means a handgun as defined in subsection (a) of Code Section 16-11-125.1.

(b) It shall be unlawful for a person intentionally, knowingly, or recklessly to sell or furnish a pistol or revolver to a minor, except that it shall be lawful for a parent or legal guardian to permit possession of a pistol or revolver by a minor for the purposes specified in subsection (c) of Code Section 16-11-132 unless otherwise expressly limited by subsection (c) of this Code section.

(c)

    (1) It shall be unlawful for a parent or legal guardian to permit possession of a pistol or revolver by a minor if the parent or legal guardian knows of a minor's conduct which violates the provisions of Code Section 16-11-132 and fails to make reasonable efforts to prevent any such violation of Code Section 16-11-132.

    (2) Notwithstanding any provisions of subsection (c) of Code Section 16-11-132 or any other law to the contrary, it shall be unlawful for any parent or legal guardian intentionally, knowingly, or recklessly to furnish to or permit a minor to possess a pistol or revolver if such parent or legal guardian is aware of a substantial risk that such minor will use a pistol or revolver to commit a felony offense or if such parent or legal guardian who is aware of such substantial risk fails to make reasonable efforts to prevent commission of the offense by the minor.

    (3) In addition to any other act which violates this subsection, a parent or legal guardian shall be deemed to have violated this subsection if such parent or legal guardian furnishes to or permits possession of a pistol or revolver by any minor who has been convicted of a forcible felony or forcible misdemeanor, as defined in Code Section 16-1-3, or who has been adjudicated for committing a delinquent act under the provisions of Article 6 of Chapter 11 of Title 15 for an offense which would constitute a forcible felony or forcible misdemeanor, as defined in Code Section 16-1-3, if such minor were an adult.

(d) Upon conviction of a violation of subsection (b) or (c) of this Code section, a person shall be guilty of a felony and punished by a fine not to exceed $5,000.00 or by imprisonment for not less than three nor more than five years, or both.

## O.C.G.A. § 16-11-102
### Pointing or aiming gun or pistol at another

A person is guilty of a misdemeanor when he intentionally and without legal justification points or aims a gun or pistol at another, whether the gun or pistol is loaded or unloaded.

## O.C.G.A. § 16-11-103
### Discharge of gun or pistol near public highway; penalty

(a) As used in this Code section, the term:

(1) "Firearm" means any handgun, rifle, or shotgun.

(2) "Public highway" means every public street, road, and highway in this state.

(3) "Sport shooting range" means an area designated and operated by a person or entity for the sport shooting of firearms, target practice, trapshooting, skeet shooting, or shooting sporting clays and not available for such use by the general public without payment of a fee, membership contribution, or dues or without the invitation of an authorized person, or any area so designated and operated by a unit of government, regardless of the terms of admission thereto.

(4) "Unit of government" means any of the departments, agencies, authorities, or political subdivisions of the state, cities, municipal corporations, townships, or villages and any of their respective departments, agencies, or authorities.

(b) Except as provided in subsection (c) of this Code section, it shall be unlawful for any person, without legal justification, to discharge a firearm on or within 50 yards of a public highway.

(c) This Code section shall not apply to a discharge of a firearm which occurs within 50 yards of a public highway if such discharge is shielded from the view of a traveler on the public highway and occurs at:

(1) An indoor or outdoor sport shooting range;

(2) Facilities used for firearm or hunting safety courses spon-

sored by a unit of government, nonprofit corporation, or commercial enterprise; or

(3) The business location of any person, firm, retail dealer, wholesale dealer, pawnbroker, or corporation licensed as a firearm dealer pursuant to Chapter 16 of Title 43.

(d) Any person who violates subsection (b) of the Code section shall be guilty of a misdemeanor.

## O.C.G.A. § 16-11-104
### Discharge of firearms on property of another

(a) It shall be unlawful for any person to fire or discharge a firearm on the property of another person, firm, or corporation without having first obtained permission from the owner or lessee of the property. This Code section shall not apply to:

(1) Persons who fire or discharge a firearm in defense of person or property; and

(2) Law enforcement officers.

(b) Any person who violates subsection (a) of this Code section is guilty of a misdemeanor.

## O.C.G.A. § 16-11-106
### Possession of firearm or knife during commission of or attempt to commit certain crimes

(a) For the purposes of this Code section, the term "firearm" shall include stun guns and tasers. A stun gun or taser is any device that is powered by electrical charging units such as batteries and emits an electrical charge in excess of 20,000 volts or is otherwise capable of incapacitating a person by an electrical charge.

(b) Any person who shall have on or within arm's reach of his or her person a firearm or a knife having a blade of three or more inches in length during the commission of, or the attempt to commit:

(1) Any crime against or involving the person of another;

(2) The unlawful entry into a building or vehicle;

(3) A theft from a building or theft of a vehicle;

(4) Any crime involving the possession, manufacture, delivery, distribution, dispensing, administering, selling, or possession with intent to distribute any controlled substance or marijuana as provided in Code Section 16-13-30, any counterfeit sub-

stance as defined in Code Section 16-13-21, or any noncontrolled substance as provided in Code Section 16-13-30.1; or (5) Any crime involving the trafficking of cocaine, marijuana, or illegal drugs as provided in Code Section 16-13-31,

and which crime is a felony, commits a felony and, upon conviction thereof, shall be punished by confinement for a period of five years, such sentence to run consecutively to any other sentence which the person has received.

(c) Upon the second or subsequent conviction of a person under this Code section, the person shall be punished by confinement for a period of ten years. Notwithstanding any other law to the contrary, the sentence of any person which is imposed for violating this Code section a second or subsequent time shall not be suspended by the court and probationary sentence imposed in lieu thereof.

(d) The punishment prescribed for the violation of subsections (b) and (c) of this Code section shall not be reducible to misdemeanor punishment as is provided by Code Section 17-10-5.

(e) Any crime committed in violation of subsections (b) and (c) of this Code section shall be considered a separate offense.

## O.C.G.A. § 16-11-113
### Offense of transferring firearm to individual other than actual buyer
Any person who attempts to solicit, persuade, encourage, or entice any dealer to transfer or otherwise convey a firearm other than to the actual buyer, as well as any other person who willfully and intentionally aids or abets such person, shall be guilty of a felony. This Code section shall not apply to a federal law enforcement officer or a peace officer, as defined in Code Section 16-1-3, in the performance of his or her official duties or other person under such officer's direct supervision.

## O.C.G.A. § 16-11-121
### Possession of Dangerous Weapons: Definitions
As used in this part, the term:
(1) "Dangerous weapon" means any weapon commonly known as a "rocket launcher," "bazooka," or "recoilless rifle"

which fires explosive or nonexplosive rockets designed to injure or kill personnel or destroy heavy armor, or similar weapon used for such purpose. The term shall also mean a weapon commonly known as a "mortar" which fires high explosive from a metallic cylinder and which is commonly used by the armed forces as an antipersonnel weapon or similar weapon used for such purpose. The term shall also mean a weapon commonly known as a "hand grenade" or other similar weapon which is designed to explode and injure personnel or similar weapon used for such purpose.

(2) "Machine gun" means any weapon which shoots or is designed to shoot, automatically, more than six shots, without manual reloading, by a single function of the trigger.

(3) "Person" means any individual, partnership, company, association, or corporation.

(4) "Sawed-off rifle" means a weapon designed or redesigned, made or remade, and intended to be fired from the shoulder; and designed or redesigned, made or remade, to use the energy of the explosive in a fixed metallic cartridge to fire only a single projectile through a rifle bore for each single pull of the trigger; and which has a barrel or barrels of less than 16 inches in length or has an overall length of less than 26 inches.

(5) "Sawed-off shotgun" means a shotgun or any weapon made from a shotgun whether by alteration, modification, or otherwise having one or more barrels less than 18 inches in length or if such weapon as modified has an overall length of less than 26 inches.

(6) "Shotgun" means a weapon designed or redesigned, made or remade, and intended to be fired from the shoulder; and designed or redesigned, and made or remade, to use the energy of the explosive in a fixed shotgun shell to fire through a smooth bore either a number of ball shot or a single projectile for each single pull of the trigger.

(7) "Silencer" means any device for silencing or diminishing the report of any portable weapon such as a rifle, carbine, pistol, revolver, machine gun, shotgun, fowling piece, or other device from which a shot, bullet, or projectile may be discharged by an explosive.

## O.C.G.A. § 16-11-122
**Possession of sawed-off shotgun or rifle, machine gun, silencer, or dangerous weapon prohibited.**

No person shall have in his possession any sawed-off shotgun, sawed-off rifle, machine gun, dangerous weapon, or silencer except as provided in Code Section 16-11-124.

## O.C.G.A. § 16-11-123
**Unlawful possession of firearms or weapons**

A person commits the offense of unlawful possession of firearms or weapons when he or she knowingly has in his or her possession any sawed-off shotgun, sawed-off rifle, machine gun, dangerous weapon, or silencer, and, upon conviction thereof, he or she shall be punished by imprisonment for a period of five years.

## O.C.G.A. § 16-11-124
**Exemptions from application of part**

This part shall not apply to:

(1) A peace officer of any duly authorized police agency of this state or of any political subdivision thereof, or a law enforcement officer of any department or agency of the United States who is regularly employed and paid by the United States, this state, or any such political subdivision, or an employee of the Department of Corrections of this state who is authorized in writing by the commissioner of corrections to transfer or possess such firearms while in the official performance of his duties;

(2) A member of the National Guard or of the armed forces of the United States to wit: the army, navy, marine corps, air force, or coast guard who, while serving therein, possesses such firearm in the line of duty;

(3) Any sawed-off shotgun, sawed-off rifle, machine gun, dangerous weapon, or silencer which has been modified or changed to the extent that it is inoperative. Examples of the requisite modification include weapons with their barrel or barrels filled with lead, hand grenades filled with sand, or other nonexplosive materials;

(4) Possession of a sawed-off shotgun, sawed-off rifle, machine gun, dangerous weapon, or silencer by a person who is authorized to possess the same because he has registered the sawed-off shotgun, sawed-off rifle, machine gun, dangerous

weapon, or silencer in accordance with the dictates of the National Firearms Act, 68A Stat. 725 (26 U.S.C. Sections 5841-5862); and

(5) A security officer employed by a federally licensed nuclear power facility or a licensee of such facility, including a contract security officer, who is trained and qualified under a security plan approved by the United States Nuclear Regulatory Commission or other federal agency authorized to regulate nuclear facility security; provided, however, that this exemption shall apply only while such security officer is acting in connection with his or her official duties on the premises of such nuclear power facility or on properties outside the facility property pursuant to a written agreement entered into with the local law enforcement agency having jurisdiction over the facility. The exemption under this paragraph does not include the possession of silencers.

## O.C.G.A. § 16-11-125.1
## Carrying and possession of firearms: Definitions
As used in this part, the term:

(1) "Handgun" means a firearm of any description, loaded or unloaded, from which any shot, bullet, or other missile can be discharged by an action of an explosive where the length of the barrel, not including any revolving, detachable, or magazine breech, does not exceed 12 inches; provided, however, that the term "handgun" shall not include a gun which discharges a single shot of .46 centimeters or less in diameter.

(2) "Knife" means a cutting instrument designed for the purpose of offense and defense consisting of a blade that is greater than five inches in length which is fastened to a handle.

(3) "License holder" means a person who holds a valid weapons carry license.

(4) "Long gun" means a firearm with a barrel length of at least 18 inches and overall length of at least 26 inches designed or made and intended to be fired from the shoulder and designed or made to use the energy of the explosive in a fixed:

(A) Shotgun shell to fire through a smooth bore either a number of ball shot or a single projectile for each single pull of the trigger or from which any shot, bullet, or other missile can be discharged; or

(B) Metallic cartridge to fire only a single projectile through a

rifle bore for each single pull of the trigger;provided, however, that the term "long gun" shall not include a gun which discharges a single shot of .46 centimeters or less in diameter.
(5) "Weapon" means a knife or handgun.
(6) "Weapons carry license" or "license" means a license issued pursuant to Code Section 16-11-129.

## O.C.G.A. § 16-11-126
### Having or carrying handguns, long guns, or other weapons; license requirement; exceptions for homes, motor vehicles, private property, and other locations and conditions

(a) Any person who is not prohibited by law from possessing a handgun or long gun may have or carry on his or her person a weapon or long gun on his or her property or inside his or her home, motor vehicle, or place of business without a valid weapons carry license.

(b) Any person who is not prohibited by law from possessing a handgun or long gun may have or carry on his or her person a long gun without a valid weapons carry license, provided that if the long gun is loaded, it shall only be carried in an open and fully exposed manner.

(c) Any person who is not prohibited by law from possessing a handgun or long gun may have or carry any handgun provided that it is enclosed in a case and unloaded.

(d) Any person who is not prohibited by law from possessing a handgun or long gun who is eligible for a weapons carry license may transport a handgun or long gun in any private passenger motor vehicle; provided, however, that private property owners or persons in legal control of private property through a lease, rental agreement, licensing agreement, contract, or any other agreement to control access to such private property shall have the right to exclude or eject a person who is in possession of a weapon or long gun on their private property in accordance with paragraph (3) of subsection (b) of Code Section 16-7-21, except as provided in Code Section 16-11-135.

(e) Any person licensed to carry a handgun or weapon in any other state whose laws recognize and give effect to a license issued pursuant to this part shall be authorized to carry a weapon in this state, but only while the licensee is not a resident of this state; provided, however, that such licensee shall carry the weapon in compliance with the laws of this state.

(f) Any person with a valid hunting or fishing license on his or her person, or any person not required by law to have a hunting or fishing license, who is engaged in legal hunting, fishing, or sport shooting when the person has the permission of the owner of the land on which the activities are being conducted may have or carry on his or her person a handgun or long gun without a valid weapons carry license while hunting, fishing, or engaging in sport shooting.

(g) Notwithstanding Code Sections 12-3-10, 27-3-1.1, 27-3-6, and 16-12-122 through 16-12-127, any person with a valid weapons carry license may carry a weapon in all parks, historic sites, or recreational areas, as such term is defined in Code Section 12-3-10, including all publicly owned buildings located in such parks, historic sites, and recreational areas, in wildlife management areas, and on public transportation; provided, however, that a person shall not carry a handgun into a place where it is prohibited by federal law.

(h)
(1) No person shall carry a weapon without a valid weapons carry license unless he or she meets one of the exceptions to having such license as provided in subsections (a) through (g) of this Code section.
(2) A person commits the offense of carrying a weapon without a license when he or she violates the provisions of paragraph (1) of this subsection.

(i) Upon conviction of the offense of carrying a weapon without a valid weapons carry license, a person shall be punished as follows:
(1) For the first offense, he or she shall be guilty of a misdemeanor; and
(2) For the second offense within five years, as measured from the dates of previous arrests for which convictions were obtained to the date of the current arrest for which a conviction is obtained, and for any subsequent offense, he or she shall be guilty of a felony and, upon conviction thereof, shall be imprisoned for not less than two years and not more than five years.

(j) Nothing in this Code section shall in any way operate or be construed to affect, repeal, or limit the exemptions provided for under Code Section 16-11-130.

## O.C.G.A. § 16-11-127
### Carrying weapons in unauthorized locations

(a) As used in this Code section, the term:

    (1) Courthouse" means a building occupied by judicial courts and containing rooms in which judicial proceedings are held.

    (2) "Government building" means:

        (A) The building in which a government entity is housed;

        (B) The building where a government entity meets in its official capacity; provided, however, that if such building is not a publicly owned building, such building shall be considered a government building for the purposes of this Code section only during the time such government entity is meeting at such building; or

        (C) The portion of any building that is not a publicly owned building that is occupied by a government entity.

    (3) "Government entity" means an office, agency, authority, department, commission, board, body, division, instrumentality, or institution of the state or any county, municipal corporation, consolidated government, or local board of education within this state.

    (4) "Parking facility" means real property owned or leased by a government entity, courthouse, jail, prison, or place of worship that has been designated by such government entity, courthouse, jail, prison, or place of worship for the parking of motor vehicles at a government building or at such courthouse, jail, prison, or place of worship.

(b) Except as provided in Code Section 16-11-127.1 and subsection (d) or (e) of this Code section, a person shall be guilty of carrying a weapon or long gun in an unauthorized location and punished as for a misdemeanor when he or she carries a weapon or long gun while:

    (1) In a government building as a nonlicense holder;

    (2) In a courthouse;

    (3) In a jail or prison;

    (4) In a place of worship, unless the governing body or author-

ity of the place of worship permits the carrying of weapons or
long guns by license holders;

(5) In a state mental health facility as defined in Code Section 37-1-1 which admits individuals on an involuntary basis
for treatment of mental illness, developmental disability, or
addictive disease; provided, however, that carrying a weapon
or long gun in such location in a manner in compliance with
paragraph (3) of subsection (d) of this Code section shall not
constitute a violation of this subsection;

(6) On the premises of a nuclear power facility, except as
provided in Code Section 16-11-127.2, and the punishment
provisions of Code Section 16-11-127.2 shall supersede the
punishment provisions of this Code section; or

(7) Within 150 feet of any polling place when elections are being conducted and such polling place is being used as a polling
place as provided for in paragraph (27) of Code Section 21-2-2,
except as provided in subsection (i) of Code Section.

(c) A license holder or person recognized under subsection (e) of
Code Section 16-11-126 shall be authorized to carry a weapon as
provided in Code Section 16-11-135 and in every location in this
state not listed in subsection (b) or prohibited by subsection (e) of
this Code section; provided, however, that private property owners
or persons in legal control of private property through a lease, rental agreement, licensing agreement, contract, or any other agreement to control access to such private property shall have the right
to exclude or eject a person who is in possession of a weapon or
long gun on their private property in accordance with paragraph
(3) of subsection (b) of Code Section 16-7-21, except as provided in
Code Section 16-11-135. A violation of subsection (b) of this Code
section shall not create or give rise to a civil action for damages.

(d) Subsection (b) of this Code section shall not apply:

(1) To the use of weapons or long guns as exhibits in a legal
proceeding, provided such weapons or long guns are secured
and handled as directed by the personnel providing courtroom
security or the judge hearing the case;

(2) To a license holder who approaches security or management personnel upon arrival at a location described in subsection (b) of this Code section and notifies such security or management personnel of the presence of the weapon or long gun

and explicitly follows the security or management personnel's direction for removing, securing, storing, or temporarily surrendering such weapon or long gun; and
(3) To a weapon or long gun possessed by a license holder which is under the possessor's control in a motor vehicle or is in a locked compartment of a motor vehicle or one which is in a locked container in or a locked firearms rack which is on a motor vehicle and such vehicle is parked in a parking facility.

(e)

(1) A license holder shall be authorized to carry a weapon in a government building when the government building is open for business and where ingress into such building is not restricted or screened by security personnel. A license holder who enters or attempts to enter a government building carrying a weapon where ingress is restricted or screened by security personnel shall be guilty of a misdemeanor if at least one member of such security personnel is certified as a peace officer pursuant to Chapter 8 of Title 35; provided, however, that a license holder who immediately exits such building or immediately leaves such location upon notification of his or her failure to clear security due to the carrying of a weapon shall not be guilty of violating this subsection or paragraph (1) of subsection (b) of this Code section. A person who is not a license holder and who attempts to enter a government building carrying a weapon shall be guilty of a misdemeanor.
(2) Any license holder who violates subsection (b) of this Code section in a place of worship shall not be arrested but shall be fined not more than $100.00. Any person who is not a license holder who violates subsection (b) of this Code section in a place of worship shall be punished as for a misdemeanor.

(f) Nothing in this Code section shall in any way operate or be construed to affect, repeal, or limit the exemptions provided for under Code Section 16-11-130.

## O.C.G.A. § 16-11-127.1
**Carrying weapons within school safety zones, at school functions, or on a bus or other transportation furnished by a school**
(a) As used in this Code section, the term:

(1) "Bus or other transportation furnished by a school" means a bus or other transportation furnished by a public or private elementary or secondary school.

(2) "School function" means a school function or related activity that occurs outside of a school safety zone and is for a public or private elementary or secondary school.

(10) Those employees of the State Board of Pardons and Paroles when specifically designated and authorized in writing by the members of the State Board of Pardons and Paroles to carry a weapon;

(11) The Attorney General and those members of his or her staff whom he or she specifically authorizes in writing to carry a weapon;

(12) Community supervision officers employed by and under the authority of the Department of Community Supervision when specifically designated and authorized in writing by the commissioner of community supervision;

(13) Public safety directors of municipal corporations;

(14) State and federal trial and appellate judges;

(15) United States attorneys and assistant United States attorneys;

(16) Clerks of the superior courts;

(17) Teachers and other personnel who are otherwise authorized to possess or carry weapons, provided that any such weapon is in a locked compartment of a motor vehicle or one which is in a locked container in or a locked firearms rack which is on a motor vehicle;

(18) Constables of any county of this state; or

(19) Any person who is 18 years of age or older or currently enrolled in classes on the campus in question and carrying, possessing, or having under such person's control an electroshock weapon while in or on any building or real property owned by or leased to such public technical school, vocational school, college or university or other public institution of post-secondary education; provided, however, that, if such person makes use of such electroshock weapon, such use shall be in defense of self or others. The exemption under this paragraph shall apply only to such person in regard to such electroshock weapon. As used in this paragraph, the term "electroshock weapon" means any commercially available device that is powered by electrical charging units and designed exclusively

to be capable of incapacitating a person by electrical charge, including, but not limited to, a stun gun or taser as defined in subsection (a) of Code Section 16-11-106.

(d)

(1) This Code section shall not prohibit any person who resides or works in a business or is in the ordinary course transacting lawful business or any person who is a visitor of such resident located within a school safety zone from carrying, possessing, or having under such person's control a weapon within a school safety zone; provided, however, that it shall be unlawful for any such person to carry, possess, or have under such person's control while at a school building or school function or on school property or a bus or other transportation furnished by a school any weapon or explosive compound, other than fireworks the possession of which is regulated by Chapter 10 of Title 25.

(2) Any person who violates this subsection shall be subject to the penalties specified in subsection (b) of this Code section.

(e) It shall be no defense to a prosecution for a violation of this Code section that:

(1) School was or was not in session at the time of the offense;

(2) The real property was being used for other purposes besides school purposes at the time of the offense; or

(3) The offense took place on a bus or other transportation furnished by a school.

(f) In a prosecution under this Code section, a map produced or reproduced by any municipal or county agency or department for the purpose of depicting the location and boundaries of the area of the real property of a school board or a private or public elementary or secondary school that is used for school purposes or the area of any public or private technical school, vocational school, college, university, or other institution of postsecondary education, or a true copy of the map, shall, if certified as a true copy by the custodian of the record, be admissible and shall constitute prima-facie evidence of the location and boundaries of the area, if the governing body of the municipality or county has approved the map as an official record of the location and boundaries of the area. A map approved under this Code section may be revised from time to time by the governing body of the municipality or county. The original of every map approved or revised under this subsection or a true copy of such original map shall be filed with the municipality or county and shall be maintained as an official record of the municipality or county. This subsection shall not preclude the prosecution from introducing or relying upon any other evidence or testimony to establish any element of this offense. This subsection shall not preclude the use or admissibility of a map or diagram other than the one which has been approved by the municipality or county.

(g) A county school board may adopt regulations requiring the posting of signs designating the areas of school boards and private or public elementary and secondary schools as "Weapon-free and Violence-free School Safety Zones."

(h) Nothing in this Code section shall in any way operate or be construed to affect, repeal, or limit the exemptions provided for under Code Section 16-11-130.

## O.C.G.A. § 16-11-129
### Weapons carry license; temporary renewal permit; mandamus; verification of license

(a) Application for weapons carry license or renewal license; term. The judge of the probate court of each county shall, on application under oath, on payment of a fee of $30.00, and on investigation of applicant pursuant to subsections (b) and (d) of this Code section, issue a weapons carry license or renewal license valid for a period of five years to any person whose domicile is in that county or who is on active duty with the United States armed forces and who is not a domiciliary of this state but who either resides in that county or on a military reservation located in whole or in part in that county at the time of such application. Such license or renewal license shall authorize that person to carry any weapon in any county of this state notwithstanding any change in that person's county of residence or state of domicile. Applicants shall submit the application for a weapons carry license or renewal license to the judge of the probate court on forms prescribed and furnished free of charge to persons wishing to apply for the license or renewal license. An application shall be considered to be for a renewal license if the applicant has a weapons carry license or renewal license with 90 or fewer days remaining before the expiration of such weapons carry license or renewal license or 30 or fewer days since the expiration of such weapons carry license or renewal license regardless of the county of issuance of the applicant's expired or expiring weapons carry license or renewal license. An applicant who is not a United States citizen shall provide sufficient personal identifying data, including without limitation his or her place of birth and United States issued alien or admission number, as the Georgia Bureau of Investigation may prescribe by rule or regulation. An applicant who is in nonimmigrant status shall provide proof of his or her qualifications for an exception to the federal firearm prohibition pursuant to 18 U.S.C. Section 922(y). Forms shall be designed to elicit information from the applicant pertinent to his or her eligibility under this Code section, including citizenship, but shall not require data which is nonpertinent or irrelevant, such as serial numbers or other identification capable of being used as a de facto registration of firearms owned by the applicant. The Department of Public Safety shall furnish application forms and license forms required by this Code section. The forms shall be furnished to each judge of each probate court within this state at no cost.

(b) Licensing exceptions.
    (1) As used in this subsection, the term:
        (A) "Armed forces" means active duty or a reserve component of the United States Army, United States Navy, United States Marine Corps, United States Coast Guard, United States Air Force, United States National Guard, Georgia Army National Guard, or Georgia Air National Guard.
        (B) "Controlled substance" means any drug, substance, or immediate precursor included in the definition of controlled substances in paragraph (4) of Code Section 16-13-21.
        (C) "Convicted" means an adjudication of guilt. Such term shall not include an order of discharge and exoneration pursuant to Article 3 of Chapter 8 of Title 42.
        (D) "Dangerous drug" means any drug defined as such in Code Section 16-13-71.
    (2) No weapons carry license shall be issued to:
        (A) Any person younger than 21 years of age unless he or she:
            (i) Is at least 18 years of age;
            (ii) Provides proof that he or she has completed basic

training in the armed forces of the United States; and
(iii) Provides proof that he or she is actively serving in the armed forces of the United States or has been honorably discharged from such service;

(B) Any person who has been convicted of a felony by a court of this state or any other state; by a court of the United States, including its territories, possessions, and dominions; or by a court of any foreign nation and has not been pardoned for such felony by the President of the United States, the State Board of Pardons and Paroles, or the person or agency empowered to grant pardons under the constitution or laws of such state or nation;

(C) Any person against whom proceedings are pending for any felony;

(D) Any person who is a fugitive from justice;

(E) Any person who is prohibited from possessing or shipping a firearm in interstate commerce pursuant to subsections (g) and (n) of 18 U.S.C. Section 922;

(F) Any person who has been convicted of an offense arising out of the unlawful manufacture or distribution of a controlled substance or other dangerous drug;

(G) Any person who has had his or her weapons carry license revoked pursuant to subsection (e) of this Code section within three years of the date of his or her application;

(H) Any person who has been convicted of any of the following:
(i) Carrying a weapon without a weapons carry license in violation of Code Section 16-11-126; or
(ii) Carrying a weapon or long gun in an unauthorized location in violation of Code Section 16-11-127and has not been free of all restraint or supervision in connection therewith and free of any other conviction for at least five years immediately preceding the date of the application;

(I) Any person who has been convicted of any misdemeanor involving the use or possession of a controlled substance and has not been free of all restraint or supervision in connection therewith or free of:
(i) A second conviction of any misdemeanor involving the use or possession of a controlled substance; or
(ii) Any conviction under subparagraphs (E) through (G)

of this paragraph for at least five years immediately preceding the date of the application;

(J) Except as provided for in subsection (b.1) of this Code section, any person who has been hospitalized as an inpatient in any mental hospital or alcohol or drug treatment center within the five years immediately preceding the application. The judge of the probate court may require any applicant to sign a waiver authorizing any mental hospital or treatment center to inform the judge whether or not the applicant has been an inpatient in any such facility in the last five years and authorizing the superintendent of such facility to make to the judge a recommendation regarding whether the applicant is a threat to the safety of others and whether a license to carry a weapon should be issued. When such a waiver is required by the judge, the applicant shall pay a fee of $3.00 for reimbursement of the cost of making such a report by the mental health hospital, alcohol or drug treatment center, or the Department of Behavioral Health and Developmental Disabilities, which the judge shall remit to the hospital, center, or department. The judge shall keep any such hospitalization or treatment information confidential. It shall be at the discretion of the judge, considering the circumstances surrounding the hospitalization and the recommendation of the superintendent of the hospital or treatment center where the individual was a patient, to issue the weapons carry license or renewal license;

(K) Except as provided for in subsection (b.1) of this Code section, any person who has been adjudicated mentally incompetent to stand trial; or

(L) Except as provided for in subsection (b.1) of this Code section, any person who has been adjudicated not guilty by reason of insanity at the time of the crime pursuant to Part 2 of Article 6 of Chapter 7 of Title 17.

(b.1) Petitions for relief from certain licensing exceptions.

(1) Persons provided for under subparagraphs (b)(2)(J), (b)(2)(K), and (b)(2)(L) of this Code section may petition the court in which such adjudication, hospitalization, or treatment proceedings, if any, under Chapter 3 or 7 of Title 37 occurred for relief. A copy of such petition for relief shall be served as notice upon the opposing civil party or the prosecuting attor-

ney for the state, as the case may be, or their successors, who appeared in the underlying case. Within 30 days of the receipt of such petition, such court shall hold a hearing on such petition for relief. Such prosecuting attorney for the state may represent the interests of the state at such hearing.

(2) At the hearing provided for under paragraph (1) of this subsection, the court shall receive and consider evidence in a closed proceeding concerning:

(A) The circumstances which caused the person to be subject to subparagraph (b)(2)(J), (b)(2)(K), or (b)(2)(L) of this Code section;

(B) The person's mental health and criminal history records, if any. The judge of such court may require any such person to sign a waiver authorizing the superintendent of any mental hospital or treatment center to make to the judge a recommendation regarding whether such person is a threat to the safety of others. When such a waiver is required by the judge, the applicant shall pay a fee of $3.00 for reimbursement of the cost of making such a report by the mental health hospital, alcohol or drug treatment center, or the Department of Behavioral Health and Developmental Disabilities, which the judge shall remit to the hospital, center, or department;

(C) The person's reputation which shall be established through character witness statements, testimony, or other character evidence; and

(D) Changes in the person's condition or circumstances since such adjudication, hospitalization, or treatment proceedings under Chapter 3 or 7 of Title 37. The judge shall issue an order of his or her decision no later than 30 days after the hearing.

(3) The court shall grant the petition for relief if such court finds by a preponderance of the evidence that the person will not likely act in a manner dangerous to public safety in carrying a weapon and that granting the relief will not be contrary to the public interest. A record shall be kept of the hearing; provided, however, that such records shall remain confidential and be disclosed only to a court or to the parties in the event of an appeal. Any appeal of the court's ruling on the petition for relief shall be de novo review.

(4) If the court grants such person's petition for relief, the

applicable subparagraph (b)(2)(J), (b)(2)(K), or (b)(2)(L) of this Code section shall not apply to such person in his or her application for a weapons carry license or renewal; provided, however, that such person shall comply with all other requirements for the issuance of a weapons carry license or renewal license. The clerk of such court shall report such order to the Georgia Crime Information Center immediately, but in no case later than ten business days after the date of such order.

(5) A person may petition for relief under this subsection not more than once every two years. In the case of a person who has been hospitalized as an inpatient, such person shall not petition for relief prior to being discharged from such treatment.

(c) Fingerprinting. Following completion of the application for a weapons carry license, the judge of the probate court shall require the applicant to proceed to an appropriate law enforcement agency in the county or to any vendor approved by the Georgia Bureau of Investigation for fingerprint submission services with the completed application so that such agency or vendor can capture the fingerprints of the applicant. The law enforcement agency shall be entitled to a fee of $5.00 from the applicant for its services in connection with fingerprinting and processing of an application. Fingerprinting shall not be required for applicants seeking temporary renewal licenses or renewal licenses.

(d) Investigation of applicant; issuance of weapons carry license; renewal.

(1)

(A) For weapons carry license applications, the judge of the probate court shall within five business days following the receipt of the application or request direct the law enforcement agency to request a fingerprint based criminal history records check from the Georgia Crime Information Center and Federal Bureau of Investigation for purposes of determining the suitability of the applicant and return an appropriate report to the judge of the probate court. Fingerprints shall be in such form and of such quality as prescribed by the Georgia Crime Information Center and under standards adopted by the Federal Bureau of Investigation. The Georgia Bureau of Investigation may charge such fee as is necessary to cover the cost of the records search.

(B) For requests for license renewals, the presentation of a weapons carry license issued by any probate judge in this state shall be evidence to the judge of the probate court to whom a request for license renewal is made that the finger-prints of the weapons carry license holder are on file with the judge of the probate court who issued the weapons carry license, and the judge of the probate court to whom a request for license renewal is made shall, within five business days following the receipt of the request, direct the law enforcement agency to request a nonfingerprint based criminal history records check from the Georgia Crime Information Center and Federal Bureau of Investigation for purposes of determining the suitability of the applicant and return an appropriate report to the judge of the probate court to whom a request for license renewal is made.

(2) For both weapons carry license applications and requests for license renewals, the judge of the probate court shall within five business days following the receipt of the application or request also direct the law enforcement agency, in the same manner as provided for in subparagraph (B) of paragraph (1) of this subsection, to conduct a background check using the Federal Bureau of Investigation's National Instant Criminal Background Check System and return an appropriate report to the probate judge.

(3) When a person who is not a United States citizen applies for a weapons carry license or renewal of a license under this Code section, the judge of the probate court shall direct the law enforcement agency to conduct a search of the records maintained by United States Immigration and Customs En-forcement and return an appropriate report to the probate judge. As a condition to the issuance of a license or the renew-al of a license, an applicant who is in nonimmigrant status shall provide proof of his or her qualifications for an exception to the federal firearm prohibition pursuant to 18 U.S.C. Sec-tion 922(y).

(4) The law enforcement agency shall report to the judge of the probate court within 30 days, by telephone and in writing, of any findings relating to the applicant which may bear on his or her eligibility for a weapons carry license or renewal license under the terms of this Code section. When no derogatory

information is found on the applicant bearing on his or her eligibility to obtain a license or renewal license, a report shall not be required. The law enforcement agency shall return the application directly to the judge of the probate court within such time period. Not later than ten days after the judge of the probate court receives the report from the law enforcement agency concerning the suitability of the applicant for a license, the judge of the probate court shall issue such applicant a license or renewal license to carry any weapon unless facts establishing ineligibility have been reported or unless the judge determines such applicant has not met all the qualifications, is not of good moral character, or has failed to comply with any of the requirements contained in this Code section. The judge of the probate court shall date stamp the report from the law enforcement agency to show the date on which the report was received by the judge of the probate court.

(e) Revocation, loss, or damage to license.

(1) If, at any time during the period for which the weapons carry license was issued, the judge of the probate court of the county in which the license was issued shall learn or have brought to his or her attention in any manner any reasonable ground to believe the licensee is not eligible to retain the license, the judge may, after notice and hearing, revoke the license of the person upon a finding that such person is not eligible for a weapons carry license pursuant to subsection (b) of this Code section or an adjudication of falsification of application, mental incompetency, or chronic alcohol or narcotic usage. The judge of the probate court shall report such revocation to the Georgia Crime Information Center immediately but in no case later than ten days after such revocation. It shall be unlawful for any person to possess a license which has been revoked pursuant to this paragraph, and any person found in possession of any such revoked license, except in the performance of his or her official duties, shall be guilty of a misdemeanor.

(2) If a person is convicted of any crime or involved in any matter which would make the maintenance of a weapons carry license by such person unlawful pursuant to subsection (b) of this Code section, the judge of the superior court or state court hearing such case or presiding over such matter

shall inquire whether such person is the holder of a weapons carry license. If such person is the holder of a weapons carry license, then the judge of the superior court or state court shall inquire of such person the county of the probate court which issued such weapons carry license, or if such person has ever had his or her weapons carry license renewed, then of the county of the probate court which most recently issued such person a renewal license. The judge of the superior court or state court shall notify the judge of the probate court of such county of the matter which makes the maintenance of a weapons carry license by such person to be unlawful pursuant to subsection (b) of this Code section. The Council of Superior Court Judges of Georgia and The Council of State Court Judges of Georgia shall provide by rule for the procedures which judges of the superior court and the judges of the state courts, respectively, are to follow for the purposes of this paragraph. (3) Loss of any license issued in accordance with this Code section or damage to the license in any manner which shall render it illegible shall be reported to the judge of the probate court of the county in which it was issued within 48 hours of the time the loss or damage becomes known to the license holder. The judge of the probate court shall thereupon issue a replacement for and shall take custody of and destroy a damaged license; and in any case in which a license has been lost, he or she shall issue a cancellation order. The judge shall charge the fee specified in subsection (k) of Code Section 15-9-60 for such services.

(f)

(1) Weapons carry license specifications. Weapons carry licenses issued prior to January 1, 2012, shall be in the format specified by the former provisions of this paragraph as they existed on June 30, 2013.
(2) On and after January 1, 2012, newly issued or renewal weapons carry licenses shall incorporate overt and covert security features which shall be blended with the personal data printed on the license to form a significant barrier to imitation, replication, and duplication. There shall be a minimum of three different ultraviolet colors used to enhance the security of the license incorporating variable data, color shifting characteristics, and front edge only perimeter visibility. The

weapons carry license shall have a color photograph viewable under ambient light on both the front and back of the license. The license shall incorporate custom optical variable devices featuring the great seal of the State of Georgia as well as matching demetalized optical variable devices viewable under ambient light from the front and back of the license incorporating microtext and unique alphanumeric serialization specific to the license holder. The license shall be of similar material, size, and thickness of a credit card and have a holographic laminate to secure and protect the license for the duration of the license period.

(3) Using the physical characteristics of the license set forth in paragraph (2) of this subsection, The Council of Probate Court Judges of Georgia shall create specifications for the probate courts so that all weapons carry licenses in this state shall be uniform and so that probate courts can petition the Department of Administrative Services to purchase the equipment and supplies necessary for producing such licenses. The department shall follow the competitive bidding procedure set forth in Code Section 50-5-102.

(g) Alteration or counterfeiting of license; penalty. A person who deliberately alters or counterfeits a weapons carry license or who possesses an altered or counterfeit weapons carry license with the intent to misrepresent any information contained in such license shall be guilty of a felony and, upon conviction thereof, shall be punished by imprisonment for a period of not less than one nor more than five years.

(h) Licenses for former law enforcement officers. Except as otherwise provided in Code Section 16-11-130, any person who has served as a law enforcement officer for at least ten of the 12 years immediately preceding the retirement of such person as a law enforcement officer shall be entitled to be issued a weapons carry license as provided for in this Code section without the payment of any of the fees provided for in this Code section. Such person shall comply with all the other provisions of this Code section relative to the issuance of such licenses. As used in this subsection, the term "law enforcement officer" means any peace officer who is employed by the United States government or by the State of Georgia or any political subdivision thereof and who is required by the terms of his or her employment, whether by election or appointment, to give his or her full time to the preservation of public order or the protection of life and property or the prevention of crime. Such term shall include conservation rangers.

(i) Temporary renewal licenses.

(1) Any person who holds a weapons carry license under this Code section may, at the time he or she applies for a renewal of the license, also apply for a temporary renewal license if less than 90 days remain before expiration of the license he or she then holds or if the previous license has expired within the last 30 days.

(2) Unless the judge of the probate court knows or is made aware of any fact which would make the applicant ineligible for a five-year renewal license, the judge shall at the time of application issue a temporary renewal license to the applicant.

(3) Such a temporary renewal license shall be in the form of a paper receipt indicating the date on which the court received the renewal application and shall show the name, address, sex, age, and race of the applicant and that the temporary renewal license expires 90 days from the date of issue.

(4) During its period of validity the temporary renewal license, if carried on or about the holder's person together with the holder's previous license, shall be valid in the same manner and for the same purposes as a five-year license.

(5) A $1.00 fee shall be charged by the probate court for issuance of a temporary renewal license.

(6) A temporary renewal license may be revoked in the same manner as a five-year license.

(j) Applicant may seek relief. When an eligible applicant fails to receive a license, temporary renewal license, or renewal license within the time period required by this Code section and the application or request has been properly filed, the applicant may bring an action in mandamus or other legal proceeding in order to obtain a license, temporary renewal license, or renewal license. When an applicant is otherwise denied a license, temporary renewal license, or renewal license and contends that he or she is qualified to be issued a license, temporary renewal license, or renewal license, the applicant may bring an action in mandamus or other legal proceeding in order to obtain such license. Additionally, the applicant may request a hearing before the judge of the probate court relative to the applicant's fitness to be issued such license. Upon the issuance of a denial, the judge of the probate court shall inform the applicant of his or her rights pursuant to this subsection. If such applicant is the prevailing party, he or she shall be entitled to recover his or her costs in such action, including reasonable attorney's fees.

(k) Data base prohibition. A person or entity shall not create or maintain a multijurisdictional data base of information regarding persons issued weapons carry licenses.

(l) Verification of license. The judge of a probate court or his or her designee shall be authorized to verify the legitimacy and validity of a weapons carry license of a license holder pursuant to a subpoena or court order, for public safety purposes to law enforcement agencies pursuant to paragraph (40) of subsection (a) of Code Section 50-18-72, and for licensing to a judge of a probate court or his or her designee pursuant to paragraph (40) of subsection (a) of Code Section 50-18-72; provided, however, that the judge of a probate court or his or her designee shall not be authorized to provide any further information regarding license holders.

### O.C.G.A. § 16-11-130
### Exemptions from Code Sections 16-11-126 through 16-11-127.2
(a) Code Sections 16-11-126 through 16-11-127.2 shall not apply to or affect any of the following persons if such persons are employed in the offices listed below or when authorized by federal or state law, regulations, or order:

(1) Peace officers, as such term is defined in paragraph (11) of Code Section 16-1-3, and retired peace officers so long as they remain certified whether employed by the state or a political subdivision of the state or another state or a political subdivision of another state but only if such other state provides a similar privilege for the peace officers of this state;

(2) Wardens, superintendents, and keepers of correctional institutions, jails, or other institutions for the detention of persons accused or convicted of an offense;

(3) Persons in the military service of the state or of the United States;

(4) Persons employed in fulfilling defense contracts with the

government of the United States or agencies thereof when possession of the weapon or long gun is necessary for manufacture, transport, installation, and testing under the requirements of such contract;

(5) District attorneys, investigators employed by and assigned to a district attorney's office, assistant district attorneys, attorneys or investigators employed by the Prosecuting Attorneys' Council of the State of Georgia, and any retired district attorney, assistant district attorney, district attorney's investigator, or attorney or investigator retired from the Prosecuting Attorneys' Council of the State of Georgia, if such employee is retired in good standing and is receiving benefits under Title 47 or is retired in good standing and receiving benefits from a county or municipal retirement system;

(6) State court solicitors-general; investigators employed by and assigned to a state court solicitor-general's office; assistant state court solicitors-general; the corresponding personnel of any city court expressly continued in existence as a city court pursuant to Article VI, Section X, Paragraph I, subparagraph (5) of the Constitution; and the corresponding personnel of any civil court expressly continued as a civil court pursuant to said provision of the Constitution;

(7) Those employees of the State Board of Pardons and Paroles when specifically designated and authorized in writing by the members of the State Board of Pardons and Paroles to carry a weapon or long gun;

(8) The Attorney General and those members of his or her staff whom he or she specifically authorizes in writing to carry a weapon or long gun;

(9) Community supervision officers employed by and under the authority of the Department of Community Supervision when specifically designated and authorized in writing by the commissioner of community supervision;

(10) Public safety directors of municipal corporations;

(11) Explosive ordnance disposal technicians, as such term is defined by Code Section 16-7-80, and persons certified as provided in Code Section 35-8-13 to handle animals trained to detect explosives, while in the performance of their duties;

(12) Federal judges, Justices of the Supreme Court, Judges of the Court of Appeals, judges of superior, state, probate, juvenile, and magistrate courts, full-time judges of municipal and

city courts, permanent part-time judges of municipal and city courts, and administrative law judges;

(12.1) Former federal judges, Justices of the Supreme Court, Judges of the Court of Appeals, judges of superior, state, probate, juvenile, and magistrate courts, full-time judges of municipal and city courts, permanent part-time judges of municipal courts, and administrative law judges who are retired from their respective offices, provided that such judge or Justice would otherwise be qualified to be issued a weapons carry license;

(12.2) Former federal judges, Justices of the Supreme Court, Judges of the Court of Appeals, judges of superior, state, probate, juvenile, and magistrate courts, full-time judges of municipal and city courts, permanent part-time judges of municipal courts, and administrative law judges who are no longer serving in their respective office, provided that he or she served as such judge or Justice for more than 24 months; and provided, further, that such judge or Justice would otherwise be qualified to be issued a weapons carry license;

(13) United States Attorneys and Assistant United States Attorneys;

(14) County medical examiners and coroners and their sworn officers employed by county government;

(15) Clerks of the superior courts; and

(16) Constables employed by a magistrate court of this state.

(b) Code Sections 16-11-126 through 16-11-127.2 shall not apply to or affect persons who at the time of their retirement from service with the Department of Community Supervision were community supervision officers, when specifically designated and authorized in writing by the commissioner of community supervision.

(c) Code Sections 16-11-126 through 16-11-127.2 shall not apply to or affect any:

(1) Sheriff, retired sheriff, deputy sheriff, or retired deputy sheriff if such retired sheriff or deputy sheriff is eligible to receive or is receiving benefits under the Peace Officers' Annuity and Benefit Fund provided under Chapter 17 of Title 47, the Sheriffs' Retirement Fund of Georgia provided under Chapter 16 of Title 47, or any other public retirement system established under the laws of this state for service as a law enforcement officer;

(2) Member of the Georgia State Patrol or agent of the Georgia Bureau of Investigation or retired member of the Georgia State Patrol or agent of the Georgia Bureau of Investigation if such retired member or agent is receiving benefits under the Employees' Retirement System;

(3) Full-time law enforcement chief executive engaging in the management of a county, municipal, state, state authority, or federal law enforcement agency in the State of Georgia, including any college or university law enforcement chief executive that is registered or certified by the Georgia Peace Officer Standards and Training Council; or retired law enforcement chief executive that formerly managed a county, municipal, state, state authority, or federal law enforcement agency in the State of Georgia, including any college or university law enforcement chief executive that was registered or certified at the time of his or her retirement by the Georgia Peace Officer Standards and Training Council, if such retired law enforcement chief executive is receiving benefits under the Peace Officers' Annuity and Benefit Fund provided under Chapter 17 of Title 47 or is retired in good standing and receiving benefits from a county, municipal, State of Georgia, state authority, or federal retirement system; or

(4) Police officer of any county, municipal, state, state authority, or federal law enforcement agency in the State of Georgia, including any college or university police officer that is registered or certified by the Georgia Peace Officer Standards and Training Council, or retired police officer of any county, municipal, state, state authority, or federal law enforcement agency in the State of Georgia, including any college or university police officer that was registered or certified at the time of his or her retirement by the Georgia Peace Officer Standards and Training Council, if such retired employee is receiving benefits under the Peace Officers' Annuity and Benefit Fund provided under Chapter 17 of Title 47 or is retired in good standing and receiving benefits from a county, municipal, State of Georgia, state authority, or federal retirement system.

In addition, any such sheriff, retired sheriff, deputy sheriff, retired deputy sheriff, active or retired law enforcement chief executive, or other law enforcement officer referred to in this subsection shall be authorized to carry a handgun on or off duty anywhere within the state and the provisions of Code

Sections 16-11-126 through 16-11-127.2 shall not apply to the carrying of such firearms.

(d) A prosecution based upon a violation of Code Section 16-11-126 or 16-11-127 need not negative any exemptions.

## O.C.G.A. § 16-11-130.2
### Carrying a weapon or long gun at a commercial service airport

(a) No person shall enter the restricted access area of a commercial service airport, in or beyond the airport security screening checkpoint, knowingly possessing or knowingly having under his or her control a weapon or long gun. Such area shall not include an airport drive, general parking area, walkway, or shops and areas of the terminal that are outside the screening checkpoint and that are normally open to unscreened passengers or visitors to the airport. Any restricted access area shall be clearly indicated by prominent signs indicating that weapons are prohibited in such area.

(b) A person who is not a license holder and who violates this Code section shall be guilty of a misdemeanor. A license holder who violates this Code section shall be guilty of a misdemeanor; provided, however, that a license holder who is notified at the screening checkpoint for the restricted access area that he or she is in possession of a weapon or long gun and who immediately leaves the restricted access area following such notification and completion of federally required transportation security screening procedures shall not be guilty of violating this Code section.

(c) Any person who violates this Code section with the intent to commit a separate felony offense shall be guilty of a felony and, upon conviction thereof, shall be punished by a fine of not less than $1,000.00 nor more than $15,000.00, imprisonment for not less than one nor more than ten years, or both.

(d) Any ordinance, resolution, regulation, or policy of any county, municipality, or other political subdivision of this state which is in conflict with this Code section shall be null, void, and of no force and effect, and this Code section shall preempt any such ordinance, resolution, regulation, or policy.

**O.C.G.A. § 16-11-131**
**Possession of firearms by convicted felons and first offender probationers**
(a) As used in this Code section, the term:

(1) "Felony" means any offense punishable by imprisonment for a term of one year or more and includes conviction by a court-martial under the Uniform Code of Military Justice for an offense which would constitute a felony under the laws of the United States.

(2) "Firearm" includes any handgun, rifle, shotgun, or other weapon which will or can be converted to expel a projectile by the action of an explosive or electrical charge.

(b) Any person who is on probation as a felony first offender pursuant to Article 3 of Chapter 8 of Title 42 or who has been convicted of a felony by a court of this state or any other state; by a court of the United States including its territories, possessions, and dominions; or by a court of any foreign nation and who receives, possesses, or transports any firearm commits a felony and, upon conviction thereof, shall be imprisoned for not less than one nor more than five years; provided, however, that if the felony as to which the person is on probation or has been previously convicted is a forcible felony, then upon conviction of receiving, possessing, or transporting a firearm, such person shall be imprisoned for a period of five years.

(b.1) Any person who is prohibited by this Code section from possessing a firearm because of conviction of a forcible felony or because of being on probation as a first offender for a forcible felony pursuant to this Code section and who attempts to purchase or obtain transfer of a firearm shall be guilty of a felony and shall be punished by imprisonment for not less than one nor more than five years.

(c) This Code section shall not apply to any person who has been pardoned for the felony by the President of the United States, the State Board of Pardons and Paroles, or the person or agency empowered to grant pardons under the constitutions or laws of the several states or of a foreign nation and, by the terms of the pardon, has expressly been authorized to receive, possess, or transport a firearm.

(d) A person who has been convicted of a felony, but who has been granted relief from the disabilities imposed by the laws of the United States with respect to the acquisition, receipt, transfer, shipment, or possession of firearms by the secretary of the United States Department of the Treasury pursuant to 18 U.S.C. Section 925, shall, upon presenting to the Board of Public Safety proof that the relief has been granted and it being established from proof submitted by the applicant to the satisfaction of the Board of Public Safety that the circumstances regarding the conviction and the applicant's record and reputation are such that the acquisition, receipt, transfer, shipment, or possession of firearms by the person would not present a threat to the safety of the citizens of Georgia and that the granting of the relief sought would not be contrary to the public interest, be granted relief from the disabilities imposed by this Code section. A person who has been convicted under federal or state law of a felony pertaining to antitrust violations, unfair trade practices, or restraint of trade shall, upon presenting to the Board of Public Safety proof, and it being established from said proof, submitted by the applicant to the satisfaction of the Board of Public Safety that the circumstances regarding the conviction and the applicant's record and reputation are such that the acquisition, receipt, transfer, shipment, or possession of firearms by the person would not present a threat to the safety of the citizens of Georgia and that the granting of the relief sought would not be contrary to the public interest, be granted relief from the disabilities imposed by this Code section. A record that the relief has been granted by the board shall be entered upon the criminal history of the person maintained by the Georgia Crime Information Center and the board shall maintain a list of the names of such persons which shall be open for public inspection.

(e) As used in this Code section, the term "forcible felony" means any felony which involves the use or threat of physical force or violence against any person and further includes, without limitation, murder; murder in the second degree; burglary in any degree; robbery; armed robbery; home invasion in any degree; kidnapping; hijacking of an aircraft or motor vehicle; aggravated stalking; rape; aggravated child molestation; aggravated sexual battery; arson in the first degree; the manufacturing, transporting, distribution, or possession of explosives with intent to kill, injure, or intimidate individuals or destroy a public building; terroristic threats; or acts of treason or insurrection.

(f) Any person placed on probation as a first offender pursuant to Article 3 of Chapter 8 of Title 42 and subsequently discharged without court adjudication of guilt as a matter of law pursuant to Code Section 42-8-60 shall, upon such discharge, be relieved from the disabilities imposed by this Code section.

**O.C.G.A. § 16-11-132 Possession of handgun by person under the age of 18 years**

(a) For the purposes of this Code section, a handgun is considered loaded if there is a cartridge in the chamber or cylinder of the handgun.

(b) Notwithstanding any other provisions of this part and except as otherwise provided in this Code section, it shall be unlawful for any person under the age of 18 years to possess or have under such person's control a handgun. A person convicted of a first violation of this subsection shall be guilty of a misdemeanor and shall be punished by a fine not to exceed $1,000.00 or by imprisonment for not more than 12 months, or both. A person convicted of a second or subsequent violation of this subsection shall be guilty of a felony and shall be punished by a fine of $5,000.00 or by imprisonment for a period of three years, or both.

(c) Except as otherwise provided in subsection (d) of this Code section, the provisions of subsection (b) of this Code section shall not apply to:
    (1) Any person under the age of 18 years who is:
        (A) Attending a hunter education course or a firearms safety course;
        (B) Engaging in practice in the use of a firearm or target shooting at an established range authorized by the governing body of the jurisdiction where such range is located;
        (C) Engaging in an organized competition involving the use of a firearm or participating in or practicing for a performance by an organized group under 26 U.S.C. Section 501(c)(3) which uses firearms as a part of such performance;
        (D) Hunting or fishing pursuant to a valid license if such person has in his or her possession such a valid hunting or fishing license if required; is engaged in legal hunting or fishing; has permission of the owner of the land on which

the activities are being conducted; and the handgun, whenever loaded, is carried only in an open and fully exposed manner; or

(E) Traveling to or from any activity described in subparagraphs (A) through (D) of this paragraph if the handgun in such person's possession is not loaded;

(2) Any person under the age of 18 years who is on real property under the control of such person's parent, legal guardian, or grandparent and who has the permission of such person's parent or legal guardian to possess a handgun; or

(3) Any person under the age of 18 years who is at such person's residence and who, with the permission of such person's parent or legal guardian, possesses a handgun for the purpose of exercising the rights authorized in Code Section 16-3-21 or 16-3-23.

(d) Subsection (c) of this Code section shall not apply to any person under the age of 18 years who has been convicted of a forcible felony or forcible misdemeanor, as defined in Code Section 16-1-3, or who has been adjudicated for committing a delinquent act under the provisions of Article 6 of Chapter 11 of Title 15 for an offense which would constitute a forcible felony or forcible misdemeanor, as defined in Code Section 16-1-3, if such person were an adult.

## O.C.G.A. § 16-11-134 Discharging firearm while under the influence of alcohol or drugs

(a) It shall be unlawful for any person to discharge a firearm while:

(1) Under the influence of alcohol or any drug or any combination of alcohol and any drug to the extent that it is unsafe for the person to discharge such firearm except in the defense of life, health, and property;

(2) The person's alcohol concentration is 0.08 grams or more at any time while discharging such firearm or within three hours after such discharge of such firearm from alcohol consumed before such discharge ended; or

(3) Subject to the provisions of subsection (b) of this Code section, there is any amount of marijuana or a controlled substance, as defined in Code Section 16-13-21, present in the person's blood or urine, or both, including the metabolites and derivatives of each or both without regard to whether or not any alcohol is present in the person's breath or blood.

(b) The fact that any person charged with violating this Code section is or has been legally entitled to use a drug shall not constitute a defense against any charge of violating this Code section; provided, however, that such person shall not be in violation of this Code section unless such person is rendered incapable of possessing or discharging a firearm safely as a result of using a drug other than alcohol which such person is legally entitled to use.

(c) Any person convicted of violating subsection (a) of this Code section shall be guilty of a misdemeanor of a high and aggravated nature.

## O.C.G.A. § 16-11-135
**Public or private employer's parking lots; right of privacy in vehicles in employer's parking lot or invited guests on lot; severability; rights of action**
(a) Except as provided in this Code section, no private or public employer, including the state and its political subdivisions, shall establish, maintain, or enforce any policy or rule that has the effect of allowing such employer or its agents to search the locked privately owned vehicles of employees or invited guests on the employer's parking lot and access thereto.

(b) Except as provided in this Code section, no private or public employer, including the state and its political subdivisions, shall condition employment upon any agreement by a prospective employee that prohibits an employee from entering the parking lot and access thereto when the employee's privately owned motor vehicle contains a firearm or ammunition, or both, that is locked out of sight within the trunk, glove box, or other enclosed compartment or area within such privately owned motor vehicle, provided that any applicable employees possess a Georgia weapons carry license.
(c) Subsection (a) of this Code section shall not apply:
    (1) To searches by certified law enforcement officers pursuant to valid search warrants or valid warrantless searches based upon probable cause under exigent circumstances;
    (2) To vehicles owned or leased by an employer;
    (3) To any situation in which a reasonable person would believe that accessing a locked vehicle of an employee is necessary to prevent an immediate threat to human health, life, or safety; or

(4) When an employee consents to a search of his or her locked privately owned vehicle by licensed private security officers for loss prevention purposes based on probable cause that the employee unlawfully possesses employer property.

(d) Subsections (a) and (b) of this Code section shall not apply:

(1) To an employer providing applicable employees with a secure parking area which restricts general public access through the use of a gate, security station, security officers, or other similar means which limit public access into the parking area, provided that any employer policy allowing vehicle searches upon entry shall be applicable to all vehicles entering the property and applied on a uniform and frequent basis;

(2) To any penal institution, correctional institution, detention facility, jail, or similar place of confinement or confinement alternative;

(3) To facilities associated with electric generation owned or operated by a public utility;

(4) To any United States Department of Defense contractor, if such contractor operates any facility on or contiguous with a United States military base or installation or within one mile of an airport;

(5) To an employee who is restricted from carrying or possessing a firearm on the employer's premises due to a completed or pending disciplinary action;

(6) Where transport of a firearm on the premises of the employer is prohibited by state or federal law or regulation;

(7) To parking lots contiguous to facilities providing natural gas transmission, liquid petroleum transmission, water storage and supply, and law enforcement services determined to be so vital to the State of Georgia, by a written determination of the Georgia Department of Homeland Security, that the incapacity or destruction of such systems and assets would have a debilitating impact on public health or safety; or

(8) To any area used for parking on a temporary basis.

(e) No employer, property owner, or property owner's agent shall be held liable in any criminal or civil action for damages resulting from or arising out of an occurrence involving the transportation, storage, possession, or use of a firearm, including, but not limited to, the theft of a firearm from an employee's automobile, pursuant to this Code section unless such employer commits a criminal act involving the use of a firearm or unless the employer knew that the person using such firearm would commit such criminal act on the employer's premises. Nothing contained in this Code section shall create a new duty on the part of the employer, property owner, or property owner's agent. An employee at will shall have no greater interest in employment created by this Code section and shall remain an employee at will.

(f) In any action relating to the enforcement of any right or obligation under this Code section, an employer, property owner, or property owner's agent's efforts to comply with other applicable federal, state, or local safety laws, regulations, guidelines, or ordinances shall be a complete defense to any employer, property owner, or property owner's agent's liability.

(g) In any action brought against an employer, employer's agent, property owner, or property owner's agent relating to the criminal use of firearms in the workplace, the plaintiff shall be liable for all legal costs of such employer, employer's agent, property owner, or property owner's agent if such action is concluded in such employer, employer's agent, property owner, or property owner's agent's favor.

(h) This Code section shall not be construed so as to require an employer, property owner, or property owner's agent to implement any additional security measures for the protection of employees, customers, or other persons. Implementation of remedial security measures to provide protection to employees, customers, or other persons shall not be admissible in evidence to show prior negligence or breach of duty of an employer, property owner, or property owner's agent in any action against such employer, its officers or shareholders, or property owners.

(i) All actions brought based upon a violation of subsection (a) of this Code section shall be brought exclusively by the Attorney General.

(j) In the event that subsection (e) of this Code section is declared or adjudged by any court to be invalid or unconstitutional for any reason, the remaining portions of this Code section shall be invalid and of no further force or effect. The General Assembly declares that it would not have enacted the remaining provisions of this Code section if it had known that such portion hereof would be declared or adjudged invalid or unconstitutional.

(k) Nothing in this Code section shall restrict the rights of private property owners or persons in legal control of property through a lease, a rental agreement, a contract, or any other agreement to control access to such property. When a private property owner or person in legal control of property through a lease, a rental agreement, a contract, or any other agreement is also an employer, his or her rights as a private property owner or person in legal control of property shall govern.

### O.C.G.A. § 16-11-136
### Restrictions on possession, manufacture, sale, or transfer of knives
(a) As used in this Code section, the term:
    (1) "Courthouse" shall have the same meaning as set forth in Code Section 16-11-127.
    (2) "Government building" shall have the same meaning as set forth in Code Section 16-11-127.
    (3) "Knife" means any cutting instrument with a blade and shall include, without limitation, a knife as such term is defined in Code Section 16-11-125.1.

(b) Except for restrictions in courthouses and government buildings, no county, municipality, or consolidated government shall, by rule or ordinance, constrain the possession, manufacture, sale, or transfer of a knife more restrictively than the provisions of this part.

### O.C.G.A. § 16-11-137
### Required possession of weapons carry license or proof of exemption when carrying a weapon; detention for investigation of carrying permit
(a) Every license holder shall have his or her valid weapons carry license in his or her immediate possession at all times when carrying a weapon, or if such person is exempt from having a weapons carry license pursuant to Code Section 16-11-130 or subsection (c) of Code Section 16-11-127.1, he or she shall have proof of his or her exemption in his or her immediate possession at all times when carrying a weapon, and his or her failure to do so shall be prima-fa-

cie evidence of a violation of the applicable provision of Code Sections 16-11-126 through 16-11-127.2.

(b) A person carrying a weapon shall not be subject to detention for the sole purpose of investigating whether such person has a weapons carry license.

(c) A person convicted of a violation of this Code section shall be fined not more than $10.00 if he or she produces in court his or her weapons carry license, provided that it was valid at the time of his or her arrest, or produces proof of his or her exemption.

### O.C.G.A. § 16-11-138
**Defense of self or others as absolute defense**
Defense of self or others, as contemplated by and provided for under Article 2 of Chapter 3 of this title, shall be an absolute defense to any violation under this part.

### O.C.G.A. § 16-11-160
**Use of machine guns, sawed-off rifles, sawed-off shotguns, or firearms with silencers during commission of certain offenses; enhanced criminal penalties**
(a) It shall be unlawful for any person to possess or to use a machine gun, sawed-off rifle, sawed-off shotgun, or firearm equipped with a silencer, as those terms are defined in Code Section 16-11-121, during the commission or the attempted commission of any of the following offenses:
    (A) Aggravated assault as defined in Code Section 16-5-21;
    (B) Aggravated battery as defined in Code Section 16-5-24;
    (C) Robbery as defined in Code Section 16-8-40;
    (D) Armed robbery as defined in Code Section 16-8-41;
    (D.1) Home invasion in any degree as defined in Code Section 16-7-5;
    (E) Murder or felony murder as defined in Code Section 16-5-1;
    (F) Voluntary manslaughter as defined in Code Section 16-5-2;
    (G) Involuntary manslaughter as defined in Code Section 16-5-3;
    (H) Sale, possession for sale, transportation, manufacture, offer for sale, or offer to manufacture controlled substances in violation of any provision of Article 2 of Chapter 13 of this

title, the "Georgia Controlled Substances Act";

(I) Terroristic threats or acts as defined in Code Section 16-11-37;

(J) Arson as defined in Code Section 16-7-60, 16-7-61, or 16-7-62 or arson of lands as defined in Code Section 16-7-63;

(K) Influencing witnesses as defined in Code Section 16-10-93; and

(L) Participation in criminal gang activity as defined in Code Section 16-15-4.

(2)(A) As used in this paragraph, the term "bulletproof vest" means a bullet-resistant soft body armor providing, as a minimum standard, the level of protection known as "threat level I," which means at least seven layers of bullet-resistant material providing protection from at least three shots of 158-grain lead ammunition fired from a .38 caliber handgun at a velocity of 850 feet per second.

(B) It shall be unlawful for any person to wear a bulletproof vest during the commission or the attempted commission of any of the following offenses:

(i) Any crime against or involving the person of another in violation of any of the provisions of this title for which a sentence of life imprisonment may be imposed;

(ii) Any felony involving the manufacture, delivery, distribution, administering, or selling of controlled substances or marijuana as provided in Code Section 16-13-30; or

(iii) Trafficking in cocaine, illegal drugs, marijuana, or methamphetamine as provided in Code Section 16-13-31.

(b) Any person who violates paragraph (1) of subsection (a) of this Code section shall be guilty of a felony, and, upon conviction thereof, shall be punished by confinement for a period of ten years, such sentence to run consecutively to any other sentence which the person has received. Any person who violates paragraph (2) of subsection (a) of this Code section shall be guilty of a felony, and, upon conviction thereof, shall be punished by confinement for a period of one to five years, such sentence to run consecutively to any other sentence which the person has received.

(c) Upon the second or subsequent conviction of a person under this Code section, the person shall be punished by life imprisonment. Notwithstanding any other law to the contrary, the sentence of any person which is imposed for violating this Code section a second or subsequent time shall not be suspended by a court or a probationary sentence imposed in lieu thereof.

(d) The punishment prescribed for the violation of subsections (a) and (c) of this Code section shall not be probated or suspended as is provided by Code Section 17-10-7.

(e) Any crime committed in violation of this Code section shall be considered a separate offense.

**O.C.G.A. § 16-11-173 Legislative findings; preemption of local regulation and lawsuits; exceptions**
(a)(1) It is declared by the General Assembly that the regulation of firearms and other weapons is properly an issue of general, statewide concern.
(2) The General Assembly further declares that the lawful design, marketing, manufacture, and sale of firearms and ammunition and other weapons to the public is not unreasonably dangerous activity and does not constitute a nuisance *per se*.

(b)
(1) Except as provided in subsection (c) of this Code section, no county or municipal corporation, by zoning, by ordinance or resolution, or by any other means, nor any agency, board, department, commission, political subdivision, school district, or authority of this state, other than the General Assembly, by rule or regulation or by any other means shall regulate in any manner:
(A) Gun shows;
(B) The possession, ownership, transport, carrying, transfer, sale, purchase, licensing, or registration of firearms or other weapons or components of firearms or other weapons;
(C) Firearms dealers or dealers of other weapons; or
(D) Dealers in components of firearms or other weapons
(2) The authority to bring suit and right to recover against any weapons, firearms, or ammunition manufacturer, trade association, or dealer by or on behalf of any governmental unit created by or pursuant to an Act of the General Assembly or the Constitution, or any department, agency, or authority thereof,

for damages, abatement, or injunctive relief resulting from or relating to the lawful design, manufacture, marketing, or sale of weapons, firearms, or ammunition to the public shall be reserved exclusively to the state. This paragraph shall not prohibit a political subdivision or local government authority from bringing an action against a weapons, firearms, or ammunition manufacturer or dealer for breach of contract or express warranty as to weapons, firearms, or ammunition purchased by the political subdivision or local government authority.

(c)(1) A county or municipal corporation may regulate the transport, carrying, or possession of firearms by employees of the local unit of government, or by unpaid volunteers of such local unit of government, in the course of their employment or volunteer functions with such local unit of government; provided, however, that the sheriff or chief of police shall be solely responsible for regulating and determining the possession, carrying, and transportation of firearms and other weapons by employees under his or her respective supervision so long as such regulations comport with state and federal law.

(2) The commanding officer of any law enforcement agency shall regulate and determine the possession, carrying, and transportation of firearms and other weapons by employees under his or her supervision so long as such regulations comport with state and federal law.

(3) The district attorney, and the solicitor-general in counties where there is a state court, shall regulate and determine the possession, carrying, and transportation of firearms and other weapons by county employees under his or her supervision so long as such regulations comport with state and federal law.

(d) Nothing contained in this Code section shall prohibit municipalities or counties, by ordinance or resolution, from requiring the ownership of guns by heads of households within the political subdivision.

(e) Nothing contained in this Code section shall prohibit municipalities or counties, by ordinance or resolution, from reasonably limiting or prohibiting the discharge of firearms within the boundaries of the municipal corporation or county.

(f) As used in this Code section, the term "weapon" means any device designed or intended to be used, or capable of being used, for offense or defense, including but not limited to firearms, bladed devices, clubs, electric stun devices, and defense sprays.

(g) Any person aggrieved as a result of a violation of this Code section may bring an action against the person who caused such aggrievement. The aggrieved person shall be entitled to reasonable attorney's fees and expenses of litigation and may recover or obtain against the person who caused such damages any of the following:
    (1) Actual damages or $100.00, whichever is greater;
    (2) Equitable relief, including, but not limited to, an injunction or restitution of money and property; and
    (3) Any other relief which the court deems proper.

## O.C.G.A. § 16-12-122
### Transportation Passenger Safety Act: Definitions
As used in this part, the term:
    (1) "Aircraft" means any machine, whether heavier or lighter than air, used or designed for navigation of or flight in the air.
    (2) "Avoid a security measure" means to take any action that is intended to result in any person, baggage, container, or item of any type being allowed into a secure area without being subjected to security measures or the assembly of items into an object or substance that is prohibited under the laws of this state or of the United States or any of their agencies, political subdivisions, or authorities after such items have passed through a security measure into a secure area.
    (3) "Bus" means any passenger bus or coach or other motor vehicle having a seating capacity of not less than 15 passengers operated by a transportation company for the purpose of carrying passengers or freight for hire.
    (4) "Charter" means a group of persons, pursuant to a common purpose and under a single contract and at a fixed charge for the vehicle in accordance with a transportation company's tariff, who have acquired the exclusive use of an aircraft, bus, or rail vehicle to travel together as a group to a specified destination.
    (5) "Interfere with a security measure" means to take any action that is intended to defeat, disable, or prevent the full operation of equipment or procedures designed or intended

to detect any object or substance, including, but not limited to, disabling of any device so that it cannot fully function, creation of any diversion intended to defeat a security measure, or packaging of any item or substance so as to avoid detection by a security measure.

(6) "Passenger" means any person served by the transportation company; and, in addition to the ordinary meaning of passenger, the term shall include any person accompanying or meeting another person who is transported by such company, any person shipping or receiving freight, and any person purchasing a ticket or receiving a pass.

(7) "Rail vehicle" means any railroad or rail transit car, carriage, coach, or other vehicle, whether self-propelled or not and designed to be operated upon a rail or rails or other fixed right of way by a transportation company for the purpose of carrying passengers or freight or both for hire.

(8) "Secure area" means any enclosed or unenclosed area within a terminal whereby access is restricted in any manner or the possession of items subject to security measures is prohibited. Access to a secure area may be restricted to persons specifically authorized by law, regulation, or policy of the governing authority or transportation company operating said terminal, and such access into a secure area may be conditioned on passing through security measures, and possession of items may be restricted to designated persons who are acting in the course of their official duties.

(9) "Security measure" means any process or procedure by which employees, agents, passengers, persons accompanying passengers, containers, baggage, freight, or possessions of passengers or persons accompanying passengers are screened, inspected, or examined by any means for the purpose of ensuring the safety and welfare of aircraft, bus, or rail vehicles and the employees, agents, passengers, and freight of any transportation company. The security measures may be operated by or under the authority of any governmental entity, transportation company, or any entity contracting therewith.

(10) "Terminal" means an aircraft, bus, or rail vehicle station, depot, any such transportation facility, or infrastructure relating thereto operated by a transportation company or governmental entity or authority. This term includes a reasonable

area immediately adjacent to any designated stop along the route traveled by any coach or rail vehicle operated by a trans-portation company or governmental entity operating aircraft, bus, or rail vehicle transportation facility and parking lots or parking areas adjacent to a terminal.

(11) "Transportation company" or "company" means any person, group of persons, or corporation providing for-hire transportation to passengers or freight by aircraft, by bus upon the highways in this state, by rail vehicle upon any public or private right of way in this state, or by all, including pas-sengers and freight in interstate or intrastate travel. This term shall also include transportation facilities owned or operated by local public bodies; by municipalities; and by public corpo-rations, authorities, boards, and commissions established un-der the laws of this state, any of the several states, the United States, or any foreign nation.

## O.C.G.A. § 16-12-123 Bus or rail vehicle hijacking; boarding with concealed weapon; company use of reasonable security measures

(a)  (1) A person commits the offense of bus or rail vehicle hijack-ing when he or she:

> (A) Seizes or exercises control by force or violence or threat of force or violence of any bus or rail vehicle within the jurisdiction of this state;
>
> (B) By force or violence or by threat of force or violence seizes or exercises control of any transportation company or all or any part of the transportation facilities owned or operated by any such company; or
>
> (C) By force or violence or by threat of force or violence substantially obstructs, hinders, interferes with, or other-wise disrupts or disturbs the operation of any transporta-tion company or all or any part of a transportation facility.

(2) Any person convicted of the offense of bus or rail hijacking shall be guilty of a felony and, upon conviction thereof, shall be punished by imprisonment for life or by imprisonment for not less than one nor more than 20 years.

(b) Any person who boards or attempts to board an aircraft, bus, or rail vehicle with any explosive, destructive device, or hoax device as such term is defined in Code Section 16-7-80; firearm for which such person does not have on his or her person a valid weapons carry license issued pursuant to Code Section 16-11-129 unless possessing such firearm is prohibited by federal law; hazardous substance as defined by Code Section 12-8-92; or knife or other device designed or modified for the purpose of offense and defense concealed on or about his or her person or property which is or would be accessible to such person while on the aircraft, bus, or rail vehicle shall be guilty of a felony and, upon conviction thereof, shall be sentenced to imprisonment for not less than one nor more than ten years. The prohibition of this subsection shall not apply to any law enforcement officer, peace officer retired from a state or federal law enforcement agency, person in the military service of the state or of the United States, or commercial security personnel employed by the transportation company who is in possession of weapons used within the course and scope of employment; nor shall the prohibition apply to persons transporting weapons contained in baggage which is not accessible to passengers if the presence of such weapons has been declared to the transportation company and such weapons have been secured in a manner prescribed by state or federal law or regulation for the purpose of transportation or shipment. The provisions of this subsection shall not apply to any privately owned aircraft, bus, or rail vehicle if the owner of such aircraft or vehicle has given his or her express permission to board the aircraft or vehicle with the item.

(c) The company may employ reasonable security measures, including any method or device, to detect concealed weapons, explosives, or hazardous material in baggage or freight or upon the person of the passenger. Upon the discovery of any such item or material in the possession of a person, unless the item is a weapon in the possession of a person exempted under subsection (b) of this Code section from the prohibition of that subsection (b), the company shall obtain possession and retain custody of such item or materials until they are transferred to the custody of law enforcement officers.

**O.C.G.A. § 16-12-127 Prohibition on firearms, hazardous substances, knives, or other devices; penalty; affirmative defenses**

(a) It shall be unlawful for any person, with the intention of avoiding or interfering with a security measure or of introducing into a terminal any explosive, destructive device, or hoax device as defined in Code Section 16-7-80; firearm for which such person does not have on his or her person a valid weapons carry license issued pursuant to Code Section 16-11-129 unless possessing such firearm is prohibited by federal law; hazardous substance as defined by Code Section 12-8-92; or knife or other device designed or modified for the purpose of offense and defense, to:

(1) Have any such item on or about his or her person, or

(2) Place or cause to be placed or attempt to place or cause to be placed any such item:

(A) In a container or freight of a transportation company;

(B) In the baggage or possessions of any person or any transportation company without the knowledge of the passenger or transportation company; or

(C) Aboard such aircraft, bus, or rail vehicle.

(b) A person violating the provisions of this Code section shall be guilty of a felony and shall, upon conviction, be sentenced to imprisonment for not less than one year nor more than 20 years, a fine not to exceed $15,000.00, or both. A prosecution under this Code section shall not be barred by the imposition of a civil penalty imposed by any governmental entity.

(c) It is an affirmative defense to a violation of this Code section if a person notifies a law enforcement officer or other person employed to provide security for a transportation company of the presence of such item as soon as possible after learning of its presence and surrenders or secures such item as directed by the law enforcement officer or other person employed to provide security for a transportation company.

## O.C.G.A. § 16-12-129
### Defense of self or others; absolute defense

Defense of self or others, as contemplated by and provided for under Article 2 of Chapter 3 of this title, shall be an absolute defense to any violation under this part.

## O.C.G.A. § 27-3-1.1
### Acts prohibited on wildlife management areas

It shall be unlawful for any person on any wildlife management area owned or operated by the department:

(1) To possess a firearm other than a handgun, as such term is defined in Code Section 16-11-125.1, during a closed hunting season for that area unless such firearm is unloaded and stored in a motor vehicle so as not to be readily accessible

or to possess a handgun during a closed hunting season for that area unless such person possesses a valid weapons carry license issued pursuant to Code Section 16-11-129;

(2) To possess a loaded firearm other than a handgun, as such term is defined in Code Section 16-11-125.1, in a motor vehicle during a legal open hunting season for that area or to possess a loaded handgun in a motor vehicle during a legal open hunting season for that area unless such person possesses a valid weapons carry license issued pursuant to Code Section 16-11-129;

(3) To be under the influence of drugs, intoxicating liquors, beers, or wines. The determination of whether any person is under the influence of drugs or intoxicating liquors, beers, or wines may be made in accordance with Code Section 27-3-7;

(4) To hunt within 50 yards of any road which receives regular maintenance for the purpose of public vehicular access;

(5) To target practice, except where an authorized shooting range is made available by the department, and then only in a manner consistent with the rules for shooting ranges promulgated by the board;

(6) To drive a vehicle around a closed gate, cable, sign, or other structure or device intended to prevent vehicular access to a road entering onto or within such an area;

(7) To hunt within any posted safety zone;

(8) To camp upon or drive a motor vehicle over any permanent pasture or area planted in crops;

(9) While hunting bears in any such area opened to bear hunting, to kill a female bear with a cub or cubs or to kill a cub weighing less than 75 pounds;

(10) To fail to report if he or she kills a deer, bear, or turkey in the manner specified by the rules of the department for that wildlife management area on the date killed to the state game and fish checking station on the area;

(11) To construct any tree stand or to hunt from any tree stand except a portable or natural tree stand; or

(12) To trap except with a special trapping permit issued by the department.

## O.C.G.A. § 27-3-7
### Hunting under the influence of alcohol or drugs

(a) As used in this Code section, the term "hunt" or "hunting" means the act of hunting, as such term is defined in Code Section 27-1-2, while in possession of or using a firearm, bow, or any other device which serves to launch a projectile.

(b) A person shall not hunt while:
(1) Under the influence of alcohol to the extent that it is less safe for the person to hunt;
(2) Under the influence of any drug to the extent that it is less safe for the person to hunt;
(3) Under the combined influence of alcohol and any drug to the extent that it is less safe for the person to hunt;
(4) The person's alcohol concentration is 0.08 grams or more at any time within three hours after such hunting from alcohol consumed before such hunting ended; or
(5) Subject to the provisions of subsection (c) of this Code section, there is any amount of marijuana or a controlled substance, as defined in Code Section 16-13-21, present in the person's blood or urine, or both, including the metabolites and derivatives of each or both without regard to whether or not any alcohol is present in the person's breath or blood.

(c) The fact that any person charged with violating this Code section is or has been legally entitled to use a drug shall not constitute a defense against any charge of violating this Code section; provided, however, that such person shall not be in violation of this Code section unless such person is rendered incapable of hunting safely as a result of using a drug other than alcohol which such person is legally entitled to use.

(d) Upon the trial of any civil or criminal action or proceeding arising out of acts alleged to have been committed by any person in violation of subsection (b) of this Code section, evidence of the amount of alcohol or drug in a person's blood, urine, breath, or other bodily substance at the alleged time, as determined by a chemical analysis of the person's blood, urine, breath, or other bodily substance shall be admissible. Where such a chemical test is made, the following provisions shall apply:
(1) Chemical analysis of the person's blood, urine, breath, or other bodily substance, to be considered valid under this Code section, shall have been performed according to methods approved by the Division of Forensic Sciences of the Georgia Bu-

reau of Investigation on a machine which was operated with all the electronic and operating components prescribed by its manufacturer properly attached and in good working order and by an individual possessing a valid permit issued by the Division of Forensic Sciences for this purpose. The Division of Forensic Sciences of the Georgia Bureau of Investigation shall approve satisfactory techniques or methods to ascertain the qualifications and competence of individuals to conduct analyses and to issue permits, along with requirements for properly operating and maintaining any testing instruments, and to issue certificates certifying that instruments have met those requirements, which certificates and permits shall be subject to termination or revocation at the discretion of the Division of Forensic Sciences;

(2) When a person undergoes a chemical test at the request of a law enforcement officer, only a physician, registered nurse, laboratory technician, emergency medical technician, or other qualified person may withdraw blood for the purpose of determining the alcoholic content therein, provided that this limitation shall not apply to the taking of breath or urine specimens. No physician, registered nurse, or other qualified person or employer thereof shall incur any civil or criminal liability as a result of the medically proper obtaining of such blood specimens when requested in writing by a law enforcement officer;

(3) The person tested may have a physician or a qualified technician, chemist, registered nurse, or other qualified person of his or her own choosing administer a chemical test or tests in addition to any administered at the direction of a law enforcement officer. The justifiable failure or inability to obtain an additional test shall not preclude the admission of evidence relating to the test or tests taken at the direction of a law enforcement officer; and

(4) Upon the request of the person who shall submit to a chemical test or tests at the request of a law enforcement officer, full information concerning the test or tests shall be made available to such person or such person's attorney. The arresting officer at the time of arrest shall advise the person arrested of his or her rights to a chemical test or tests according to this Code section.

(e) In the event of a hunting accident involving a fatality, the investigating coroner or medical examiner having jurisdiction shall direct that a chemical blood test to determine the blood alcohol concentration or the presence of drugs be performed on the dead person and that the results of such test be properly recorded on his or her report.

(f) Upon the trial of any civil or criminal action or proceeding arising out of acts alleged to have been committed by any person hunting in violation of subsection (b) of this Code section, the amount of alcohol in the person's blood at the time alleged, as shown by chemical analysis of the person's blood, urine, breath, or other bodily substance, shall give rise to the following presumptions:

(1) If there was at that time a blood alcohol concentration of 0.05 grams or less, it shall be presumed that the person was not under the influence of alcohol, as prohibited by paragraphs (1), (2), and (3) of subsection (b) of this Code section;

(2) If there was at that time a blood alcohol concentration in excess of 0.05 grams but less than 0.08 grams, such fact shall not give rise to any presumption that the person was or was not under the influence of alcohol, as prohibited by paragraphs (1), (2), and (3) of subsection (b) of this Code section, but such fact may be considered with other competent evidence in determining whether the person was under the influence of alcohol, as prohibited by paragraphs (1), (2), and (3) of subsection (b) of this Code section; and

(3) If there was at that time or within three hours after hunting, from alcohol consumed before such hunting ended, a blood alcohol concentration of 0.08 or more grams, the person shall be in violation of paragraph (4) of subsection (b) of this Code section.

(g)

(1) Any person who exercises the privilege of hunting in this state shall be deemed to have given consent, subject to subsection (d) of this Code section, to a chemical test or tests of his or her blood, breath, urine, or other bodily substances for the purpose of determining the presence of alcohol or any other drug, if arrested for any offense arising out of acts alleged to have been committed while such person was hunting in violation of subsection (b) of this Code section. Subject to subsection (d) of this Code section, the requesting law enforcement officer shall designate which test or tests shall be administered.

(2) At the time a chemical test or tests are requested, the arresting officer shall read to the person the following implied consent warning:

"Georgia law requires you to submit to state administered chemical tests of your blood, breath, urine, or other bodily substances for the purpose of determining if you are under the influence of alcohol or drugs. If you refuse this testing and you are convicted of hunting while under the influence of alcohol or drugs, your privilege to hunt in this state will be suspended for a period of two years. Your refusal to submit to the required testing may be offered into evidence against you at trial. If you submit to testing and the results indicate an alcohol concentration of 0.08 grams or more and if you are subsequently convicted of hunting under the influence of alcohol by having an alcohol concentration of 0.08 grams or more at any time within three hours after hunting from alcohol consumed before such hunting ended, your privilege to hunt in this state will be suspended for a period of one year. After first submitting to the required state tests, you are entitled to additional chemical tests of your blood, breath, urine, or other bodily substances at your own expense and from qualified personnel of your own choosing. Will you submit to the state administered chemical tests of your ( designate which tests ) under the implied consent law?"

(h) Any person who is dead, unconscious, or otherwise in a condition rendering such person incapable of refusal shall be deemed not to have withdrawn the consent provided by subsection (g) of this Code section, and the test or tests may be administered, subject to subsection (d) of this Code section.

(i)

(1) If a person refuses, upon the request of a law enforcement officer, to submit to a chemical test designated by the law enforcement officer as provided in subsection (g) of this Code section, no test shall be given; provided, however, that subject to the provisions of paragraphs (2) and (3) of this subsection, such refusal shall be admissible in any legal action; and provided, further, that upon conviction of a violation of subsection (b) of this Code section, in addition to any other punishment imposed, such person's privileges to hunt in this state shall be

suspended by operation of law for a period of two years. The fact that such person was not in possession of a valid hunting license at the time of the violation shall have no effect on the suspension of his or her hunting privilege.

(2) If in any legal action a party desires to present evidence of the refusal of a person charged with violating subsection (b) of this Code section to submit to a chemical test designated by a law enforcement officer as provided in subsection (g) of this Code section, the party desiring to present such evidence shall request the judge presiding over such legal proceeding to hold a hearing to determine the admissibility of such evidence after notice to the person alleged to have refused to submit to such testing and to the law enforcement officer.

(3) The scope of the hearing shall be limited to the following issues:

(A) Whether the law enforcement officer had reasonable grounds to believe the person was hunting while under the influence of alcohol or a controlled substance and was lawfully placed under arrest for violating subsection (b) of this Code section;

(B) Whether at the time of the request for the test or tests the officer informed the person of the person's implied consent rights and the consequence of submitting or refusing to submit to such test; and

(C) Whether the person refused to submit to the test.

(4) It shall be unlawful during any period of a person's hunting privilege suspension for such person to:

(A) Hunt without a license in violation of Code Section 27-2-1;

(B) Possess a current Georgia hunting license; or

(C) Hunt in any situation where a hunting license is not required.

(5) Any person convicted of hunting while intoxicated while his or her hunting privileges are suspended pursuant to this subsection shall be guilty of a misdemeanor.

(j) Nothing in this Code section shall be deemed to preclude the acquisition or admission of evidence of a violation of this Code section if the evidence was obtained by voluntary consent or a search warrant as authorized by the Constitution or the laws of this state or the United States.

(k) Upon the request of a law enforcement officer, if a person consents to submit to a chemical test designated by such officer as provided in subsection (g) of this Code section, and the results of such test indicate an alcohol concentration of 0.08 grams or more, upon a conviction of a violation of paragraph (4) of subsection (b) of this Code section, in addition to any other punishment imposed, such person's privileges to hunt in this state shall be suspended by operation of law for a period of one year. Even if such person did not possess a valid hunting license at the time of the violation, such person's hunting privileges shall be suspended for one year.

(l) Following the period of suspension set forth in subsection (i) or (k) of this Code section, such person may apply to the department for reinstatement of his or her hunting privileges. Any suspension pursuant to this Code section shall remain in effect until such person submits proof of completion of a DUI Alcohol or Drug Use Risk Reduction Program certified by the Department of Driver Services and pays a restoration fee of $200.00, unless such conviction was a recidivist conviction, in which case the restoration fee shall be $500.00.

### O.C.G.A. § 27-4-11.1
**Possession of firearms and intoxication on public fishing areas; fishing in closed fishing areas; other restrictions in public fishing areas**
(a) It shall be unlawful for any person on any public fishing area owned or operated by the department:
    (1) To possess a firearm other than a handgun, as such term is defined in Code Section 16-11-125.1, during a closed hunting season for that area unless such firearm is unloaded and stored in a motor vehicle so as not to be readily accessible or to possess a handgun during a closed hunting season for that area unless such person possesses a valid weapons carry license issued pursuant to Code Section 16-11-129;
    (2) To possess a loaded firearm other than a handgun, as such term is defined in Code Section 16-11-125.1, in a motor vehicle during a legal open hunting season for that area or to possess a loaded handgun in a motor vehicle during a legal open hunting season for that area unless such person possesses a valid weapons carry license issued pursuant to Code Section 16-11-129; or

(3) To be under the influence of drugs, intoxicating liquors, beers, or wines. The determination of whether any person is under the influence of drugs or intoxicating liquors, beers, or wines may be made in accordance with the provisions of Chapter 3 of this title relating to hunting while under the influence of drugs or alcohol.

(b) It shall be unlawful for any person to fish at any time in any pond or lake on a public fishing area owned or operated by the department which has been posted "closed" by the department for purposes of fisheries management or to take or possess any species or any size of any species or to exceed the creel limit of any species at any time from any pond or lake on a public fishing area which has been posted with a sign which states that that species or size may not be taken or that creel limit exceeded. Creel and size limits posted as permissible must be within the limits set forth in Code Section 27-4-10 and, if applicable, the limits set by the board pursuant to subsection (c) of this Code section.

(c) It shall be unlawful for any person to take in one day or to possess at any one time any number of fish caught from public fishing areas except in compliance with limits set by rule and regulation of the board, which limits shall not be more than the maximum limit for that species set forth in Code Section 27-4-10.

(d) It shall be unlawful for any person to fish or to be present on any public fishing area except in accordance with rules and regulations established by the board for the use of such area. The board shall have the authority to adopt rules and regulations governing methods of fishing; to regulate the operation and use of vessels; to close the area or certain ponds or lakes of the area to vessels; and to regulate other matters that the board deems necessary for the safe operation and sound management of the area.

(e) It shall be unlawful on any public fishing area for any person to drive or otherwise operate a vehicle on any road posted "closed" to vehicular access, to drive around a closed gate or cable blocking a road, or to drive on any road that is not improved in that it is not receiving maintenance for the purpose of vehicular access. It shall be unlawful for any person to park a vehicle at any place within a public fishing area, including upon the right of way of any county, state, or federal highway which traverses the public fishing area, where signs placed at the direction of the commissioner or his or her designee prohibit parking.

(f) It shall be unlawful for any person to camp anywhere on any public fishing area except in those areas designated by appropriate signs as camping areas.

(g) It shall be unlawful for persons under 14 years of age to enter or remain upon any public fishing area unless such person is under adult supervision. It shall be unlawful for any person to cause or knowingly to permit his or her ward who is under 14 years of age to enter or remain upon any public fishing area unless such child or ward is under adult supervision.

(h) It shall be unlawful for any person who has fished at a public fishing area to refuse to allow department personnel to count, measure, and weigh his or her catch.

### O.C.G.A. § 38-3-37 Prohibited actions by government official or employee during declared state of emergency

(a) As used in this Code section, the term:
    (1) "Firearm" means any handgun, rifle, shotgun, or similar device or weapon which will or can be converted to expel a projectile by the action of an explosive or electrical charge.
    (2) "License holder" shall have the same meaning as set forth in Code Section 16-11-125.1.
    (3) "Weapon" shall have the same meaning as set forth in Code Section 16-11-125.1.

(b) No official or employee of the state or any political subdivision thereof, member of the National Guard in the service of the state, or any person operating pursuant to or under color of state law, while acting during or pursuant to a declared state of emergency, shall:
    (1) Temporarily or permanently seize, or authorize the seizure of, any firearm or ammunition or any component thereof the possession of which was not prohibited by law at the time immediately prior to the declaration of a state of emergency, other than as provided by the criminal or forfeiture laws of this state;
    (2) Prohibit possession of any firearm or ammunition or any

component thereof or promulgate any rule, regulation, or order prohibiting possession of any firearm or ammunition or any component thereof if such possession was not otherwise prohibited by law at the time immediately prior to the declaration of a state of emergency;

(3) Prohibit any license holder from carrying any weapon or promulgate any rule, regulation, or order prohibiting such carrying if such carrying was not otherwise prohibited by law at the time immediately prior to the declaration of a state of emergency; or

(4) Require the registration of any firearm.

## O.C.G.A. § 42-5-15
### Crossing of guard lines with weapons, intoxicants, or drugs without consent of warden or superintendent

(a) It shall be unlawful for any person to come inside the guard lines established at any state or county correctional institution with a gun, pistol, or any other weapon or with or under the influence of any intoxicating liquor, amphetamines, biphetamines, or any other hallucinogenic or other drugs, without the knowledge or consent of the warden, superintendent, or his designated representative.

(b) Any person who violates this Code section shall be guilty of a felony and, upon conviction thereof, shall be punished by imprisonment for not less than one year nor more than four years.

## O.C.G.A. § 51-11-9 Immunity from civil liability for threat or use of force in defense of habitation

A person who is justified in threatening or using force against another under the provisions of Code Section 16-3-21, relating to the use of force in defense of self or others, Code Section 16-3-23, relating to the use of force in defense of a habitation, or Code Section 16-3-24, relating to the use of force in defense of property other than a habitation, has no duty to retreat from the use of such force and shall not be held liable to the person against whom the use of force was justified or to any person acting as an accomplice or assistant to such person in any civil action brought as a result of the threat or use of such force.

# APPENDIX B

## SELECTED FEDERAL FORMS

*ATF Form 4473, page 1*

| | OMB No. 1140-0020 |
|---|---|
| **U.S. Department of Justice**<br>Bureau of Alcohol, Tobacco, Firearms and Explosives | |

**Firearms Transaction Record**

| **WARNING:** You may not receive a firearm if prohibited by Federal or State law. The information you provide will be used to determine whether you are prohibited from receiving a firearm. Certain violations of the Gun Control Act, 18 U.S.C. 921 et. seq., are punishable by up to 10 years imprisonment and/or up to a $250,000 fine. | Transferor's/Seller's Transaction Serial Number *(If any)* |
|---|---|

Read the Notices, Instructions, and Definitions on this form. Prepare in original only at the licensed premises *("licensed premises" includes business temporarily conducted from a qualifying gun show or event in the same State in which the licensed premises is located)* unless the transaction qualifies under 18 U.S.C. 922(c). All entries must be handwritten in ink. **"PLEASE PRINT."**

**Section A - Must Be Completed Personally By Transferee/Buyer**

1. Transferee's/Buyer's Full Name *(If legal name contains an initial only, record "IO" after the initial. If no middle initial or name, record "NMN".)*

| Last Name *(Including suffix (e.g., Jr, Sr, II, III))* | First Name | Middle Name |
|---|---|---|

2. Current State of Residence and Address **(U.S. Postal abbreviations are acceptable. Cannot be a post office box.)**

| Number and Street Address | City | County | State | ZIP Code |
|---|---|---|---|---|

| 3. Place of Birth<br>U.S. City and State     -OR-   Foreign Country | 4. Height<br>Ft. ____<br>In. ____ | 5. Weight<br>*(Lbs.)* | 6. Sex<br>☐ Male<br>☐ Female | 7. Birth Date<br>Month   Day   Year |
|---|---|---|---|---|

| 8. Social Security Number *(Optional, but will help prevent misidentification)* | 9. Unique Personal Identification Number *(UPIN)* if applicable *(See Instructions for Question 9.)* |
|---|---|

| 10.a. Ethnicity | 10.b. Race *(In addition to ethnicity, select one or more race in 10.b. Both 10.a. and 10.b. must be answered.)* | |
|---|---|---|
| ☐ Hispanic or Latino | ☐ American Indian or Alaska Native   ☐ Black or African American | ☐ White |
| ☐ Not Hispanic or Latino | ☐ Asian   ☐ Native Hawaiian or Other Pacific Islander | |

| 11. Answer the following questions by checking or marking *"yes"* or *"no"* in the boxes to the right of the questions. | Yes | No |
|---|---|---|
| a. Are you the actual transferee/buyer of the firearm(s) listed on this form? **Warning: You are not the actual transferee/buyer if you are acquiring the firearm(s) on behalf of another person. If you are not the actual transferee/buyer, the licensee cannot transfer the firearm(s) to you. Exception: If you are picking up a repaired firearm(s) for another person, you are *not* required to answer 11.a. and may proceed to question 11.b. (See Instructions for Question 11.a.)** | ☐ | ☐ |
| b. Are you under indictment or information in any court for a **felony**, or any other crime for which the judge could imprison you for more than one year? *(See Instructions for Question 11.b.)* | ☐ | ☐ |
| c. Have you ever been convicted in any court of a **felony**, or any other crime for which the judge could have imprisoned you for more than one year, even if you received a shorter sentence including probation? *(See Instructions for Question 11.c.)* | ☐ | ☐ |
| d. Are you a fugitive from justice? *(See Instructions for Question 11.d.)* | ☐ | ☐ |
| e. Are you an unlawful user of, or addicted to, marijuana or any depressant, stimulant, narcotic drug, or any other controlled substance? **Warning: The use or possession of marijuana remains unlawful under Federal law regardless of whether it has been legalized or decriminalized for medicinal or recreational purposes in the state where you reside.** | ☐ | ☐ |
| f. Have you ever been adjudicated as a mental defective **OR** have you ever been committed to a mental institution? *(See Instructions for Question 11.f.)* | ☐ | ☐ |
| g. Have you been discharged from the Armed Forces under **dishonorable** conditions? | ☐ | ☐ |
| h. Are you subject to a court order restraining you from harassing, stalking, or threatening your child or an intimate partner or child of such partner? *(See Instructions for Question 11.h.)* | ☐ | ☐ |
| i. Have you ever been **convicted** in any court of a misdemeanor crime of domestic violence? *(See Instructions for Question 11.i.)* | ☐ | ☐ |

12.a. Country of Citizenship: *(Check/List more than one, if applicable. Nationals of the United States may check U.S.A.)*
☐ United States of America *(U.S.A)*   ☐ Other Country/Countries *(Specify):*

| | | Yes | No |
|---|---|---|---|
| 12.b. | Have you ever renounced your United States citizenship? | ☐ | ☐ |
| 12.c. | Are you an alien **illegally** or **unlawfully** in the United States? | ☐ | ☐ |
| 12.d.1. | Are you an alien who has been admitted to the United States under a nonimmigrant visa? *(See Instructions for Question 12.d.)* | ☐ | ☐ |
| 12.d.2. | If "yes", do you fall within any of the exceptions stated in the instructions?     ☐ N/A | ☐ | ☐ |

13. If you are an alien, record your U.S.-Issued Alien or Admission number *(AR#, USCIS#, or I94#)*:

| Previous Editions Are Obsolete | **Transferee/Buyer Continue to Next Page** | ATF Form 4473 (5300.9) |
|---|---|---|
| Page 1 of 6 | **STAPLE IF PAGES BECOME SEPARATED** | Revised October 2016 |

## ATF Form 4473, page 2

I certify that my answers in Section A are true, correct, and complete. I have read and understand the Notices, Instructions, and Definitions on ATF Form 4473. I understand that answering "yes" to question 11.a. if I am not the actual transferee/buyer is a crime punishable as a felony under Federal law, and may also violate State and/or local law. I understand that a person who answers "yes" to any of the questions 11.b. through 11.i and/or 12.b. through 12.c. is prohibited from purchasing or receiving a firearm. I understand that a person who answers "yes" to question 12.d.1. is prohibited from receiving or possessing a firearm, unless the person answers "yes" to question 12.d.2. and provides the documentation required in 18.c. I also understand that making any false oral or written statement, or exhibiting any false or misrepresented identification with respect to this transaction, is a crime punishable as a felony under Federal law, and may also violate State and/or local law. I further understand that the repetitive purchase of firearms for the purpose of resale for livelihood and profit without a Federal firearms license is a violation of Federal law. (See Instructions for Question 14.)

| 14. Transferee's/Buyer's Signature | 15. Certification Date |
|---|---|

### Section B - Must Be Completed By Transferor/Seller

16. Type of firearm(s) to be transferred (check or mark all that apply): Handgun / Long Gun (rifles or shotguns) / Other Firearm (frame, receiver, etc. See Instructions for Question 16.)

17. If transfer is at a qualifying gun show or event: Name of Function: ___ City, State: ___

18.a. Identification (e.g., Virginia Driver's license (VA DL) or other valid government-issued photo identification.) (See Instructions for Question 18.a.)

Issuing Authority and Type of Identification | Number on Identification | Expiration Date of Identification (if any) Month Day Year

18.b. Supplemental Government Issued Documentation (if identification document does not show current residence address) (See Instructions for Question 18.b.)

18.c. Exception to the Nonimmigrant Alien Prohibition: If the transferee/buyer answered "YES" to 12.d.2. the transferor/seller must record the type of documentation showing the exception to the prohibition and attach a copy to this ATF Form 4473. (See Instructions for Question 18.c.)

### Questions 19, 20, or 21 Must Be Completed Prior To The Transfer Of The Firearm(s) (See Instructions for Questions 19, 20 and 21.)

19.a. Date the transferee's/buyer's identifying information in Section A was transmitted to NICS or the appropriate State agency: Month Day Year

19.b. The NICS or State transaction number (if provided) was:

19.c. The response initially (first) provided by NICS or the appropriate State agency was: Proceed / Delayed [The firearm(s) may be transferred on ___ if State law permits (optional)] / Denied / Cancelled

19.d. The following response(s) was/were later received from NICS or the appropriate State agency: Proceed ___ (date) / Denied ___ (date) / Cancelled ___ (date) / Overturned / No response was provided within 3 business days.

19.e. (Complete if applicable.) After the firearm was transferred, the following response was received from NICS or the appropriate State agency on: ___ (date). Proceed / Denied / Cancelled

19.f. The name and Brady identification number of the NICS examiner. (Optional) ___ (name) ___ (number)

19.g. Name of FFL Employee Completing NICS check. (Optional)

20. ☐ No NICS check was required because a background check was completed during the NFA approval process on the individual who will receive the NFA firearm(s), as reflected on the approved NFA application. (See Instructions for Question 20.)

21. ☐ No NICS check was required because the transferee/buyer has a valid permit from the State where the transfer is to take place, which qualifies as an exemption to NICS. (See Instructions for Question 21.)

Issuing State and Permit Type | Date of Issuance (if any) | Expiration Date (if any) | Permit Number (if any)

### Section C - Must Be Completed Personally By Transferee/Buyer

If the transfer of the firearm(s) takes place on a different day from the date that the transferee/buyer signed Section A, the transferee/buyer must complete Section C immediately prior to the transfer of the firearm(s). (See Instructions for Question 22 and 23.)

I certify that my answers to the questions in Section A of this form are still true, correct, and complete.

| 22. Transferee's/Buyer's Signature | 23. Recertification Date |
|---|---|

Transferor/Seller Continue to Next Page
**STAPLE IF PAGES BECOME SEPARATED**

Page 2 of 6

ATF Form 4473 (5300.9)
Revised October 2016

## ATF Form 4473, page 3

| | | | | | |
|---|---|---|---|---|---|
| **Section D - Must Be Completed By Transferor /Seller Even If The Firearm(s) is Not Transferred** | | | | | |
| 24.<br>Manufacturer and Importer *(If any) (If the manufacturer and importer are different, the FFL must include both.)* | 25.<br>Model<br>*(If Designated)* | 26.<br>Serial Number | | 27.<br>Type *(See Instructions for Question 27.)* | 28.<br>Caliber or Gauge |
| 1. | | | | | |
| 2. | | | | | |
| 3. | | | | | |
| 4. | | | | | |

**REMINDER - By the Close of Business Complete ATF Form 3310.4 For Multiple Purchases of Handguns Within 5 Consecutive Business Days**

29. Total Number of Firearms Transferred *(Please handwrite by printing e.g., zero, one, two, three, etc. Do not use numerals.)*

30. Check if any part of this transaction is a pawn redemption.
☐ Line Number(s) From Question 24 Above:

31. For Use by Licensee *(See Instructions for Question 31.)*

32. Check if this transaction is to facilitate a private party transfer.
☐ *(See Instructions for Question 32.)*

33. Trade/corporate name and address of transferor/seller and Federal Firearm License Number *(Must contain at least first three and last five digits of FFL Number X-XX-XXXXX.) (Hand stamp may be used.)*

---

**The Person Transferring The Firearm(s) Must Complete Questions 34-37.**
**For Denied/Cancelled Transactions, the Person Who Completed Section B Must Complete Questions 34-36.**

I certify that: (1) I have read and understand the Notices, Instructions, and Definitions on this ATF Form 4473; (2) the information recorded in Sections B and D is true, correct, and complete; and (3) this entire transaction record has been completed at my licensed business premises ("licensed premises" includes business temporarily conducted from a qualifying gun show or event in the same State in which the licensed premises is located) unless this transaction has met the requirements of 18 U.S.C. 922(c). Unless this transaction has been denied or cancelled, I further certify on the basis of — (1) the transferee's/buyer's responses in Section A (and Section C, if applicable); (2) my verification of the identification recorded in question 18 (and my re-verification at the time of transfer, *if Section C was completed*); and (3) State or local law applicable to the firearms business — it is my belief that it is not unlawful for me to sell, deliver, transport, or otherwise dispose of the firearm(s) listed on this form to the person identified in Section A.

| 34. Transferor's/Seller's Name *(Please print)* | 35. Transferor's/Seller's Signature | 36. Transferor's/Seller's Title | 37. Date Transferred |
|---|---|---|---|
| | | | |

### NOTICES, INSTRUCTIONS, AND DEFINITIONS

**Purpose of the Form:** The information and certification on this form are designed so that a person licensed under 18 U.S.C. 923 may determine if he/she may lawfully sell or deliver a firearm to the person identified in Section A, and to alert the transferee/buyer of certain restrictions on the receipt and possession of firearms. The transferor/seller of a firearm must determine the lawfulness of the transaction and maintain proper records of the transaction. Consequently, the transferor/seller must be familiar with the provisions of 18 U.S.C. 921-931 and the regulations in 27 CFR Parts 478 and 479. In determining the lawfulness of the sale or delivery of a rifle or shotgun to a resident of another State, the transferor/seller is presumed to be aware of the applicable State laws and published ordinances in both the transferor's/seller's State and the transferee's/buyer's State. *(See ATF Publication 5300.5, State Laws and Published Ordinances.)*

Generally, ATF Form 4473 must be completed at the licensed business premises when a firearm is transferred over-the-counter. Federal law, 18 U.S.C. 922(c), allows a licensed importer, manufacturer, or dealer to sell a firearm to a nonlicensee who does not appear in person at the licensee's business premises only if the transferee/buyer meets certain requirements. These requirements are set forth in section 922(c), 27 CFR 478.96(b), and ATF Procedure 2013-2.

After the transferor/seller has completed the firearms transaction, he/she must make the completed, original ATF Form 4473 *(which includes the Notices, General Instructions, and Definitions)*, and any supporting documents, part of his/her permanent records. Such Forms 4473 must be retained for at least 20 years and after that period may be submitted to ATF. Filing may be chronological *(by date of disposition)*, alphabetical *(by name of purchaser)*, or numerical *(by transaction serial number)*, as long as all of the transferor's/seller's completed Forms 4473 are filed in the same manner.

FORMS 4473 FOR DENIED/CANCELLED TRANSFERS MUST BE RETAINED: If the transfer of a firearm is denied/cancelled by NICS, or if for any other reason the transfer is not completed after a NICS check is initiated, the licensee must retain the ATF Form 4473 in his/her records for at least 5 years. Forms 4473 with respect to which a sale, delivery, or transfer did not take place shall be separately retained in alphabetical *(by name of transferee)* or chronological *(by date of transferee's certification)* order.

If the transferor/seller or the transferee/buyer discovers that an ATF Form 4473 is incomplete or improperly completed after the firearm has been transferred, and the transferor/seller or the transferee/buyer wishes to correct the omission(s) or error(s), photocopy the inaccurate form and make any necessary additions or revisions to the photocopy. The transferor/seller should only make changes to Sections B and D. The transferee/buyer should only make changes to Section A and C. Whoever made the changes should initial and date the changes. The corrected photocopy should be attached to the original Form 4473 and retained as part of the transferor's/seller's permanent records.

**Exportation of Firearms:** The State or Commerce Departments may require a firearms exporter to obtain a license prior to export. **Warning:** Any person who exports a firearm without proper authorization may be fined not more than $1,000,000 and/or imprisoned for not more than 20 years. See 22 U.S.C. 2778(c).

#### Section A

The transferee/buyer must personally complete Section A of this form and certify *(sign)* that the answers are true, correct, and complete. However, if the transferee/buyer is unable to read and/or write, the answers *(other than the signature)* may be completed by another person, excluding the transferor/seller. Two persons *(other than the transferor/seller)* must then sign as witnesses to the transferee's/buyer's answers and signature/certification in question 14.

Page 3 of 6

ATF Form 4473 (5300.9)
Revised October 2016

## ATF Form 4, page 1

**U.S. Department of Justice**
Bureau of Alcohol, Tobacco, Firearms and Explosives

OMB No. 1140-0014 (06/30/2019)

**Application for Tax Paid Transfer and Registration of Firearm**

**ATF Control Number**

**National Firearms Act Branch**
SUBMIT in DUPLICATE to: Bureau of Alcohol, Tobacco, Firearms and Explosives, P.O. Box 530298, Atlanta, GA 30353-0298

1. Type of Transfer *(Check one)*

☐ $5   ☐ $200

Submit the appropriate tax payment with the application. The tax may be paid by credit or debit card, check, or money order. Please complete item 20. Upon approval of the application, we will affix and cancel the required National Firearms Act stamp. *(See instructions 2b, 2i and 3)*

2a. Transferee's Name and Address *(Include trade name, if any) (See instruction 2d)*

☐ INDIVIDUAL   ☐ TRUST or LEGAL ENTITY

2b. County

3a. Transferor's Name and Address *(Include trade name, if any) (Executors: see instruction 2k)*

3b. e-mail address *(optional)*

3c. Transferor's Telephone *(Area Code and Number)*

3d. If Applicable: Decedent's Name, Address, and Date of Death

3e. Number, Street, City, State and Zip Code of Residence *(or Firearms Business Premises)* If Different from Item 3a.

The above-named and undersigned transferor hereby makes application as required by Section 5812 of the National Firearms Act to transfer and register the firearm described below to the transferee.

4. Description of Firearm *(Complete items a through h) (See instruction 2m)*

| a. Name and Address of Maker, Manufacturer and/or Importer of Firearm | b. Type of Firearm *(See definitions)* | c. Caliber or Gauge | d. Model |
| --- | --- | --- | --- |
| | | | e. Length (Inches) of Barrel:   f. Overall: |
| | | | g. Serial Number |

h. Additional Description or Data Appearing on Firearm *(Attach additional sheet if necessary)*

5. Transferee's Federal Firearms License *(If any)*
*(Give complete 15-digit number) (See instruction 2c)*

| First 6 digits | 2 digits | 2 digits | 5 digits |
| --- | --- | --- | --- |

6. Transferee's Special (Occupational) Tax Status *(If any)*
a. Employer Identification Number   b. Class

7. Transferor's Federal Firearms License *(If any)*

| First 6 digits | 2 digits | 2 digits | 5 digits |
| --- | --- | --- | --- |

8. Transferor's Special (Occupational) Tax Status *(If any)*
a. Employer Identification Number   b. Class

Under Penalties of Perjury, I Declare that I have examined this application, and to the best of my knowledge and belief it is true, correct and complete, and that the transfer of the described firearm to the transferee and receipt and possession of it by the transferee are not prohibited by the provisions of Title 18, United States Code; Chap 44; Title 26, United States Code; Chap 53; or any provisions of State or local law.

9. Signature of Transferor *(Or authorized official)*

10. Name and Title of Authorized Official *(Print or type)*

11. Date

**The Space Below is for the use of the Bureau of Alcohol, Tobacco, Firearms and Explosives**

By Authority of The Director, This Application Has Been Examined, and the Transfer and Registration of the Firearm Described Herein and the Interstate Movement of that Firearm, When Applicable to the Transferee are:

Stamp Denomination

☐ Approved *(With the following conditions, if any)*

☐ Disapproved *(For the following reasons)*

Signature of Authorized ATF Official

Date

Previous Editions are Obsolete

ATF Copy

ATF E-Form 4 (5320.4)
Revised May 2016

## ATF Form 4, page 2

**Transferee Certification**

12. Law Enforcement Notification *(See instruction 2f)*

The transferee is to provide notification of the proposed acquisition and possession of the firearm described on this Form 4 by providing a copy of the completed form to the chief law enforcement officer in the agency identified below:

Agency or Department Name | Name and Title of Official

Address (Street address or P.O. Box, City, State and Zip Code) to which sent (mailed or delivered))

**Information for the Chief Law Enforcement Officer**

This form provides notification of the transferee's intent to acquire and possess a National Firearms Act (NFA) firearm. No action on your part is required. However, should you have information that may disqualify this person from acquiring or possessing a firearm, please contact the NFA Branch at (304) 616-4500 or NFA @atf.gov. A "Yes" answer to items 14.a through 14.h or 16.a or 16.b could disqualify a person from acquiring or possessing a firearm. Also, ATF will not approve an application if the transfer or possession of the firearm is in violation of State or local law.

13. Transferee Necessity Statement *(See instruction 2e)*

I, _____ , have a reasonable necessity to possess the machinegun, short-barreled rifle,
   *(Name and Title of Transferee)*

short-barreled shotgun, or destructive device described on this application for the following reason(s) _____

and my possession of the device or weapon would be consistent with public safety (18 U.S.C. § 922(b) (4) and 27 CFR § 478.98).

Transferee Questions (Complete Only When Transferee is An Individual)

14. Answer questions 14.a. through 14.h. Answer questions 16 through 17 if applicable. For any "Yes" answer the transferee shall provide details on a separate sheet. *(See instruction 7b and definitions)*

| | | Yes | No | 15. Photograph |
|---|---|---|---|---|
| a. | Are you under indictment or information in any court for a felony, or any other crime, for which the judge could imprison you for more than one year? *(See definition 1m)* | | | |
| b. | Have you ever been convicted in any court for a felony, or any other crime, for which the judge could have imprisoned you for more than one year, even if you received a shorter sentence including probation? *(See definition 1m)* | | | Affix Recent Photograph Here *(Approximately 2" x 2")* *(See instruction 2g)* |
| c. | Are you a fugitive from justice? *(See definitions 1s)* | | | |
| d. | Are you an unlawful user of, or addicted to, marijuana or any depressant, stimulant, narcotic drug, or any other controlled substance? **Warning: The use or possession of marijuana remains unlawful under Federal law regardless of whether it has been legalized or decriminalized for medicinal or recreational purposes in the state where you reside.** | | | |
| e. | Have you ever been adjudicated as a mental defective OR have you ever been committed to a mental institution? *(See definitions 1n and 1o)* | | | |
| f. | Have you been discharged from the Armed Forces under dishonorable conditions? | | | |
| g. | Are you subject to a court order restraining you from harassing, stalking, or threatening your child or an intimate partner or child of such partner? *(See definition 1p)* | | | |
| h. | Have you ever been convicted in any court of a misdemeanor crime of domestic violence? *(See definition 1q)* | | | |

16a. Country of Citizenship *(Check/List more than one, if applicable. Nationals of the United States may check U.S.A.) (See definition 1r)*

☐ United States of America    ☐ Other Country/Countries *(specify):* _____

| | | Yes | No |
|---|---|---|---|
| b. | Have you ever renounced your United States citizenship? | | |
| c. | Are you an alien Illegally or unlawfully in the United States? | | |
| d.1. | Are you an alien who has been admitted to the United States under a nonimmigrant visa? | | |
| d.2. | If "yes", do you fall within any of the exceptions stated in the instructions? Attach the documentation to the application | ☐ N/A | |

17. If you are an alien, record your U.S.-Issued Alien or Admission number (AR#, USCIS#, or 194#): _____

**CERTIFICATION:** Under penalties imposed by 18 U.S.C. § 924 and 26 U.S.C. § 5861, I certify that, upon submission of this form to ATF, a completed copy of this form will be directed to the chief law enforcement officer (CLEO) shown in item 12, that the statements, as applicable, contained in this certification, and any attached documents in support thereof, are true and correct to the best of my knowledge and belief. NOTE: See instructions 2.d(2) and 2.d(3) for the items to be completed depending on the type of transferee.

Signature of Transferee                              Date

ATF Copy

ATF E-Form 4 (5320.4)
Revised May 2016

## ATF Form 4, page 3

18. Number of Responsible Persons (see definitions) associated with the transferee trust or legal entity _____

19. Provide the full name (printed or typed) below for each Responsible Person associated with the applicant trust or legal entity (if there are more Responsible Persons than can be listed on the form, attach a separate sheet listing the additional Responsible Person(s)). Please note that a completed Form 5320.23, National Firearms Act (NFA) Responsible Person Questionnaire, must be submitted with the Form 4 application for each Responsible Person.

Full Name

Full Name

_____

_____

_____

_____

_____

_____

20. **Method of Payment** (Check one) (See Instruction 2i) (if paying by credit/debit card, complete the sections below)

☐ Check (Enclosed)   ☐ Cashier's Check or Money Order (Enclosed)   ☐ Visa   ☐ Mastercard   ☐ American Express   ☐ Discover   ☐ Diners Club

| Credit/Debit Card Number (No dashes) | Name as Printed on the Credit/Debit Card | Expiration Date (Month & year) |
|---|---|---|

| Credit/Debit Card Billing Address: | Address: | | |
|---|---|---|---|
| | City: | State: | Zip Code: |
| | | | Total Amount: $ |

I Authorize ATF to Charge my Credit/Debit Card the Tax Amount.

_____          _____
Signature of Cardholder                                    Date

Your credit/debit card will be charged the above stated amount upon receipt of the application. The charge will be reflected on your credit/debit card statement. In the event your application is NOT approved, the above amount will be credited to the credit/debit card noted above.

**Important Information for Currently Registered Firearms**

If you are the current registrant of the firearm described on this form, please note the following information.

**Estate Procedures:** For procedures regarding the transfer of firearms in an estate resulting from the death of the registrant identified in item 2a, the executor should contact the NFA Branch, Bureau of Alcohol, Tobacco, Firearms and Explosives, 244 Needy Road, Martinsburg, WV 25405.

**Change of Address:** Unless currently licensed under the Gun Control Act, the registrant shall notify the NFA Branch, Bureau of Alcohol, Tobacco, Firearms, and Explosives, 244 Needy Road, Martinsburg, WV 25405, in writing, of any change to the address in item 2a.

**Change of Description:** The registrant shall notify the NFA Branch, Bureau of Alcohol, Tobacco, Firearms and Explosives, 244 Needy Road, Martinsburg, WV 25405, in writing, of any change to the description of the firearm(s) in item 4.

**Interstate Movement:** If the firearm identified in item 4 is a **machinegun, short-barreled rifle, short-barreled shotgun,** or **destructive device,** the registrant may be required by 18 U.S.C. § 922(a)(4) to obtain permission from ATF prior to any transportation in interstate or foreign commerce. ATF E-Form 5320.20 can be used to request this permission.

**Restrictions on Possession:** Any restriction (see approval block on face of form) on the possession of the firearm identified in item 4 continues with the further transfer of the firearm.

**Persons Prohibited from Possessing Firearms:** If the registrant becomes prohibited from possessing a firearm, please contact the NFA Branch for procedures on how to dispose of the firearm.

**Proof of Registration:** A person possessing a firearm registered as required by the NFA shall retain proof of registration which shall be made available to any ATF officer upon request.

**Paperwork Reduction Act Notice**

This form meets the clearance requirements of the Paperwork Reduction Act of 1995. The information you provide is used in applying to transfer serviceable firearms taxpaid. Data is used to identify transferor, transferee, and firearm, and to ensure legality for transfer under Federal, State and local laws. The furnishing of this information is mandatory (26 U.S.C. § 5812).

The estimated average burden associated with this collection of information is 3.78 hours per respondent or recordkeeper, depending on individual circumstances. Comments concerning the accuracy of this burden estimate and suggestion for reducing this burden should be addressed to Reports Management Officer, Information Technology Coordination Staff, Bureau of Alcohol, Tobacco, Firearms and Explosives, Washington, DC 20226.

An agency may not conduct or sponsor, and a person is not required to respond to, a collection of information unless it displays a currently valid OMB control number.

ATF Copy

ATF E-Form 4 (5320.4)
Revised May 2016

## ATF Form 1, page 1

U.S. Department of Justice
Bureau of Alcohol, Tobacco, Firearms and Explosives

OMB No. 1140-0011 (06/30/2019)

# Application to Make and Register a Firearm

**ATF Control Number**

**To:** National Firearms Act Branch, Bureau of Alcohol, Tobacco, Firearms and Explosives, P.O. Box 530298, Atlanta, GA 30353-0298

*(Submit in duplicate. See instructions attached.)*

As required by Sections 5821(b), 5822, and 5841 of the National Firearms Act, Title 26 U.S.C., Chapter 53, the undersigned hereby submits application to make and register the firearm described below.

**1.** Type of Application *(Check one)*

2. Application is made by:

☐ INDIVIDUAL ☐ TRUST or LEGAL ENTITY ☐ GOVERNMENT ENTITY

3a. Trade name *(If any)*

☐ a. Tax Paid. Submit your tax payment of $200 with the application.. The tax may be paid by credit or debit card, check, or money order. Please complete item 17. Upon approval of the application, we will affix and cancel the required National Firearms Act Stamp. *(See instruction 2c and 3)*

3b. Applicant's name and mailing address *(Type or print below and between the dots) (See instruction 2d)*

• •

☐ b. Tax Exempt because firearm is being made on behalf of the United States, or any department, independent establishment, or agency thereof.

3c. If P.O. Box is shown above, street address must be given here

☐ c. Tax Exempt because firearm is being made by or on behalf of any State or possession of the United States, or any political subdivision thereof, or any official police organization of such a government entity engaged in criminal investigations.

3d. County | 3e. Telephone area code and number | 3f. e-mail address (optional)

**4** Description of Firearm *(complete items a through k) (See instruction 2j)*

a. Name and Address of Original Manufacturer and/or Importer of Firearm *(if any)*

b. Type of Firearm to be made *(See definition 1c) If a destructive device, complete item 4j*

c. Caliber or Gauge *(Specify one)*

d. Model

Length *(Inches)* | e. Of Barrel: | f. Overall

g. Serial Number

h. Additional Description *(Include all numbers and other identifying data to include maker's name, city and state which will appear on the firearm) (use additional sheet if necessary)*

i. State Why You Intend To Make Firearm *(Use additional sheet if necessary)*

j. Type of destructive device (check one box): ☐ Firearm ☐ Explosives *(If the Explosives box is checked, complete item 5 and see instruction 2l)*

If an explosive type destructive device, identify the type of explosive(s):

k. Is this firearm being reactivated? ☐ Yes ☐ No *(See definition 1k)*

5. Applicant's Federal Firearms License *(If any)* or Explosives License or Permit Number

*(Give complete 15-digit Number)*

6. Special *(Occupational)* Tax Status *(If applicable) (See definitions)*

a. Employer Identification Number | b. Class

**Under Penalties of Perjury, I Declare** that I have examined this application, including accompanying documents, and to the best of my knowledge and belief it is true, accurate and complete and the making and possession of the firearm described above would not constitute a violation of Title 18, U.S.C., Chapter 44, Title 26, U.S.C., Chapter 53; or any provisions of State or local law.

7. Signature of Applicant | 8. Name and Title of Authorized Official | 9. Date

**The space below is for the use of the Bureau of Alcohol, Tobacco, Firearms, and Explosives**

By authority of the Director, Bureau of Alcohol, Tobacco, Firearms and Explosives, this application has been examined and the applicant's making and registration of the firearms described above is:

☐ Approved *(With the following conditions, if any)*

☐ Disapproved *(For the following reasons)*

Authorized ATF Official | Date

Previous Editions are Obsolete

ATF Copy

ATF E-Form 1 (5320.1) Revised May 2016

## ATF Form 1, page 2

**MAKER'S CERTIFICATION** *(not completed by a GOVERNMENT ENTITY)*

**10. Law Enforcement Notification** *(See instruction 2g)*

Each applicant is to provide notification of the proposed making and possession of the firearm described on this Form 1 by providing a copy of the completed form to the chief law enforcement officer in the agency identified below:

Agency or Department Name                                    Name and Title of Official

Address (Street address or P.O. Box, City, State and Zip Code) to which sent (mailed or delivered)

### Information for the Chief Law Enforcement Officer

This form provides notification of the applicant's intent to make and register a National Firearms Act (NFA) firearm. No action on your part is required. However, should you have information that may disqualify this person from making or possessing a firearm, please contact the NFA Branch at (304) 616-4500 or NFA@atf.gov. A "Yes" answer to items 11.a through 11.h or 13.b or 13.c could disqualify a person from acquiring or possessing a firearm. Also, ATF will not approve an application if the making or possession of the firearm is in violation of State or local law.

**Maker's Questions** *(complete only when the maker is an individual)*

A maker who is an individual must complete this Section.

11. Answer questions 11.a. through 11.h. Answer questions 13 and 14, if applicable. For any "Yes" answer the applicant shall provide details on a separate sheet. *(See instruction 7c and definitions)*

|  | Yes | No | 12. Photograph |
|---|---|---|---|
| a. Are you under indictment or information in any court for a felony, or any other crime, for which the judge could imprison you for more than one year? *(See definition 1n)* | ○ | ○ | |
| b. Have you ever been convicted in any court for a felony, or any other crime, for which the judge could have imprisoned you for more than one year, even if you received a shorter sentence including probation? *(See definition 1o)* | ○ | ○ | |
| c. Are you a fugitive from justice? *(See definition 1t)* | ○ | ○ | Affix |
| d. Are you an unlawful user of, or addicted to, marijuana or any depressant, stimulant, narcotic drug, or any other controlled substance? **Warning: The use or possession of marijuana remains unlawful under Federal law regardless of whether it has been legalized or decriminalized for medicinal or recreational purposes in the state where you reside.** | ○ | ○ | Recent Photograph Here *(Approximately 2" x 2")* *(See instruction 2e)* |
| e. Have you ever been adjudicated as a mental defective **OR** have you ever been committed to a mental institution? *(See definition 1o and 1p)* | ○ | ○ | |
| f. Have you been discharged from the Armed Forces under **dishonorable** conditions? | ○ | ○ | |
| g. Are you subject to a court order restraining you from harassing, stalking, or threatening your child or an intimate partner or child of such a partner? *(See definition 1q)* | ○ | ○ | |
| h. Have you ever been convicted in any court of a misdemeanor crime of domestic violence? *(See definition 1r)* | ○ | ○ | |

13a. Country of Citizenship: *(Check/List more than one, if applicable. Nationals of the United States may check U.S.A.) (See definition 1s)*

☐ United States of America      ☐ Other Country/Countries *(specify)*: _____

|  | Yes | No |
|---|---|---|
| b. Have you ever renounced your United States citizenship? | ○ | ○ |
| c. Are you an alien illegally or unlawfully in the United States? | ○ | ○ |
| d.1. Are you an alien who has been admitted to the United States under a nonimmigrant visa? | ○ | ○ |
| d.2. If "yes", do you fall within any of the exceptions stated in the instructions? Attach the documentation to the application | ☐ N/A | ○ | ○ |

14. If you are an alien, record your U.S.-Issued Alien or Admission number (AR#, USCIS#, or I94#): _____

**CERTIFICATION:** Under penalties imposed by 18 U.S.C. § 924 and 26 U.S.C. § 5861, I certify that, upon submission of this form to ATF, a completed copy of this form will be directed to the chief law enforcement officer (CLEO) shown in item 10, that the statements, as applicable, contained in this certification, and any attached documents in support thereof, are true and correct to the best of my knowledge and belief. NOTE: See instructions 2.d(2) and 2.d(3) for the items to be completed depending on the type of applicant.

Signature of Maker                                    Date

ATF Copy

ATF E-Form 1 (5320.1)
Revised May 2016

## ATF Form 1, page 3

15. Number of Responsible Persons (*see definitions*) associated with the applicant trust or legal entity _____

16. Provide the full name (printed or typed) below for each Responsible Person associated with the applicant trust or legal entity (if there are more Responsible Persons than can be listed on the form, attach a separate sheet listing the additional Responsible Person(s)). Please note that a completed Form 5320.23, National Firearms Act (NFA) Responsible Person Questionnaire, must be submitted with the Form 1 application for each Responsible Person.

Full Name                                                      Full Name

_____                              _____

_____                              _____

_____                              _____

17. **Method of Payment** (*Check one*) (*See instruction 2h*) (*if paying by credit/debit card, complete the sections below*)

☐ Check (*Enclosed*)   ☐ Cashier's Check or Money Order (*Enclosed*)   ☐ Visa   ☐ Mastercard   ☐ American Express   ☐ Discover   ☐ Diners Club

| Credit/Debit Card Number (*No dashes*) | | Name as Printed on the Credit/Debit Card | Expiration Date (*Month & year*) |
|---|---|---|---|
| Credit/Debit Card Billing Address: | Address: | | |
| | City: | State: | Zip Code: |
| | | | Total Amount: $ |

I Authorize ATF to Charge my Credit/Debit Card the Above Amount.

_____                              _____
Signature of Cardholder                                               Date

Your credit/debit card will be charged the above stated amount upon receipt of your application. The charge will be reflected on your credit/debit card statement. In the event your application is NOT approved, the above amount will be credited to the credit/debit card noted above.

### Important Information for Currently Registered Firearms

If you are the current registrant of the firearm described on this form, please note the following information.

**Estate Procedures:** For procedures regarding the transfer of firearms in an estate resulting from the death of the registrant identified in item 3b, the executor should contact the NFA Branch, Bureau of ATF, 244 Needy Road, Martinsburg, WV 25405.

**Interstate Movement:** If the firearm identified in item 4 is a **machinegun, short-barreled rifle, short-barreled shotgun,** or **destructive device,** the registrant may be required by 18 U.S.C. § 922(a)(4) to obtain permission from ATF prior to any transportation in interstate or foreign commerce. ATF E-Form 5320.20 can be used to request this permission.

**Change of Description or Address:** The registrant shall notify the NFA Branch, Bureau of Alcohol, Tobacco, Firearms and Explosives, 244 Needy Road, Martinsburg, WV 25405, in writing, of any change to the description of the firearm in Item 4, or any change to the address of the registrant.

**Restrictions on Possession:** Any restriction (*see approval block on face of form*) on the possession of the firearm identified in item 4 continues with the further transfer of the firearm.

**Persons Prohibited from Possessing Firearms:** If the registrant becomes prohibited from possessing a firearm, please contact the NFA Branch for procedures on how to dispose of the firearm.

**Proof of Registration:** A person possessing a firearm registered as required by the NFA shall retain proof of registration which shall be made available to any ATF officer upon request.

### Paperwork Reduction Act Notice

This form is in accordance with the Paperwork Reduction Act of 1995. The information you provide is used to establish that the applicant's making and possession of the firearm would be in conformance with Federal, State, and local law. The data is used as proof of lawful registration of a firearm to the manufacturer. The furnishing of this information is mandatory (*26 U.S.C. § 5822*).

The estimated average burden associated with this collection of information is 4.0 hours per respondent or recordkeeper, depending on individual circumstances. Comments concerning the accuracy of this burden estimate and suggestion for reducing this burden should be addressed to Reports Management Officer, Information Technology Coordination Staff, Bureau of Alcohol, Tobacco, Firearms and Explosives, Washington, DC 20226.

An agency may not conduct or sponsor, and a person is not required to respond to, a collection of information unless it displays a currently valid OMB control number.

ATF Copy

ATF E-Form 1 (5320.1)
Revised May 2016

## ATF Form 5320.23, page 1

---

**U.S. Department of Justice**
Bureau of Alcohol, Tobacco, Firearms and Explosives

OMB No. 1140-0107 (06/30/2019)

**National Firearms Act *(NFA)***
**Responsible Person Questionnaire**

Complete the form in duplicate. The ATF copy of the form, with fingerprints on Form FD-258 and photograph, will be submitted with the ATF Form 1, 4, or 5 (to the address shown on the specific form) and the other copy will be directed to the responsible person's chief law enforcement officer. *(See Instructions)*

1. Please check the appropriate box to indicate with which ATF form this questionnaire will be submitted.

☐ ATF Form 1    ☐ ATF Form 4    ☐ ATF Form 5

2. Name and Address of Applicant or Transferee *(as shown on the ATF Form 1, 4 or 5) (see instruction 2)*

| 3a. Name and Home Address of Responsible Person | 3b. Telephone *(Area code and Number)* |
| | 3c. e-mail address *(optional)* |
| | 3d. Other names used *(including maiden name)* |

4a. Type of Firearm *(see definition 5)*

3e. Photograph

4b. Name and Address of Maker, Manufacturer and/or Importer of Firearm

Affix recent
Photograph Here

*(Approximately 2" x 2")*
*(See instruction 3b)*

| 4c. Firearm Model | 4d. Caliber or Gauge | 4e. Firearm Serial Number |

5. Law Enforcement Notification *(See instruction 5)*

As a responsible person (see definition 4) of the trust or legal entity identified in Item 2 of this form, I am required to provide notification of the proposed making or acquisition and possession of the firearm described in item 4 of this form by providing a copy of the completed form to the chief law enforcement officer (CLEO) in the agency identified below:

Agency or Department Name      Name and Title of Official

Address (Street address or P.O. Box, City, State and Zip Code) to which sent (mailed or delivered)

---

**Information for the Chief Law Enforcement Officer**

This form provides notification of the maker or transferee's intent to make or acquire and possess a National Firearms Act (NFA) firearm. No action on your part is required. However, should you have information that may disqualify this person from making or possessing a firearm, please contact the NFA Branch at (304) 616-4500 or NFA@atf.gov. A "Yes" answer to items 6h or item 7b or 7c could disqualify a person from acquiring or possessing a firearm. Also, ATF may not approve an application if the transfer or possession of the firearm would be in violation of State or local law.

ATF Copy

ATF E-Form 5320.23
Revised May 2016

# ATF Form 5320.23, page 2

6. Answer questions 6.a through 6.h. Answer questions 7 and 8 if applicable. For any "Yes" answer the transferee shall provide details on a separate sheet. *(See definitions 8-12)*

| | Yes | No |
|---|---|---|
| a. Are you under indictment or information in any court for a felony, or any other crime, for which the judge could imprison you for more than one year? *(See definition 8)* | ○ | ○ |
| b. Have you ever been convicted in any court for a felony, or any other crime, for which the judge could have imprisoned you for more than one year, even if you received a shorter sentence including probation? *(See definition 8)* | ○ | ○ |
| c. Are you a fugitive from justice? *(See definition 13)* | ○ | ○ |
| d. Are you an unlawful user of, or addicted to, marijuana or any depressant, stimulant, narcotic drug, or any other controlled substance? **Warning: The use or possession of marijuana remains unlawful under Federal law regardless of whether is has been legalized or decriminalized for medicinal or recreational purposes in the state where you reside.** | ○ | ○ |
| e. Have you ever been adjudicated as a mental defective **OR** have you ever been committed to a mental institution? *(See definitions 9 and 10)* | ○ | ○ |
| f. Have you been discharged from the Armed Forces under **dishonorable** conditions? | ○ | ○ |
| g. Are you subject to a court order restraining you from harassing, stalking, or threatening your child or an intimate partner or child of such partner? *(See definition 11)* | ○ | ○ |
| h. Have you ever been convicted in any court of a misdemeanor crime of domestic violence? *(See definition 14)* | ○ | ○ |

7a. Country of Citizenship: *(Check/List more than one, if applicable. Nationals of the United States may check U.S.A.) (See definition 12)*

☐ United States of America     ☐ Other Country/Countries (specify): _____

| | Yes | No |
|---|---|---|
| b. Have you ever renounced your United States citizenship? | ○ | ○ |
| c. Are you an alien illegally or unlawfully in the United States? | ○ | ○ |
| d.1. Are you an alien who has been admitted to the United States under a nonimmigrant visa? | ○ | ○ |
| d.2. If "yes", do you fall within any of the exceptions stated in the instructions? Attach the documentation to the questionnaire    ☐ N/A | ○ | ○ |

8. If you are an alien, record your U.S.-Issued Alien or Admission number (AR#, USCIS#, or 194#): _____

**CERTIFICATION:** Under penalties imposed by 18 U.S.C. § 924 and 26 U.S.C. § 5861, I certify that, upon submission of this form to ATF, a completed copy of this form will be directed to the chief law enforcement officer (CLEO) shown in item 5, that the statements contained in this certification, and any attached documents in support thereof, are true and correct to the best of my knowledge and belief.

_____     _____
Signature of Responsible Person           Date

### Instructions

1. Completion: Each responsible person (see definition 4) of a trust or legal entity seeking to make or acquire a National Firearms Act *(NFA)* firearm shall complete this form in duplicate. (see instruction 9)
   a. Each responsible person must submit his/her fingerprints and photograph with this form *(see below)*.
   b. Please note that this form is not required when the applicant on Form 1, 4 or 5 is an individual.
2. Item 2- Enter the name, trade name *(if any)* and address of the trust or legal entity identified on the Form 1 (items 3a and b); Form 4 *(item 2a)*; or Form 5 *(item 2a)*
3. Item 3- Responsible Person information
   a. Provide the information for the responsible person in items 3a through 3e.
   b. Item 3e - Photograph: The responsible person shall attach, in item 3e on the ATF copy of the form only, a 2-inch by 2-inch frontal view photograph taken within one year prior to the date of the filing of the form. Item 3c is obscured on the CLEO copy.
4. Firearm information
   a. Type of NFA firearm: see definition 5 and as identified in item 4b of Form 1, 4, or 5
   b. Name of maker, manufacturer and/or importer: as identified in item 4a of Form 1, 4, or 5
   c. Firearm Model: identified in item 4d of Form 1, 4, or 5
   d. Caliber or Gauge: identified in item 4c of Form 1, 4 or 5
   e. Firearm Serial Number: identified in item 4g of Form 1, 4 or 5. Item 4e is obscured on the CLEO copy.
5. Item 5- Law Enforcement Notification: Each responsible person must provide a notification on this form of the proposed making or acquisition of an NFA firearm to his/her chief law enforcement officer having jurisdiction where the responsible person is located. The chief law enforcement officer is considered to be the Chief of Police; the Sheriff; the Head of the State Police; or a State or local district attorney or prosecutor.
6. Complete items 6 through 8
7. Fingerprints: The responsible person shall submit, in duplicate with the ATF copy of this form, his or her fingerprints on FBI Form FD-258 and the fingerprints must be clear for accurate classification and taken by someone properly equipped to take them. No fingerprints are required with the copy of the form sent to the chief law enforcement officer.
8. State or Local Permit: If the State in which the responsible person resides requires the responsible person to have a State or Local permit or licensee, a copy of the permit or license must be submitted with this form.
9. Disposition: The ATF copy of the form, with the fingerprints and photograph, shall be submitted with the ATF Form 1, 4 or 5. The other copy shall be directed to the responsible person's chief law enforcement officer identified in item 5 of this form.
10. Sign and date the form. The signature must be original.

ATF Copy

ATF E-Form 5320.23
Revised May 2016

## ATF Form 5320.23, page 3

**U.S. Department of Justice**
Bureau of Alcohol, Tobacco, Firearms and Explosives

OMB No. 1140-0107 (06/30/2019)

**National Firearms Act *(NFA)***
**Responsible Person Questionnaire**

Complete the form in duplicate. The ATF copy of the form, with fingerprints on Form FD-258 and photograph, will be submitted with the ATF Form 1, 4, or 5 (to the address shown on the specific form) and the other copy will be directed to the responsible person's chief law enforcement officer. *(See Instructions)*

1. Please check the appropriate box to indicate with which ATF form this questionnaire will be submitted.
   ○ ATF Form 1    ○ ATF Form 4    ○ ATF Form 5

2. Name and Address of Applicant or Transferee *(as shown on the ATF Form 1, 4 or 5) (see instruction 2)*

| 3a. Name and Home Address of Responsible Person | 3b. Telephone *(Area code and Number)* |
|---|---|
| | 3c. e-mail address *(optional)* |
| | 3d. Other names used *(including maiden name)* |

4a. Type of Firearm *(see definition 5)*

4b. Name and Address of Maker, Manufacturer and/or Importer of Firearm

| 4c. Firearm Model | 4d. Caliber or Gauge |
|---|---|

5. Law Enforcement Notification *(See instruction 5)*

As a responsible person (see definition 4) of the trust or legal entity identified in Item 2 of this form, I am required to provide notification of the proposed making or acquisition and possession of the firearm described in item 4 of this form by providing a copy of the completed form to the chief law enforcement officer (CLEO) in the agency identified below:

Agency or Department Name                     Name and Title of Official

Address (Street address or P.O. Box, City, State and Zip Code) to which sent (mailed or delivered)

**Information for the Chief Law Enforcement Officer**

This form provides notification of the maker or transferee's intent to make or acquire and possess a National Firearms Act (NFA) firearm. No action on your part is required. However, should you have information that may disqualify this person from making or possessing a firearm, please contact the NFA Branch at (304) 616-4500 or NFA@atf.gov. A "Yes" answer to items 6h or item 7b or 7c could disqualify a person from acquiring or possessing a firearm. Also, ATF may not approve an application if the transfer or possession of the firearm would be in violation of State or local law.

CLEO Copy

ATF E-Form 5320.23
Revised May 2016

## ATF Form 5320.23, page 4

6. Answer questions 6.a through 6.h. Answer questions 7 and 8 if applicable. For any "Yes" answer the transferee shall provide details on a separate sheet. *(See definitions 8-12)*

| | Yes | No |
|---|---|---|
| a. Are you under indictment or information in any court for a felony, or any other crime, for which the judge could imprison you for more than one year? *(See definition 8)* | O | O |
| b. Have you ever been convicted in any court for a felony, or any other crime, for which the judge could have imprisoned you for more than one year, even if you received a shorter sentence including probation? *(See definition 8)* | O | O |
| c. Are you a fugitive from justice? *(See definition 13)* | O | O |
| d. Are you an unlawful user of, or addicted to, marijuana or any depressant, stimulant, narcotic drug, or any other controlled substance? **Warning: The use or possession of marijuana remains unlawful under Federal law regardless of whether is has been legalized or decriminalized for medicinal or recreational purposes in the state where you reside.** | O | O |
| e. Have you ever been adjudicated as a mental defective **OR** have you ever been committed to a mental institution? *(See definitions 9 and 10)* | O | O |
| f. Have you been discharged from the Armed Forces under **dishonorable** conditions? | O | O |
| g. Are you subject to a court order restraining you from harassing, stalking, or threatening your child or an intimate partner or child of such partner? *(See definition 11)* | O | O |
| h. Have you ever been convicted in any court of a misdemeanor crime of domestic violence? *(See definition 14)* | O | O |

7a. Country of Citizenship: *(Check/List more than one, if applicable. Nationals of the United States may check U.S.A.) (See definition 12)*

O United States of America     O Other Country/Countries (specify): _____

| | Yes | No |
|---|---|---|
| b. Have you ever renounced your United States citizenship? | O | O |
| c. Are you an alien illegally or unlawfully in the United States? | O | O |
| d.1. Are you an alien who has been admitted to the United States under a nonimmigrant visa? | O | O |
| d.2. If "yes", do you fall within any of the exceptions stated in the instructions? Attach the documentation to the questionnaire    O N/A | O | O |

8. If you are an alien, record your U.S. -Issued Alien or Admission number (AR#, USCIS#, or 194#): _____

**CERTIFICATION: Under penalties imposed by 18 U.S.C. § 924 and 26 U.S.C. § 5861, I certify that, upon submission of this form to ATF, a completed copy of this form will be directed to the chief law enforcement officer (CLEO) shown in item 5, that the statements contained in this certification, and any attached documents in support thereof, are true and correct to the best of my knowledge and belief.**

_____     _____
Signature of Responsible Person                         Date

### Instructions

1. Completion: Each responsible person (see definition 4) of a trust or legal entity seeking to make or acquire a National Firearms Act *(NFA)* firearm shall complete this form in duplicate. (see instruction 9)
   a. Each responsible person must submit his/her fingerprints and photograph with this form *(see below)*.
   b. Please note that this form is not required when the applicant on Form 1, 4 or 5 is an individual.
2. Item 2- Enter the name, trade name *(if any)* and address of the trust or legal entity identified on the Form 1 (items 3a and b); Form 4 *(item 2a)*; or Form 5 *(item 2a)*
3. Item 3- Responsible Person information
   a. Provide the information for the responsible person in items 3a through 3e.
   b. Item 3e - Photograph: The responsible person shall attach, in item 3e on the ATF copy of the form only, a 2-inch by 2-inch frontal view photograph taken within one year prior to the date of the filing of the form. Item 3c is obscured on the CLEO copy.
4. Firearm information
   a. Type of NFA firearm: see definition 5 and as identified in item 4b of Form 1, 4, or 5
   b. Name of maker, manufacturer and/or importer: as identified in item 4a of Form 1, 4, or 5
   c. Firearm Model: identified in item 4d of Form 1, 4, or 5
   d. Caliber or Gauge: identified in item 4c of Form 1, 4 or 5
   e. Firearm Serial Number: identified in item 4g of Form 1, 4 or 5. Item 4e is obscured on the CLEO copy.
5. Item 5- Law Enforcement Notification: Each responsible person must provide a notification on this form of the proposed making or acquisition of an NFA firearm to his/her chief law enforcement officer having jurisdiction where the responsible person is located. The chief law enforcement officer is considered to be the Chief of Police; the Sheriff; the Head of the State Police; or a State or local district attorney or prosecutor.
6. Complete items 6 through 8
7. Fingerprints: The responsible person shall submit, in duplicate with the ATF copy of this form, his or her fingerprints on FBI Form FD-258 and the fingerprints must be clear for accurate classification and taken by someone properly equipped to take them. No fingerprints are required with the copy of the form sent to the chief law enforcement officer.
8. State or Local Permit: If the State in which the responsible person resides requires the responsible person to have a State or Local permit or license, a copy of the permit or license must be submitted with this form.
9. Disposition: The ATF copy of the form, with the fingerprints and photograph, shall be submitted with the ATF Form 1, 4 or 5. The other copy shall be directed to the responsible person's chief law enforcement officer identified in item 5 of this form.
10. Sign and date the form. The signature must be original.

CLEO Copy                                ATF E-Form 5320.23
                                                  Revised May 2016

# ABOUT THE ATTORNEY AUTHORS

### MATTHEW KILGO
CO-AUTHOR

Matthew Kilgo is an independent firearms program attorney for U.S. Law Shield Legal Defense Program and a partner in Hawkins Spizman Kilgo, a criminal defense firm in Atlanta, Georgia. Matt earned his bachelor's degree from Auburn University in 1996, and graduated from the Georgia State College of Law in 1999, beginning practice as an attorney that same year. Matt's entire legal career has been focused in criminal law, first as a prosecutor, then as legal counsel for the Recording Industry Association of America, and for almost a decade now, in criminal defense. Matt has trained the public in almost 200 Second Amendment/Use of Force seminars, has been a guest speaker nationwide on law enforcement matters, and works in both state and federal courts to protect his clients' rights in a number of different types of criminal cases, but his true passion is in gun-rights issues. He is a baseball coach, an assistant scoutmaster, and loves to teach his sons to shoot.

### MICHAEL HAWKINS
CO-AUTHOR

Michael Hawkins is an independent firearms ŗ
torney for U.S. Law Shield Legal Defense Pr
partner in Hawkins Spizman Kilgo, a criminal defens'
ta, Georgia. Mike received his bachelor's degree fr'
ty of Alabama and J.D. from Emory University Sr
began his career as a prosecuting attorney in m
and went into private practice in 1996, spec'
of alcohol, drug, and firearms cases. He prr
vises gun owners all over the great State r
advocate for the protection of our cons'